THE POWER OF POSITIVE TALK

Words to Help Every Child Succeed

A Guide for Parents, Teachers, and Other Caring Adults

by Douglas Bloch, M.A.

author of Words That Heal and Healing from Depression

with Jon Merritt, M.S.

author of Empowering Children and A Parent's Primer

free spirit
PUBLiSHiNG®

Helping kids
help themselves™
since 1983

Free Spirit, Free Spirit Publishing, and associated logos are trademarks and/or registered trademarks of Free Spirit Publishing Inc. A complete listing of our logos and trademarks is available at *www.freespirit.com*.

Library of Congress Cataloging-in-Publication Data
Bloch, Douglas, 1949–
    The power of positive talk : words to help every child succeed / by Douglas Bloch with Jon Merritt.—Rev. and updated ed.
        p. cm.
Rev. ed. of: Positive self-talk for children. c1993.
Includes bibliographical references and index.
    ISBN 1-57542-127-5
    1. Self-esteem in children. 2. Self-talk in children. 3. Affirmations. I. Merritt, Jon. II. Bloch, Douglas, 1949– Positive self-talk for children. III. Title.
    BF723.S3B56 2003
    649'.7—dc21   2002156644

10 9 8 7 6 5 4 3
Printed in the United States of America

Free Spirit Publishing Inc.
217 Fifth Avenue North, Suite 200
Minneapolis, MN 55401-1299
(612) 338-2068
help4kids@freespirit.com
www.freespirit.com

Dedication

For my goddaughter Amy Mae, who brings love and light to my life.

Acknowledgments

The inspiration for writing a book on positive self-talk for children first came to me during a series of discussions on parenting between myself and my swimming partner, Joe Mitchell. It was my agent Natasha Kern, however, who suggested that I take my ideas and submit them for publication. Her ongoing enthusiasm, encouragement, and belief in this project have been essential to its completion.

In addition, I am indebted to my coauthor Jon Merritt. Jon's experience as a teacher, school principal, child development specialist, and parent have contributed to the child-centered orientation of *The Power of Positive Talk.*

I am also grateful to the following parents, teachers, and counselors for generously sharing their personal experiences with me:

Parents—Chris Bremeker, Bob and Jan Epolito, Robert and Audrey Fowler, Ann and Jesse Garrett, Penny Gerharter, Jayne Koehn, Tim Lindsay, Joe Mitchell, Carolyn Quigley, Linda Roberts, and Theresa Russo.

Teachers—Carole Alison, Mary Baggott, Brenda Bennett, Joan Bloch, Gary Casebeer, Anita Gamotis, Linda Hayden, Fran Lancaster, John Mears, Patricia Oriti, Tom Rzecocki, Margaret Thurman, and Priscilla Winning.

Counselors—Carolyn Cook; John Dye, N.D.; Juanita Gail; Cliff Goldman; Denice Goodheart, R.N.; Claudia Hutchison; Beverly Jensen; Kathy Keller Jones; Judy Kafoury; John Koehn; Kay Kramer; Lee Hamilton; Karen Likens; Cindy McEnroe; Joe McFarland; Rich Mitchell; Maggie Nesbitt; Donna O'Neil; Carol Pasluszny; Susan Platt; Karl Schlotterbeck, Ph.D.; Erlene Smith; Jeff Sosne, Ph.D.; Dan Sisco, N.D.; Lief Terdal, Ph.D.; Bob Thurman, Ph.D.; Nancy Tuppola; Kristin Winn; and Cynthia Wojack.

I extend my appreciation to Judy Galbraith at Free Spirit Publishing for her support of this project.

Finally, my thanks go to the late Anne Zimmerman and her colleagues at Leonard and Associates who guided me to explore my unresolved childhood issues during the writing of this book. The process of healing the child within went hand-in-hand with my quest to bring healing into the lives of actual children in the world.

Contents

Introduction

> We cannot protect our children from life.
> Therefore it is essential that we prepare them for it.
>
> Rudolf Dreikurs, Children the Challenge

Even before children learn to speak, they "talk" to themselves. In their minds, they are making choices to go after what they want—or advising themselves to hesitate if they sense danger.

A good example is the determined toddler who is self-propelled in learning to walk despite repeated failed attempts. The child's thoughts, though not yet formed into words, give her the "go" signal. Before long, she steps out into the room unsupported. If she hears a startling noise, however, she's less likely to take that first step. She is telling herself, wisely, to play it safe for now.

As someone who cares about kids, you have a big influence on whether or not the "self-talk" of the children in your life remains positive and appropriately self-protective throughout their growing years. They depend on you to help them cultivate their natural confidence, courage, and sense of well-being. Your "C'mon, you can do it!" reinforces your toddler's choice to be brave. This is one of the main ways she learns to believe in herself.

I'm glad you've picked up this book as a way to help better the lives of the children in your care. Growing up isn't easy, and your kids need lots of loving and respectful support. The purpose of *The Power of Positive Talk* is to help provide this support by teaching you and your children how to apply the creative power of positive self-talk in your lives.

In this book, the technique you will learn to use in applying the principles of positive self-talk is the affirmation—a positive statement you make about yourself or a situation. An affirmation is spoken in the first person and present tense as a way of calling into being what you are creating for yourself. As I demonstrated in my previous books *Words That Heal* and *Listening to Your Inner Voice*, affirmations have a therapeutic and transformational effect on us.

For children who already have received lots of healthy nurturing and care, affirmations support them in building and maintaining a strong sense of self. For those children who have suffered emotional injury in their homes or from negative community or cultural influences, positive self-talk can help heal the damage.

While teaching and participating in "inner child" workshops over the years, I have witnessed the immense pain, low self-esteem, and shame that many adults still carry from their childhood. I've also been greatly encouraged by the power of the spoken word to help people re-parent their own injured "inner child" and counteract negative childhood learning. The approach described in *The Power of Positive Talk* shows you how to give your own children a better start. It provides guidance and encouragement to help both you and the children you love to claim or reclaim the best that is in you.

Douglas Bloch, M.A.
with Jon Merritt, M.S.

How to Use This Book

The Power of Positive Talk is a self-help book and reference guide that is designed to:

- help *adults* speak more affirmatively to the *children* in their lives.

- help *children* speak more affirmatively to *themselves*, thereby building high self-esteem and self-confidence.

- help *children* speak more affirmatively to *other children*—siblings, playmates, and classmates, so they develop positive social skills.

- help *adults* speak more affirmatively to *themselves* so they may become more positive and effective caregivers.

The Power of Positive Talk is organized to provide the parent, teacher, caregiver, or counselor with the easiest possible access to specific areas and issues in child development. There are three ways that you can locate the information you need:

1. Look through the table of contents. Parts 2 through 4 contain affirmations for children in three important areas:

Part 2 contains positive self-talk for building *self-esteem* and *emotional well-being*.

Part 3 contains affirmations for the child at a specific *developmental stage*.

Part 4 contains affirmations for children with *special needs*.

Then, locate a chapter that deals with a specific need, goal, or challenge that the child or adult faces. Each chapter contains *specific affirmations* for the child or adult to practice as well as specific examples showing how positive self-talk was successfully used in a real-life setting.

2. Consult the two indexes. Directly following this section is the *Affirmation Index*—an alphabetical listing, by topic, of affirmations used in the book. This is the quickest and easiest way to locate affirmations to use for specific situations.

For example, let's say that you are looking for affirmations to use with Joshua, your five-year-old who is expressing anxiety about the first day of school. Locate the listing *Fears, of school* in the Affirmation Index and turn to the designated pages.

In addition to using the Affirmation Index, you can turn to the back of the book for the Subject Index, a more comprehensive index of subjects covered in the book. Here you will find helpful information on any issue or aspect of child development that is of concern.

Perhaps you are a teacher or school counselor working with Meagan, a ten-year-old child with attention deficit disorder who has been acting out in the classroom. The Subject Index contains listings for *Anger of children, Attention deficit hyperactivity disorder,* and *Making friends.* In addition, you will find it helpful to review Chapter 10 on anger management and the section in Chapter 18 on behavior disorders.

Or maybe you are a stressed-out parent on the verge of losing control with and harming your child. To give yourself support, turn to the section "Breaking the Cycle of Verbal Abuse" located in Chapter 4 as well as to the listings for *Abuse* and *Anger of adults* in the Subject Index.

3. Refer to the many experiential exercises and classroom activities that are featured throughout the book.

Ultimately, *The Power of Positive Talk* is about empowering you and the children in your care. May the information that follows assist you and the child in your life to gain clarity, insight, and direction for whatever need or challenge you are facing.

Affirmation Index

Below we have listed the major topics and subjects covered in *The Power of Positive Talk*. We hope this list assists you in locating the specific information you need for the issue at hand.

PART ONE

The Power of the Spoken Word

Colin flushed triumphantly. He had made himself believe
he was going to get well which was really
more than half the battle if he had been aware of it.

Frances Hodgson Burnett, The Secret Garden

CHAPTER **1**

Sticks and Stones
Will Break My Bones, But Words Will
Wound Me Forever

As Jodi Foster accepted an Oscar for best actress in a motion picture, she thanked her mother for telling her "that all of my finger paintings were Picassos and that there was nothing to be afraid of." Those words, spoken to Jodi at an early age, gave her the confidence and belief in herself that translated into two Academy Awards.

But what if, instead of hearing "all your finger paintings are Picassos," Jodi had been told, "Don't bother me with your paintings. Finish your homework. You'll never be an artist!" Critical words such as these likewise leave a lasting impression on a young child. In some ways the effects may be more devastating than physical abuse.[1] The sting of a spanking may wear off in hours, but the sound of "I don't love you" lasts for years.

Many of us recall the saying, "Sticks and stones can break my bones, but names can never harm me." This statement turns out to be an outright lie. Words not only hurt; they create wounds that can take a lifetime to heal.

What Children Hear Is What They Become

This book is about words—specifically about the power of the spoken word and how it affects the lives of our children. Words are influential for a simple reason—each word or phrase spoken to a child carries with it an *underlying message* about the child and his relationship to the world. Once the child internalizes this message, it becomes a "belief" that governs his future experience. Even if he is not conscious of the belief, it will nevertheless affect all aspects of his life.

Unfortunately, children have not developed the ability to filter out what enters their mental computer. They cannot say, "I *accept* this compliment, but *reject* that criticism." A child views his parents as all-knowing beings whose words are powerful decrees. Later on, the child can look back and modify his early programming. But initially, he is the captive audience of his caregivers.

In a certain tribe in Africa, children are named after days of the week on which they are born. Half the crimes committed in the village are by those born on Wednesday, a name in the local language that also means "violent." In the United States, many prisoners recall that the earliest message they heard from their parents was, "One of these days you are going to end up in jail."

Here are some other examples of how negative verbal messages can impact a child's life.

Abusive statement	Child's negative belief	Life-damaging consequence
"Don't raise your voice at me."	"My anger is bad." "I can't openly express feelings."	The child suppresses his anger and becomes a people pleaser.
"You'll be the death of me."	"I am the cause of my mom's pain."	The child feels responsible for other people's problems. As an adult, he compulsively tries to fix everyone.
"Why can't you be more like your brother?"	"I'm not acceptable."	The child compares himself to others and never feels like he is enough.
"You never get it right."	"I'm stupid." "I'm incompetent."	The child is discouraged and depressed. He believes he can't succeed, so he never tries.

The following experiment will illustrate how the effects of verbal abuse may still be operating in your own life. Think back to your childhood and recall a negative word, phrase, or sentence that was spoken to you by a parent, relative, teacher, or perhaps another child. The abuse could have been a repeated harangue or an offhand remark. The following phrases may refresh your memory.

Words That Hurt

You'll never amount to anything.

What makes you think you're so special?

You'll end up just like your father.

Can't you do anything right?

I worry about you all the time.

Don't lose it.

Your room is always a mess.

When will you ever learn?

You're clumsy.

You're lazy.

You're stupid.

You're selfish

You're fat.

You're weak.

Why can't you be more like your brother (or sister)?

If you can't say something nice, don't say anything at all.

I wish you had never been born.

Don't bother me.

Big boys don't cry.

It's all your fault.

You're a bad boy.

You're a bad girl.

Now close your eyes and repeat at least *twenty* times the phrase you have chosen. When you have finished, take inventory. How do you feel in your body? How do you see yourself? How are you feeling emotionally? Ask yourself, "Are these words still operating in my life? Am I still living out their negative messages?"

Now imagine the effects of such words on an open, impressionable young child. Is it any wonder that ten-year-old Dylan now says, "I better play it safe," whereas once he thought the sky was the limit; that Rachel tells herself, "I'm stupid and ugly," instead of feeling, "I am fine just the way I am"; that Jonathan, who once believed he was born to win, is now resigned to just getting by?

If Words Can Wound, They Can Also Heal

If words can tear down and destroy, they can also build up and encourage. Instead of being told, "One day you'll end up in jail," what if those prisoners, when they were children, had heard statements such as *I'm proud of you, You're a winner, Keep up the good work, You're a bright kid*, and *You can do it!*? No doubt their lives would have taken a very different turn.

Some children *are* fortunate enough to be affirmed by their caregivers. For example, a successful entrepreneur reported that when he was four years old, his mother sat beside him at bedtime and whispered into his ear, "You can do anything you want. There are no limits to what you can achieve." The effect of this affirmative statement is shown below.

Affirmative statement	Child's positive belief	Life-enhancing consequence
"You can do anything you want. There are no limits to what you can achieve."	"I can go after what I want and get it."	Aaron is a confident child who grows up to be a successful entrepreneur. In his mid twenties he starts his own boat-building business, which develops into a highly successful enterprise. Now, he uses the same affirmative phrases with his children.

What is particularly inspiring about this story is that just as Aaron's mother affirmed him, now he does the same with his children. Emotional health can be passed down from generation to generation just as easily as abuse and other negative patterns of behavior.

Following the example set by Aaron's mother, the remainder of this book will demonstrate how the conscious use of affirmative language can foster self-love and self-esteem in children. Henry Ford once said, *"If you think you can do a thing or think you can't do a thing, you're right."* Belief and expectation, when expressed through words, have a powerful impact on shaping character. Let us put this knowledge into the hands of our children so that they can empower themselves and future generations.

CHAPTER 2

The Power of **Positive Speaking**

> You learn things by saying them over and over
> and thinking about them until they stay in your mind forever.
> *Frances Hodgson Burnett, The Secret Garden*

In her enchanting book *The Magic Journey,* Ilse Klipper tells of a series of adventures in which children are aided by "magic words" that, when repeated out loud, give them the strength and well-being to succeed at their quests. By using these empowering phrases, the heroes and heroines of the journey tap into the power of positive self-talk.

What Is Self-Talk?

Each of us carries on a silent, internal conversation known as *self-talk.* This self-talk consists of two inner voices that engage in an ongoing dialogue. The first of these voices, known as the *"yes" voice,* offers positive, supportive self-talk. The "yes" voice is a source of peacefulness and power. It taps into the natural curiosity, wonder, vitality, spontaneity, creativity, and joy that all children possess.

The second, opposing voice is called the *"no" voice.* It expresses negative, fearful, and counterproductive views. It is the voice of doubt, worry, anxiety, limitation, shame, and self-hate.

Here are examples of ten-year-old Jesse's voices:

Jesse's "Yes" Voice	Jesse's "No" Voice
I can.	I can't.
I choose to; I want to.	I have to.
I can try.	I'm afraid to do it.
I am me, and I am enough.	I'm no good.

continued ⟶

7

Jesse's "Yes" Voice	Jesse's "No" Voice
I can handle it.	I can't do it.
I am special.	I'm a loser.
I will get through this hard time.	I will never be happy again.
I can make a difference.	I am powerless.
I am smart.	I'm a dumbbell.
I am good looking.	I am ugly.
I am afraid, but I will act anyway.	I can't act because I am too afraid.

Sooner or later, a child's self-talk becomes a self-fulfilling prophecy. What she thinks of herself is what she becomes. If her "yes" voice tells her (in words and/or pictures) that she is a success, it is only a matter of time before she will demonstrate that success in the outer world. Thus, Jodi Foster's belief that all her finger paintings were Picassos—that is, her confidence in her own greatness—translated itself into the *manifestation* of that greatness.

On the other hand, if the "no" voice takes over and complains, "What's the use! I can't do it," the child will act, or fail to act, in accordance with that belief. Many children who have grown up with lots of criticism experience precisely this despair.

Supporting the "Yes" Voice Through Affirmations

The *affirmation* is a simple tool for empowering and reinforcing a child's "yes" voice. It is a positive thought or idea that one consciously focuses on in order to produce a desired result. The result may be a specific goal or outcome (doing well in school, making new friends, improving one's health) or an improved attitude or state of mind (experiencing self-love, overcoming fear). A child can create an affirmation for virtually any need, goal, or challenge in her life.

For example, twelve-year-old Phineas had just moved to a new city and a new school system. Initially, his "no" voice filled his mind with all kinds of worries and concerns. "This school is too big. You'll never make friends," it complained.

To allay these fears, Phineas decided to talk to his school counselor. Together, they created the following affirmation for Phineas: *I am a likable person who makes new friends easily.* Each day on the way to school, Phineas repeated the affirmation, either to himself or out loud. As he spoke the words, the knot in his solar plexus untied and his body felt less tense. Whenever his "no" voice returned, Phineas simply recited the affirmation. A few weeks after school began, Phineas had achieved the outcome he wanted—new friendships with his classmates.

Here are some other affirmations that have been successfully used by children:

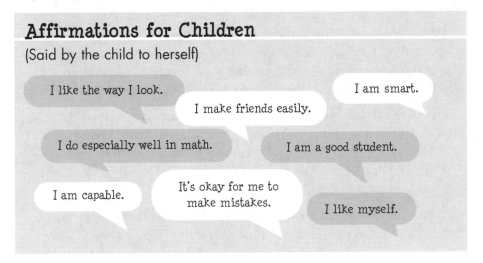

Affirmations for Children
(Said by the child to herself)

> I like the way I look.

> I make friends easily.

> I am smart.

> I do especially well in math.

> I am a good student.

> I am capable.

> It's okay for me to make mistakes.

> I like myself.

The conscious use of affirmative language can foster emotional health and self-esteem in children in a variety of ways:

1. **Positive self-talk fosters independence, autonomy, and self-responsibility** in children by encouraging them to go within and become the predominant creative force in their lives. This emphasis on moving from environmental support to self-support coincides with the work of child development pioneers such as Maria Montessori, Rudolf Dreikurs, and Erik Erikson.

2. **Through the use of positive self-talk, children can shift their self-concept from being externally to internally based.** Instead of depending on positive messages that come from the outside, kids can create their own strokes. For example, when Edward feels lonely and isolated, he looks in the mirror and repeats, "I am lovable and huggable."

3. **Positive self-talk enhances a child's self-confidence and self-esteem.** Mike was a high school dropout and recovering alcoholic. "No

one ever told me I could be anything," he lamented. After working with the simple affirmation, "I am somebody who can make a difference," Mike began to speak to other kids about his experiences with alcohol. Now he lectures full-time across the country. Additional positive self-talk for self-esteem can be found in Chapter 5.

4. **Positive self-talk can provide an antidote to unhealthy shame.** According to John Bradshaw and other therapists, toxic shame lies at the root of all addictions. By teaching children to affirm their basic self-worth, the spiral of shame can be stopped. Children can learn to *give themselves* appreciation and praise instead of criticism and condemnation. Additional positive self-talk for overcoming shame can be found in Chapter 5.

5. **Positive self-talk can help children to set and achieve personal goals** such as doing well academically, making an athletic team, or becoming a better friend. Additional positive self-talk for learning and academics can be found in Chapter 7, and for athletic performance in Chapter 6.

6. **Positive self-talk can positively affect a child's health and body image.** For example, my (Douglas Bloch's) twelve-year-old neighbor Molly, who was recovering from the flu, asked me why I hadn't gotten sick. I replied that whenever I feel myself coming down with something, I just talk myself out of it. A month later, Molly stopped by to visit.

    "It worked!" she exclaimed.

    "What worked?" I asked.

    "I did what you told me," she replied. "Last week, I started to catch the flu and I told myself, 'My flu bug is gone. I am healthy and well.' Soon, my flu went away."

    Additional positive self-talk for health can be found in Chapter 6.

7. **Positive self-talk can encourage kids to stay true to themselves and resist outer pressures** that often come from adults, peers, and the culture. For example, when a group of her friends told Jaden that her refusal to smoke was "not cool," she simply responded, "By taking care of my health, I'm helping myself—now *that* is being cool." Additional positive self-talk for resisting peer pressure can be found in Chapter 17.

8. **Positive self-talk can help kids respond to adversity in a positive and empowering manner.** After striking out with the bases loaded to end the game, Jamal blamed the entire loss on himself. "I let everyone down," he repeated to himself. With the help of his parents, Jamal slowly replaced his negative self-talk with the following affirmation: "I did the best I could. I'm still a good person. I can practice my batting and do better next time." By releasing his guilt and self-blame, Jamal was able to come back and improve his performance in the next game.

9. Finally, **positive self-talk can help children develop a greater optimism about the future** and diminish their feelings of despair and hopelessness. Tiger Woods became one of the greatest golfers of all times in large part because of his habit of positive self-talk. His refusal to let errors or failures sidetrack him has contributed mightily to his success. He said, "The road to failure is paved with negativity. If you think you can't do something, chances are you won't be able to." He also demonstrated the power of parental influence when he said, "My mom is one of those people who can find a silver lining in the darkest cloud. I guess I got my positive outlook from her, just as I got my relentless, never-ever-give-up attitude from my dad. Both require total belief in yourself and the ability to live with the outcome, whether good or bad."

How to Create Healing Affirmations

Children like using affirmations because they are simple to make and use. Essentially, an affirmation has three main characteristics:

- It is stated in the first person (using the pronoun "I").

- It is stated in the present tense.

- It is stated positively.

The following process demonstrates how to create an affirmation for any goal or need:

1. **Pick an area of your life that you wish to work on.** The topic of the affirmation can involve a relationship, health, work, finances, self-esteem, peace of mind, or any area you choose.

2. **Decide what you want to occur in that area of life.** Ask yourself, "What do I want to have happen? What is the result I am seeking?"

3. **Formulate a concise statement that expresses the desired outcome.** Use the first person (the pronoun "I"). Write the affirmation in the *present* tense. Imagine the experience happening in this moment. Saying "I love myself" feels more empowering than "I *will* love myself."

   State it *positively*. State what you do want, not what you don't want. If you say, "I am not sick," the subconscious mind screens out the word "not" and hears "sick." Hence, it works better to say, "I am healthy."

4. **Experience how the affirmation feels.** Say the affirmation over to yourself until it feels right on a gut level. When this occurs, you may feel it in your body or hear a subtle "aha!" Fine-tune the affirmation by altering a few words until it "clicks."

5. **Repeat the affirmation.** Repetition is the mother of learning. When an affirmation is repeated, its pattern is impressed on the mind, thereby anchoring the new thought. As Colin said in *The Secret Garden*, "You learn things by saying them over and over and thinking about them until they stay in your mind forever."

   In practicing an affirmation, you can say it to yourself, say it out loud, or write it down. You might even want to repeat it on a cassette tape or CD. Children especially enjoy it when affirmations are rhymed, set to music, or made into a personal rap song.

6. **Be consistent.** It is helpful to use your affirmation on a daily basis in order to benefit from the principle of spaced repetition. Set aside a specific time if you can, preferably upon awakening or before sleep. Parents report that their children enjoy practicing their affirmations at bedtime.

   Children can also carry their affirmations in their pockets or post them where they will be viewed on a daily basis. Seeing the affirmation regularly keeps the goals fixed in their minds—until the goals become a reality.

You may ask, "How do I know when the affirmation is working?" The answer is, when your desired outcome is either *felt* or *achieved*. If the result you are seeking is an outward goal, it should be evident when the goal is reached. If, on the other hand, you are seeking a change within yourself, note when your state of mind begins to shift. Once you feel a sense of completion, you can move on to the next goal or the next challenge that presents itself.

CHAPTER 3

Introducing Positive Talk
to **Children**

To whom it may concern,

My name is Erin and I'm 9 years old. Aunt Vi
has been caring for me and my sister Summer
since we were tiny.
    Aunt Vi loves kids very much. She corrects
us but doesn't scold. She reminds us to say
we're "happy, well, and grateful." Aunt Vi also
teaches us to watch our own thinking. She
says the hand can't hit if the thought is
kind. We work on art projects and we bake
cookies on holidays and other days, too. I am
going to miss Aunt Vi this summer.

Sincerely,
Erin

Erin is fortunate. Under the tutelage of her Aunt Vi, Erin learned to
direct her self-talk by the age of nine. According to Aunt Vi and others, there are three basic ways to introduce positive self-talk to children: use positive self-talk with yourself, say the affirmations directly
to children, and teach children how to create their own affirmations.

Use Positive Self-Talk with Yourself

Teaching positive self-talk to children begins with observing your own self-talk. As you learn to speak more respectfully and lovingly to yourself (and to the child within you), you will begin to speak in the same ways to your actual child. In addition, you will become a positive role model of someone who affirms himself. Chapter 4 demonstrates how parents, teachers, and counselors can incorporate positive self-talk into their daily lives.

Say the Affirmations Directly to Children

A child's self-talk does not create itself—it is born of what he hears from those around him. Long before a child consciously learns to affirm himself, he is being affirmed or negated by the words, attitudes, and actions of his primary caregivers. If a child hears words of praise and encouragement, he learns to love and to praise himself. If, on the other hand, he hears words of criticism and blame, he learns to feel ashamed and worthless.

Let us now explore how adult caregivers can *consciously* use the power of the spoken word to empower and affirm children.

When to Affirm Your Child

There are certain periods when children are especially receptive to receiving positive input. For example, children are usually more relaxed and open at bedtime when they have quieted down from the day's events. Moreover, the subconscious mind is extremely open to suggestion before sleep. Thus, before tucking your child into bed, you might want to hold him and say, "I like having you in my life" or "I'm glad that you are _____ (child's name)."

Bedtime is also a good time for children to practice using their own affirmations. Suggest to your child that he repeat his favorite affirmations or that he listen to them on tape or CD as he drifts off to sleep. If your child doesn't have an affirmation, you can help him create one by saying, "Tell me something you like about yourself or something you are good at." After repeating the affirmation together, conclude by saying, "You can say these words out loud by yourself, even when I'm not here."

The power of praise is also enhanced when you surprise your child. For example, while Samuel is doing his homework, you might say to him, "I notice that you did a really great job of sweeping out the garage. Thanks a lot." Such unsolicited comments make a powerful impact on the child. They enhance his self-esteem and create a reservoir of goodwill that can sustain your relationship during the difficult periods.

When we value something, we give it our time and attention. When you take the time to affirm a child, you are indirectly saying, "You are an important person. You matter to me." Speaking affirmatively to a child is another way of saying, "I love you."

What to Affirm in Your Child

The dictionary defines *affirm* as "to make secure, make firm, validate." There are many qualities and behaviors you can affirm in your child.

Affirm the child's basic "beingness." Every child needs to know that he is loved and accepted for the person that he is. Unconditional love is the greatest gift we can give our children. Here are some affirmations that go right to the child's core and say to him, "YOU'RE OKAY!":

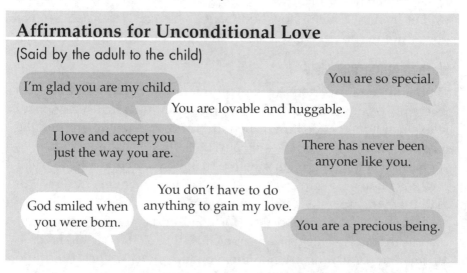

Affirmations for Unconditional Love
(Said by the adult to the child)

I'm glad you are my child.

You are so special.

You are lovable and huggable.

I love and accept you just the way you are.

There has never been anyone like you.

God smiled when you were born.

You don't have to do anything to gain my love.

You are a precious being.

Note that the above affirmations are not linked to anything a child *does*. Your child is lovable simply because *he exists*.

It is incredibly healing for children to be accepted just as they are. Think back to your childhood and imagine how wonderful it would have felt if your parents had said these words to you on a daily basis. Conversely, the greatest wound a child can receive is not being loved for the very person he is. He will then seek to matter to others by performing and achieving and seeking recognition. But no amount of "doing" can make up for a wound to the core of a child's being.

Affirm the child's right to his feelings. At the core of emotional health is the ability to feel and express feelings. Feelings are an essential aspect of what it means to be human. Feelings are primary and basic; they connect us to ourselves and to the world. Our feelings let us know what we want, what we need, what is important to us, and how to take care of ourselves.

Children initially need adults to give them the permission and the vocabulary to express their feelings. This can be done through *active listening*—reflecting the child's feeling back to him. For example, if a child is angry, we say, "I see you are mad that your sister used your toys without asking." If he is afraid, we respond, "I'll bet the first day of a new school is scary." Active listening does not evaluate, judge, or try to fix the feeling. Rather, it acknowledges and validates the child for having his reality.

When children are not allowed to experience their feelings, especially those of anger or hurt, they can erupt in inappropriate ways. Or they can be repressed and create emotional and physical distress for the child. On the other hand, when feelings of anger, fear, or hurt are freely felt, they resolve in positive ways. This principle is demonstrated in a story recounted by Swiss therapist Alice Miller in *The Drama of the Gifted Child*.[1] Apparently a girl was traumatized when her father failed to meet her at the train station. When Miller first saw the child, she was inconsolable.

> Then I said to Marianne, "Oh, but that must have been a big disappointment to you!" The child looked at me, large tears rolling down her cheeks. But soon she was stealing glances at other children, and two minutes later she was happily romping with them. *Because her deep pain was experienced and not bottled up, it could give way to happier feelings* [emphasis added].

Here are some ways that you can affirm a child's right to feel his feelings:

Affirmations for Feeling Feelings
(Said by the adult to the child)

It's okay to feel your feelings.

I like it when you share your feelings with me.

All of your feelings are important.

You can cry if you need to.

It's okay to feel sad.

It's okay to feel glad.

It's okay to feel mad.

It's okay to feel scared.

It's okay to feel however you feel.

When children are raised in an atmosphere of love, respect, and acceptance, they learn to express a wide range of emotions and feelings, including the painful feelings of anger, fear, and sadness. All too often, these feelings are put down or shamed by adults who had their own feelings shamed or denied when they were children.

In many families, feelings are considered weak or inappropriate. When children have their feelings invalidated, they will:

- stuff their feelings which fester and churn, surfacing later as rage, distrust, and acting out behavior

- stop trusting their perceptions

- lose touch with themselves and thus become much more susceptible to peer pressure, gangs, and drug abuse

The process by which a child can be shamed for his feelings by adult caregivers is as follows. The child has a "negative feeling"—anger, fear, or sadness. This triggers the adult's discomfort around his own anger, fear, or sadness. The adult then tries to eliminate what he considers to be the source of that discomfort—the child's feelings. For example:

1. If in a fit of **anger,** a child yells, "I hate you," we respond by saying, "You don't really hate your mother" or "Don't raise your voice at me."

2. If the child is **sad,** we may try to deny the grief and reply, "Don't be such a crybaby" or "It's not so bad."

3. If the child is **afraid** of going to bed with the lights out, we might respond, "Don't be silly. There's nothing to be afraid of."

4. Even **joy** can be disallowed. We tell the child, "Don't be too happy or something bad may happen to you."

If you notice yourself responding in a way that suppresses, fixes, or in any way interferes with a child's ability to feel his feelings, choose instead to engage in active listening. In addition, ask yourself, "What about this feeling makes me uncomfortable?"

IN ACTION

Thanh was inconsolable after his pet dog Spot died. His father was uncomfortable with Thanh's pain and grief, and responded in a way that minimized Thanh's feelings. He said, "Spot was old anyway. We'll get you a new dog. Let's go and buy an ice-cream cone." The dad was not conscious of how or why he was responding this way.

Because Thanh could not adequately express his grief, he began to act out in school. His school counselor arranged a meeting with the family and in the course of counseling learned that Thanh's father was raised in an authoritarian household where all feelings were seen as a sign of weakness. Meeting privately with the father, who was beginning to change his attitude toward the expression of feelings, the counselor suggested he use the following affirmations to help him reinforce that shift:

Thanh's Father's Affirmations for Validating Feelings
(Said by Thanh's father to himself)

I can allow Thanh to have his feelings.

I feel comfortable with Thanh's anger and sadness.

continued——▶

I feel comfortable with
my own anger and sadness.

I am comfortable with the full array
of my own and Thanh's feelings.

As Thanh's dad became more comfortable with his own feelings, he was more open to letting Thanh feel his grief.

Affirm the helpful things children do. We can affirm children by acknowledging the things they do. Children blossom when they're praised and appreciated. Pick out something the child did well during the day and compliment him for doing it. For example, "When we went to the store, I appreciated your putting food in the shopping cart" or "Thanks for cleaning up the playroom." Other affirmations include:

> What a nice drawing!
> Thanks for combing your hair.
> Thanks for clearing the dishes.
> That was a funny story you told.
> That was a good meal last night.
> Thanks for being patient.

Affirm the child's gifts and talents. Another set of important affirmations support the child's gifts and talents. Sample statements include:

> What a smart girl you are.
> You have good ideas.
> You are a great problem solver
> You have a lovely voice.
> What a fast runner you are.

Affirm the child's wants and desires. You can affirm a child's wants and desires by respecting his choices and by giving him options. Sample affirmations are:

> You know what feels good to you.
> You can ask for what you want.
> You can ask for what you need.
> I like your curiosity about the world;
> I'm glad you want to explore it.

Affirm the child's physical beauty. Children are terribly vulnerable to being wounded or shamed about their bodies. Affirmations can help children to feel proud of their physical appearance. Thus, while helping to dress a child you can say, "You have wonderful skin," "Your hair looks so nice," or "You are a handsome boy." Here are a few other affirmative comments:

> I like the way you look.
> You are pretty.
> You are handsome.
> You have your own special beauty.
> I like your freckles.
> I like your curly hair.
> I like your glasses.
> I like your voice.

Additional body-image affirmations are located in Chapter 6.

Affirm the goodness of the child's intent. Affirming goodness of intent can be accomplished by saying to yourself, "My child is doing the best he can." This will allow you to separate the child's intent from his behavior.

For example, suppose you walk into the kitchen and see that your child has splattered tonight's dessert on the counter and walls. Instead of yelling or calling the child a slob, you can respond, "Bobby, I know you were trying to help when you put the instant pudding in the blender, but the top wasn't on. That's why we have the rule, 'You can only use the appliances with an adult.' You are a big help in the kitchen, but remember to ask first and get an adult to help you with the blender."

Affirm the child nonverbally. There are a variety of ways to affirm children nonverbally. Positive messages can be conveyed by a hug or a loving look, or simply by spending time with the child. As important as words are, they need to be matched by an underlying attitude of love and respect for the child. Without a congruence between words, feelings, and actions, our affirmations will ring hollow and untrue.

As you affirm your child on a regular basis, he will automatically internalize the words you say and affirm himself. The underlying word behind every affirmation is the YES! and the underlying emotion is love. Using affirmations with the children in your life will make your relationship with them more loving and respectful as well as create what every caregiver wants—a happy, productive life for your child.

Teach Children How to Create Their Own Affirmations

> Give a man a fish and you feed him for a day;
> teach a man how to fish and you feed him for a lifetime.
>
> *Japanese proverb*

When children learn how to create their own affirmations, they become the source of their own positive messages, and thus the source of their own self-esteem. Here's how to get them started.

Begin by introducing the concept of self-talk. Explain that we all talk to ourselves through our inner speech. For example, if I do well on a test or hit a home run on my first at-bat, I might say, "Good going, Douglas!" On the other hand, if I strike out with the bases loaded, I might say, "I blew it. What a choke!"

Continue by explaining that "What we tell ourselves helps to determine how we feel about ourselves. Even though you may be disappointed about striking out, saying, 'What a choke!' to yourself will cause you to feel discouraged and hinder your performance next time at bat. On the other hand, saying, 'I'll do better next time' gives you the encouragement to practice your swing so you can do better."

Now you are ready to introduce the following four-step process:

1. Ask the child if there is any area of his life he would like to feel more positive about. Have him talk in *concrete terms.* If he is wanting to achieve a specific goal, have him describe what he wants in as much detail as possible. If he is facing a particular challenge (problems making friends, fears of going to school, adjusting to the death of a pet, etc.), ask him to describe the specific issue.

2. Then, go to the *feelings* associated with his goal or experience. Is the child anxious or hopeful about trying out for the soccer team? Is he hurt because no one wants to play with him? Encourage him to tell the story in his own words. With younger

children you can ask them to draw a picture of their feeling or make a sculpture with clay. Since children live in their feelings, this is an extremely important step.

3. *Reflect* and *mirror* the child's feelings and/or aspirations. Statements such as "It sounds like making the team is important to you" and "It must have been hard when Stephen said he didn't want to play with you" validate the child's feelings and assure him that he has been heard.

4. Once the child has described the situation and has identified and articulated his feelings about it, he is ready to formulate an empowering *affirmation.* Ask the child to come up with a positive statement that describes the goal, feeling, or behavior he just told you about. Wait for the child to state the affirmation in his own words, and repeat it back to him. If he is having difficulty formulating his thoughts, you can gently offer assistance. If he has a hard time believing in the affirmation, you can respond, "You may not believe what you are saying, but I believe it."

IN ACTION

Eight-year-old Lucas returned from the playground crying, "Nobody likes me." He talked to his school counselor about the incident.

1. First, the counselor asked Lucas to describe the circumstances around his being upset. What happened on the playground? Did someone call Lucas a name? Was he excluded from a group? Lucas said, "I wanted to play ball with a group of kids, but they wouldn't let me."

2. Next, the counselor asked Lucas to identify and fully experience his feelings. Lucas said he felt hurt and no good because he was turned down by the other kids. "No one will ever want to play with me," he moaned.

3. Now the counselor could help Lucas to choose a new way to respond to the situation. The counselor said, "I hear that you are disappointed that the kids wouldn't play with you. What are some things you can say to yourself that will help you feel better and to go out and find someone else to play with?"

continued——▶

4. With the help his counselor, here are some affirmations that Lucas created:

Lucas' Affirmations

I can find other kids to play with.

It is easy to meet new people.

I like myself, and so my friends like me, too.

I am a good friend.

Later on in the day, Lucas found children who wanted to play with him.

IN ACTION

Sarah had been rehearsing for her part in a sixth-grade school play. Because this was her first important role, she was feeling nervous and anxious. After school, she and her director decided to create some affirmations.

1. With the director's assistance, Sarah described her goal in concrete detail—remembering her lines and feeling relaxed and confident on stage.

2. She described how she would feel once the goal was met—excited, happy, and proud to have accomplished her goal.

3. Sarah's director reflected back to her, "I can tell you're going to be thrilled and very satisfied with yourself if you're able to perform as you've described." Sarah also did a form of "mirroring" for herself, visualizing herself being onstage and reciting her lines flawlessly.

4. Now she was ready to create her affirmations for playing her part well. Here are a few she wrote down:

continued——➤

Sarah's Affirmations

I am well-prepared for my play.

I am confident that I will do well.

I am calm and relaxed.

I remember my lines easily.

Aside from having a few jitters on opening night, Sarah was able to release her anxiety and successfully remember her lines.

Teaching Affirmations in the Classroom or a Counseling Setting

Positive self-talk in the form of affirmations is ideally suited for use in the classroom environment. Affirmations can help a student give himself positive messages about his ability to learn as well as to respond to the debilitating self-talk that says he can't learn. As one teacher told her students, "*I can* is just as important as *I.Q.*"

School is a powerful determiner of the child's self-image, especially during the elementary years. For better or worse, children are profoundly affected by their school experience. Why not make this experience as constructive as possible by teaching children to love and affirm themselves? As one teacher who uses affirmations in the class reflected, "These words are taking root and helping my students to believe in themselves." Please refer to Chapter 7 for affirmations geared to the school setting.

Affirmations can also be used as part of counseling or psychotherapy. Once the child is comfortable with the counselor, has become aware of his problem, and has identified and expressed his feelings about it, the counselor can introduce affirmations that can help the child take specific steps toward behavior change.

For example, nine-year-old Juanita entered counseling to get support in coping with her mom's cancer. Juanita said, "It's just so hard for me, especially in the afternoon when I start thinking about how sick she is."

Her school counselor replied, "It must be hard to see your mom in pain and not be able to do anything about it. One of the ways to help you feel better is to replace the worries with some other thoughts about you and your mom. Would you like to think up some different thoughts with me?"

Juanita agreed, and together she and the counselor came up with the following affirmations:

> The medicine is helping my mom to fight the cancer.
> Nice people are helping my mom.
> Nice people are helping me.
> I can find people to talk to when I am upset.
> My sadness is okay.

Saying these affirmations gave Juanita something to focus on to get through the day. Whenever she started to feel overwhelmed by her fearful thoughts, she said her affirmations as a form of self-therapy.

Because the principles of self-talk and affirmations are closely aligned with some common therapeutic approaches, many therapists already use positive self-talk with their clients. Affirmations are also particularly suited for counselors in a school setting who have neither the assignment nor the time to do long-term therapy.

A Cautionary Note to Parents, Teachers, and Counselors

In working with children who have been through traumas such as abuse, violent crime, or natural disasters, it is not appropriate to use affirmations *early on* to minimize the trauma or to cut off the child's feelings. Children need to fully feel their pain before they are ready to release it.

In addition, affirmations are not a "quick fix." Changing thinking patterns takes a long time, even with excellent therapeutic support. Nonetheless, affirmations are a tool that can promote attitudinal healing, especially when they are used with other forms of support.

Other Techniques for Introducing Affirmations to Children

There are many creative ways to share the principles of positive self-talk with children:

- **Use experiential activities to introduce positive self-talk to kids.** Many wonderful exercises and activities are available that teach children positive self-talk in a fun and engaging way. A number of them are presented throughout this book. You can share these activities with children in the home, classroom, or in a therapeutic setting.

- **Combine affirmations with visual imagery.** A picture is worth a thousand words. This is especially true for children, whose right-brained orientation makes them especially oriented to visual imagery. As one child poetically put it, "I make happy pictures with my mind." Sarah's example on pages 24–25 is a good example of how to use visualization to enhance the effectiveness of affirmations. Other examples appear in Chapters 6 and 18.

- **Set affirmations to music.** Perhaps the most powerful way to imprint affirmations on the mind is to set them to music. Music has the power to touch the soul and uplift the spirit. The following VIP song is often used in the lower elementary grades.

  > I'm a VIP in my fam-i-ly. I'm a VIP you see.
  > I'm a VIP in my fam-i-ly. And that's a pretty good thing to be.
  > A very important person. A very important person. That's me.
  > A very important person. A very important person. That's me.

  This song is especially appealing to first and second graders who love to move and dance when they hear it. The principal of one school joins in with them whenever he hears the music through his office walls.

  As a final suggestion, children can take a melody they already know, such as their favorite rap or rock song, and set affirmative words to it.

- **Record affirmations on cassette tapes or CDs.** Another powerful way to share affirmations with children is to record the words in your voice or in the child's. Add soothing music in the background to enhance the effect. Children like to play these tapes at bedtime, the first thing in the morning, or any time during the day when they need support.

- **Teach affirmations through stories.** Every child loves a story. In the classic children's book, *The Little Engine That Could,* a blue train engine was asked to transport a stranded trainload of toys to children on the other side of a high mountain. Although the engine was small and had never climbed a mountain before, it continually repeated the affirmation, "I think I can, I think I can, I think I can." Fueled by this positive thought, the engine made it over the top. As it puffed down the other side to deliver its precious cargo, it happily sang out, "I thought I could, I thought I could, I thought I could."

  A child is like that little engine—what he thinks and dreams about creates his future. If his private self-talk says, "I think I can" (or "I think I can't"), that is the reality he will face down the road.

  Older children might find inspiration for positive self-talk in the movie *Angels in the Outfield.* In that story, a baseball team had no faith in themselves and kept losing. When "angels" started helping them, they began to win. They developed faith in themselves because they thought the angels were helping them, but after the angels left, they kept winning. Believing in themselves made all the difference.

Positive Talk
for the **Adult Caregiver**

As we saw in the previous chapter, a child's self-concept does not emerge in a vacuum. A child learns about herself through the feedback and mirroring she receives from her adult caregiver(s). Ideally, a caregiver provides validation, acknowledgment, and affirmation for the child and her feelings. Therapist Alice Miller calls this supportive ally the "witness." Through the love and caring of the witness, the child learns that she matters to at least one adult, and therefore to herself.

The ideal witness, of course, is the child's parents. In addition, the witness can be a neighbor, relative, baby-sitter, minister, coach, teacher, scout master, youth leader, school counselor, psychologist, or friend.

As the reader of this book, you are no doubt an important witness in a child's life. In this chapter, we will explore how you can start the process of affirming this child by affirming yourself, that is, by talking to yourself in a more loving and compassionate way.

The chapter is divided into two sections. The first section focuses on positive self-talk for parents and can also be used by a relative, neighbor, or someone who has regular contact with the child. The second section offers positive self-talk for teachers, counselors, and other professionals who work with children.

Positive Self-Talk for Parents

In this section, we will explore the many ways that you can affirm yourself as a parent. Learning to affirm yourself has many benefits, both for yourself and your family. By learning to speak positively to yourself, you will become a positive role model for your children. In addition, you will be more likely to teach your children to create their own healing affirmations.

The affirmations that follow will empower you to give yourself positive and reassuring messages about your parenting skills. As you read over the material, note which topics and affirmations resonate most with you. Later in this chapter, you will have the opportunity to write them down so that you can practice them on a daily basis.

Trusting Yourself

In recent years, many manuals on child development have been written—more than any parent has time to read. In addition to the experts, friends and relatives offer unsolicited advice and direction to parents. Given this overwhelming amount of input, much of it contradictory, it's no wonder parents feel bewildered and confused.

Here are some affirmations that will reinforce the part of you that knows what to do:

Affirmations for Trusting Yourself
(Said by the adult to herself)

I trust my instincts as a parent.

I naturally tune in to and respond to the needs of my child.

I know more than I realize.

I am doing the best that I can.

I feel good about my decisions.

There are a number of good parenting resources I can consult.

I combine information from other sources with my own intuition.

I do it by the baby, not by the book. (for parents of newborns)

IN ACTION

Karen's mother tells her that she will spoil her infant if she picks her up or feeds her when she cries. Instinctively, Karen knows that it is impossible to spoil a three-month-old infant. To counter this advice, Karen tells herself, "I trust my instincts to nurture my child when she is in need. The more I love and nurture Amy, the better she will feel."

Please note that when parental judgments have been internalized from childhood, you don't need your mother or father to be physically present to hear these critical voices. Fortunately, affirmations work just as effectively to respond to internalized voices from the past as they do to current input.

Releasing Guilt and Accepting Your Imperfections

As much as you may try to be the perfect parent, you will make mistakes. Just as your parents made mistakes with you, there will be times when you will get impatient, overlook your child's needs, or just plain "lose it." In addition, if you and your spouse are working at a job in addition to parenting or if you are a single parent, there will be limits to the amount of time you can spend with your child. To meet *all* of a child's needs at each moment (especially if she is an infant) is clearly impossible. Here is where you need to accept and embrace your limitations.

While a certain amount of guilt is an inevitable part of being a parent, too often it turns into unhealthy guilt. When you start feeling guilty about something that you did or didn't do for your child, use this as an opportunity to love and forgive yourself. Give thanks for the incredible learning experiences that parenting offers.

Another way to release needless guilt is to remember that you are not totally responsible for how your child's life turns out. Your child has her own growth patterns and challenges that are part of her unique destiny. As one mother stated about her infant, "There are going to be days when my baby is crabby. I used to think that I had to *do something to fix* my child's pain. Now I accept that I can just *be there* with his pain, loving and supporting him just the way he is."

A knowledgeable nutritionist once said, "What you eat 80 percent of the time determines the quality of your health." In a similar manner, it is how you interact with your child *most* of the time that counts. If you are meeting her basic needs and providing the emotional nutrients of time, attention, direction, and unconditional love, your mistakes will have minimal consequences.

Accepting your right to make mistakes is accepting your humanity. Here are some affirmations that will help you make peace with your imperfections as a parent:

Affirmations to Release Guilt and Forgive Yourself
(Said by the parent to herself)

I accept my imperfections as a parent.

It's okay if I can't meet all of my child's needs all of the time.

I am loving toward myself when I make mistakes concerning my child.

I forgive myself for being less than perfect.

I learn from my mistakes and move on.

IN ACTION ➡

Jim had just lost his patience by yelling at his teenage son for getting home late. At first he started to criticize himself for having made the same mistake over again. After realizing the harm he was doing to his self-esteem, Jim sat down and created the following affirmation: "I guess I blew it again. I made a mistake, and that's okay. I can apologize to Todd and handle these situations more patiently in the future."

Self-Care

Another aspect of affirming yourself as a parent includes taking care of your own needs so that you can adequately meet your children's needs. This involves:

- being **physically** in good shape—getting adequate rest, exercise, and nutrition

- being **psychologically** in good shape—
    a) feeling good about yourself
    b) feeling good about being a parent
    c) taking care of your own "inner child" so she doesn't compete for attention with your actual child

d) making time for things you enjoy—friends, hobbies, travel, etc.

e) having enough daily private time

f) healing your past so that you don't pass on your unresolved pain to your children

- being **relationally** in a good place—with your mate or good friends and family, making sure you take time to experience high-quality time together in order to renew the relationships

Needless to say, parenting makes boot camp look like a vacation on the Riviera. To combat the normal mental and physical fatigue, wise parents take the time to nurture themselves in a variety of ways such as through seeking contact with other adults, spending quality time with their partner or a good friend, attending parenting classes and support groups, and engaging in fun activities.

Parents who neglect their own self-care start to resent their own kids and take out their frustration on them. A needy parent isn't equipped to parent a needy child. Here are some affirmations that will set the stage for you to care for and nurture yourself:

Affirmations for Self-Care
(Said by the adult to herself)

I take care of my own needs as well as my child's.

I take adequate breaks from parenting when I require them.

I create a large support network for myself.

I plan and arrange to have free time.

I take time to renew my relationship with my spouse (partner).

I take time each day for enjoyable activities.

I reach out for help when I need to.

The more I nurture myself, the better I nurture my children.

Spending Time with Your Children

Children need not only our love but also our time. The amount as well as the quality of time that children receive from their parents tell them how much they are loved.

In our over-busy society, time seems in shorter supply than ever. With the increase of single-parent families in recent decades and the frequency of both parents in two-parent homes having jobs, parents spend less time with children than in the past. Parents living in poverty may work more than one job, giving them little time with their families, and children of wealthy families also complain that they don't see their parents enough. Another sad fact is that many fathers see their children a lot less after divorce. Still, with all these constraints, most parents want to spend more time with their kids.

Here are some affirmations that will reinforce and support your desire to spend more time with your children:

Affirmations for Spending Time with Your Children
(Said by the adult to herself)

I find the time to spend with my children.

My children are my top priority.

I can give time to my children and still fulfill my other priorities.

I enjoy watching my children grow.

I have all the time I need to accomplish my goals.

IN ACTION

Wynter had a summer job giving guided tours at the zoo. She invited her parents to see her speak, but at the last minute, her father was invited out of town. Wynter was terribly disappointed.

Afterwards, her father reflected on the incident. He realized that by not taking time to see Wynter, he was in effect saying to her, "I don't value what you do." After saying the affirmation, "My child is important to me. I can find the time to see her at her job," he then negotiated to take time off work to hear Wynter speak.

Learning to Say No

Affirmations are a way of saying yes to ourselves and to others. Yet, in setting limits and providing boundaries for children, we also must say no. Parents cannot raise children successfully if they don't know how to say no lovingly.

Saying no is a way of giving children structure and security. When children know their limits, they experience the world as predictable, safe, and secure.

Admittedly, it is hard for a parent to say no. We want the child to have that candy bar she so desperately craves. But we also want her to keep her teeth healthy. In other words, saying no tells a child that we care. When a parent fails to say no, the child feels abandoned and neglected. Thus, despite their protests, children are secretly glad when we hold our position and set limits.

Saying no means that we must be secure enough within ourselves to withstand the opposition that will come. If your own parents weren't able to set limits for you, it will be difficult for you to set limits for your children. Parenting classes and counseling may prove helpful. Here are some affirmations that can also support you in saying no:

Affirmations for Saying No
(Said by the adult to herself)

I say no lovingly.

My child *wants* me to set limits.

My child feels secure when she has clearly defined limits.

I am loving and firm.

If I have not learned to set limits, I can learn now.

I am strong enough to stand my ground.

I love my child enough to say no.

Patience

A parenting instructor and mother of five children was asked what she learned from being a parent. "Patience and sacrifice" was her reply.

There are many ways in which children try our patience:

- They are messy. We pick up, clean up, and wipe up after them.

- They are noisy. They yell, scream, and cry.

- They require time-consuming tasks—cooking, doing the laundry, chauffeuring them around.

- They are self-centered and demanding.

- They push us to our limits and challenge the rules.

One of the greatest sources of irritation occurs when children don't do things on our time schedule. Here a parent can learn the difference between what *must* be done now and what actually can be done on a negotiated time schedule. Remember, young children have no conception of what "late" is.

Another source of impatience occurs when children fail to master a task or objective as fast as we would like. We ask in frustration, "When is my child going to get it right? When will she ever be a good student, ball player, pianist, etc.?"

A parent's impatience says to the child, "My needs are more important than yours. You must conform to my agenda." On the other hand, patience says to her, "I am here to serve your needs. I care about you enough to hang in there while you figure out what you need to do."

Here are some affirmations that will help to reinforce your desire to be patient with your child—and with yourself:

Affirmations for Patience
(Said by the adult to herself)

I am patient with my child.

I am patient with myself.

I let my child take the time she needs to do things.

When my child is taking extra time, I can find ways to adjust.

My child is developing at the rate that is right for her.

Anger Management

In an interview for his role in the film *Parenthood*, actor Steve Martin defined the four emotions of parenthood as rage, rage, rage, and joy. Most verbal or physical abuse arises when parents are unable to cope with their angry feelings.

Parents get angry for the same reasons children do—they feel provoked or frustrated, or they experience themselves as being treated unfairly. There are many ways children provoke parents—talking back, not cooperating, making demands, whining, getting out of control, and fighting with siblings. When your buttons get pushed, it is important to be able to express your anger in a constructive way.

Alternatives to Lashing Out at Your Kids

Everybody has negative feelings toward their children at times. You're not alone if you feel like you are verbally or physically going to "lose it" with your kids. The next time pressures build up to the point of lashing out, try one of the following alternatives:

- **Think prevention.** Don't give your four-year-old a large glass of chocolate milk if she is sitting on your brand new couch. For an older child, don't wait until she is late to meet friends to remind her of an overdue chore or deadline.

- **Recognize the situations and self-talk that trigger your anger.** Physical or verbal abuse is often a response to the feeling of powerlessness. Hitting or yelling are desperate attempts to gain some control over a child who is not cooperating. Another major trigger occurs when the parent takes her child's comments personally. Once you recognize what your triggers are, you can work to find different ways of responding.

- **When you feel yourself losing control, take a time-out.** Time-outs are good for adults as well as for kids. If you find yourself becoming too angry or frustrated with your child, it's best to put some space between the two of you to pause and get some perspective. Go into another room, take a few breaths, and count backwards from ten to one. If someone else can watch the kids, go outside and take a walk. Remember, you are the adult.

  You may also want to practice your time-outs ahead of time. You don't have to be "on the verge" to warrant some down time.

Even when you and the kids are getting along, be sure to schedule some breaks. It's good for you and good practice for the kids who learn that even parents need a moment to collect their thoughts. Plus, such practice sessions will help you and them prepare for when you really need a time-out.

- **Get your frustration out through a physical release.** Hit a pillow, stomp on a carton, yell in private. Running, jogging, and other forms of exercise will release energy and cool you down.

- **Take a hot bath,** listen to soothing music, or visualize yourself lying on a warm, ocean beach.

- In your imagination, **picture the crisis shrinking down to a manageable size,** or give yourself permission to attend to it later.

- **Write down all your frustrations on a piece of paper.** This helps to get the anger out of your system. The act of writing is therapeutic.

- **Reach for the phone instead of your child.** If you ever feel like you are about to hurt your child, call a friend, family member, or a hotline counselor. You can find someone to talk to.

- **Seek out support through parenting classes or parent support groups.** Much abuse arises from power struggles with children or futile attempts to control them. Parenting classes such as Parent Effectiveness Training (PET)[1] are available. They teach how to enlist a child's cooperation instead of trying to force it.

- **Use consistent limits.** Disciplining your child inconsistently teaches her nothing. It only leads to misbehaving children and frustrated, yelling parents.

- **Attend to your own inner wounded child by working out your feelings toward those who have harmed you.** If you consider yourself a potential abuser, most likely you were once a victim yourself. By healing the victimized child that still lives within you, you will release the unconscious compulsion to repeat the pattern with other children. This healing involves getting in touch with how you were wounded, expressing your anger toward the perpetrators (though not necessarily in person), and grieving for your wounded self. A wide variety of books (see "Suggested Reading" on pages 338–341), therapies, and support groups are available to assist you in this process.

Angry Thoughts Produce Angry Actions

Angry words and actions arise from angry thoughts and feelings. Here are specific thoughts that trigger angry responses, along with affirmations that can change your thinking:

Anger-producing thought	Corrective affirmation
"Children *shouldn't* act this way."	"They have the right to choose how they will act."
"I have to get angry to stop them."	"I can persuade them without getting angry."
"They are wrong and I am right."	"We are having a disagreement. I see it one way. My child sees it another."

IN ACTION

After a long day at work, Mark arrived home and found the dirty dishes stacked up. His daughter Sharon was on the phone with her friend, though she had agreed to do the dishes that day. Twice she ignored Mark's request to hang up and assist him with cleaning.

Realizing that he was in danger of losing control, Mark took a deep breath, stepped aside, and examined his anger-producing self-talk:

Mark's Anger-Producing Self-Talk

How dare she do that!

Children shouldn't treat their parents like this.

She *should* be more cooperative.

Realizing his old beliefs and patterns were causing his anger, Mark shifted to the self-talk he learned in his anger control class:

continued ⟶

Mark's Corrective Affirmations

> My child needs an adult who is in control and can help her.

> I can get my point across in a positive way, without resorting to violence.

> I can model how to manage my frustration.

> I can be there for my teenager.

After taking some deep breaths and getting a handle on his feelings, Mark touched Sharon on the shoulder and asked her to put her friend on hold. He then reminded Sharon of the consequences for not honoring her agreement—losing her phone privileges. Sharon was relieved and reassured that her dad did not resort to violence. By staying cool and adult in the midst of the battle, Mark was able to teach his daughter the affirmation, "We can work out conflict in a humane way, even if we are angry."

Breaking the Cycle of Verbal Abuse: Stop Using Words That Hurt

When a parent's anger gets out of control, it often takes the form of verbal abuse. Like physical abuse, verbal and emotional abuse are forms of violence. Examples of verbal abuse include:

- constant criticism, judgment
- yelling, screaming
- humiliating the child
- threatening the child (with force or abandonment)
- comparing the child to another
- invalidating and shaming feelings.

Once the verbal abuse begins, it contains a variety of components:

1. the **words** we use—a direct insult or a sarcastic remark

2. our **tone of voice**—yelling, critical

3. our **facial expression**—a scowl or an impatient look

4. the **critical thoughts** in our head that fuel all of the above

Verbal abuse is widespread and its effects are pernicious. Yet, unlike physical abuse, verbal abuse is not considered to be a major offense. If a child arrives at school with signs that she has been physically or sexually molested, the authorities are contacted. But if she complains, "Mommy told me I was no good," we shrug our shoulders.

Perhaps this indifference can be traced to the fact that abusive language is modeled daily on television, in the movies, and in political life. It is precisely the normalcy of verbal abuse that makes it so dangerous. The same child who becomes outraged when she is slapped may easily let the words "You'll never amount to anything" slip into her subconscious unchallenged. Years later that negative belief is still with her, creating unwanted consequences in her life.

How Verbal Abuse Causes Damage

Words can wound and injure our children. There is nothing so heart-breaking as watching a young child, wide-eyed and innocent, being yelled at and not knowing why.

When a child is yelled at or criticized:

•   She feels bad about herself. She reasons, "I must be a bad person if mom is always mad at me."

•   She feels scared and unsafe.

•   She feels abandoned.

•   Most importantly, she internalizes the negative words and believes what they say.

How to Stop Using Words That Hurt

Many situations can trigger us to say disparaging words to kids:

•   We are frustrated by the problems in our lives and take it out on the child.

•   We are in direct conflict with the child. She either defies us, talks back, or does not do what we want.

- We use outmoded parenting rules that fail to embody democratic and egalitarian values.

- We pass on the verbal abuse that was spoken to us by our parents.

- We react to the fact that children reflect back to us negative aspects of ourselves that we don't like and don't wish to see.

As the National Council on Child Abuse and Family Violence reminds us, what we say and the tone of voice we use can contribute to emotional abuse:

> Victims of emotional abuse are "hit" every day with the power of words which are demeaning, shaming, threatening, blaming, intimidating, unfairly critical, or sarcastic in nature.
>
> This form of abuse is destructive to a child's self-confidence and self-esteem. It can affect a child's emotional development, resulting in a sense of worthlessness and inadequacy. . . . Frequently, those who have experienced emotional abuse in childhood find it difficult to develop healthy, intimate relationships as adults. They may even develop antisocial behaviors which isolate them further.[2]

Most people do not consciously wish to abuse children. Most of the harm they do comes from unconsciously doing to kids that which was done to them. The first step in breaking this pattern is to become *aware* of the way you speak to children. This involves listening to what you say to them, and your tone of voice when you say it. This may take a bit of practice at first, since much of the time we are not *conscious* of the powerful ways in which our words cause harm.

IN ACTION

A group of twelve-year-old girls was singing in the back of the bus on the way to camp. One of them asked the adult driver, "Is Laura the best singer among us?" The driver replied, "At least she's the loudest." Laura was humiliated by this comment and it was twenty years before she sang again.

IN ACTION ➤

A mother repeatedly warned her daughter, "Don't eat too much or you'll be the fat lady in the circus." True to her mother's unconscious programming, the woman is now a compulsive overeater who is obsessed with her weight.

Once we become aware of how we use harmful words and are willing to change, we can seek out *strategies* that will bring about change. One of the simplest and most powerful is the "I" message.

Using "I" Messages

When we must communicate our displeasure to a child or group of children, we can do so without launching a verbal attack. The most commonly taught technique for achieving this is the "I" statement. "I" messages work because they allow the adult to focus on what upsets him or her about the situation instead of blaming the child. The following examples illustrate how to reframe abusive statements using "I" messages.

Adult critical statement	Replacement "I" message
Don't raise your voice at me.	I don't like it when we get in a shouting match.
Why can't you be more like your brother?	It upsets me when you come late to dinner.
You'll be the death of me.	I am frustrated with you.
You never get it right.	I would like you to try it this way.
You're a slob.	It bothers me when I come home and see newspapers all over the floor.
You're selfish and irresponsible.	I am angry that you took my tools without asking for permission.

Another helpful technique involves getting angry at the *situation or behavior*, not at the child. Thus, if young Jennifer spills milk on the floor, her mother can respond, "I get so mad when milk is all over the floor. I hate seeing it there." This is a vast improvement to the more typical response: "You are so clumsy. You can't do anything right."

Finally, if the child is being blatantly obnoxious ask yourself, "What need does the child have that she's trying to get satisfied with this behavior? Can I help her meet that need through reinforcing more positive and constructive behavior?"

There are two basic ways to communicate your displeasure to a child—one that empowers and supports her and one that debilitates and shames her. The following affirmations can help you to choose the former:

Affirmations for Managing Anger and Verbal Abuse

(Said by the adult to herself)

I can control my anger by controlling my anger-triggering thoughts.

I express my anger without shaming the child.

I get angry at the behavior, rather than the child.

I use "I" statements to express my displeasure.

I notice when I am becoming angry.

I can pause and count to ten.

I remember to breathe deeply.

I remain calm and in control.

IN ACTION

In the usual morning rush, Keisha's father left his shaving cream on the bathroom counter. When he returned home from work, he found shaving cream all over the mirror. Initially, he lost perspective and lashed out at his preschooler.

continued———➤

Abusive statement: "Bad girl, Keisha! Don't ever play with the shaving cream again."

Negative message received by child: "I'm a bad person. It's not good to explore my environment."

If we analyze what happened, we see that (1) Keisha was curious, (2) Keisha experimented, and (3) her experiment created a mess in the bathroom. By pausing a moment to gain perspective on Keisha's intent, her father can refrain from judgment and support her curiosity by saying,

Affirmative statement: "Keisha, I know that it's fun to play with the shaving cream, but the mirror is not the place to do it. Let's clean off the mirror, and then you can finger paint at the kitchen table. We'll put the paint on shiny paper and save it for daddy to see."

IN ACTION

You have just finished swimming, and your child is not getting dressed fast enough. You are already ten minutes late for an appointment.

Abusive statement: "Hurry up. You're making us late, slowpoke!"

Negative message received by child: "I'm not good enough because I'm not a fast dresser."

Affirmative statement: "Daddy's late. It would help me out if you could put on your pants a little faster. We are already late for dinner at grandma's. We sure wouldn't want to miss that good food!"

IN ACTION

You have asked your teenager to pick up her things from the bathroom floor several times. When you return, the mess is still there.

Abusive statement: "What a slob. I could hurt myself just trying to walk over your stuff."

Negative message received by teenager: "I'm lazy. I'm no good."

Affirmative statement: "Remember that I asked you to pick up your things? When you pick up, you really help me—and I appreciate that! Can you do it before you leave for practice?"

IN ACTION

While you are engaged in an important phone conversation, your child repeatedly says in a loud voice, "Look at my drawing! Look at my drawing!"

Abusive statement: "Shut up! Can't you see I'm busy?!"

Negative message received by child: "I'm bad for bothering mommy. No one cares about my picture."

Affirmative statement: Putting down the phone, you say, "I'm so glad you want to show me your drawing—and I would love to see it. But first I have to finish this phone call. Let's meet in ten minutes, okay?"

Substituting affirming words for critical words is simple but not easy. When anger is triggered, we tend to revert back to our old, conditioned behavior. To prevent this from occurring, you can adopt a technique used by Olympic athletes—*visually rehearse* your positive language. In your mind's eye, begin to see yourself responding to conflict in an affirmative manner. When an actual conflict arises, you will be more likely to respond in a nurturing way. At times, you may hear a frightened voice in your head saying, "My God! How will I ever deal with this mess?" Staying focused on your affirmation will calm that scared part of yourself and allow the adult part to stay in charge.

Making Amends After the Abuse

The fact that every perpetrator was once a victim himself does not necessarily mean that each person who was himself abused is bound later to become the abuser of his own children.

Alice Miller, psychotherapist, researcher, and author

Even with the best preparation, most likely you will fall back into old patterns of verbal abuse at times. Fortunately, you can redeem the situation and turn it into a positive experience by acknowledging both to yourself and to your child that you made a mistake. For example, after screaming at him because he was late for dinner, Perry's mother said, "Just because parents are grown-up, it doesn't mean we know everything. Sometimes we make mistakes and do things we shouldn't do. I'm sorry I yelled at you earlier. Please forgive me."

Making amends to our children is a deeply healing experience—for us and for them. When we admit to a child that we made a mistake, the child gets to see that it wasn't her fault and releases her shame. We get to release our guilt. Moreover, when we acknowledge our imperfections, we convey to the child, *Adults are human and fallible. We make mistakes and you can, too. You don't have to be perfect.*

Here are some statements you can say to yourself that will help you to acknowledge your mistakes and forgive yourself for them:

Affirmations for Making Amends

(Said by the adult to herself)

When I apologize to my child, I help to lessen the effects of the abuse.

I can admit it when I make a mistake.

Making mistakes and learning from them is part of being a parent.

I forgive myself for my unskillful behavior.

I can do better next time.

(Said by the adult to the child)

I was verbally abusive and that was wrong.

You don't deserve the abuse I gave you. I'm sorry.

It wasn't your fault.

I'm working hard to stop this type of behavior.

You're a good kid. I love you.

New habits take time to settle in. With practice, you will learn to speak to children with respect and understanding. Additional insights about verbal abuse as well as strategies for preventing potential abuse can be found in Chapter 20 on affirming the abused child.

Letting Go of Wanting to Control Your Children

If there is any one thing we can do to raise healthy children, it is to let them have their own self and be who they are. We are called to be teachers and guides for our children, not their masters. Your child is a precious, unrepeatable person who has never happened before and will never happen again. Trying to make her over in your image is a violation of her destiny. Asking her to be something she is not is like asking an oak tree to become a maple. As Kahlil Gibran so eloquently stated in *The Prophet:*

> Your children are not your children.
> They are the sons and daughters of Life's longing
>   for itself.
> They come through you but not from you.
> And though they are with you yet they belong not
>   to you.
> You may give them your love but not your thought.
> For they have their own thoughts.
> You may house their bodies, but not their souls.
> For their souls dwell in the house of tomorrow, which
>   you cannot visit, even in your dreams.
> You may strive to be like them, but seek not to make
>   them like you.
> For life goes not backward nor tarries with yesterday.

As simple as Gibran's advice sounds, it is difficult to let kids be who they are. You must give yourself permission to be who *you are* before you can do the same for your child. This means examining the expectations that you received as a child and letting go of those that do not support your deepest yearnings. If you didn't get to have your own reality when you were growing up, reparenting yourself will be both especially difficult and extremely rewarding.

Letting go means letting children learn from their mistakes. A wise man was asked, "How did you come to have such good judgment?" "Good judgment is based on experience," he said. "And what is experience based on?" the questioner said. "Bad judgment," the wise man replied.

Many parents try to protect their children from experiencing consequences by saying, "I don't want my kids to go through the pain that I went through." This statement, while well intentioned, contains a questionable assumption—that an easier life is a better life.

In the end, we can show our trust in our children and in life by not being afraid for them. Although we as parents can lend our support, ultimately our children must face their challenges by themselves. Encouraging them to be self-reliant and self-responsible makes it more likely that they will face those challenges successfully.

Here are some affirmations for letting go of expectations for your child and the need to change her:

Affirmations for Letting Go of Expectations
(Said by the adult to herself)

I let my child have her own reality.

I let my child be who she is.

I allow my child to make her own choices.

I allow my child to experience the consequences of her choices.

I release my expectations for my child's future.

I release the need to live through my own child.

I take care of my unmet needs.

The best thing I can do for my child is to work on myself.

IN ACTION

Mya, an excellent dancer at the age of twelve, wanted to sign up for several different classes—tap dance, jazz, and ballet. Her chagrined mother complained, "Mya is never going to learn focus and discipline herself. She must decide on what she wants now and stick to it."

Suddenly her mom realized that these were the exact words she heard from *her* mother. This realization helped her to let go of wanting to control her own daughter. For support she used the affirmation, "I trust my daughter's decision to follow her own interests. I realize that she is the best judge of where her passions lie. I encourage her to take the classes that interest her."

Working In-Depth with Your Affirmations

Take a moment to look back over the chapter and locate a specific section or sections that specifically speak to a need or parenting challenge you are currently facing. Then select two affirmations from the sections and write them in a journal or on a separate piece of paper.

Over the next week, write and say these affirmations as you feel the need. Allow them to reinforce and strengthen the goal or state of mind you are seeking.

As you work with your affirmations, you may notice a small voice in the back of your head that contradicts or refutes the affirmation. This is the "no" voice that we spoke of in Chapter 2. For example, shortly after Alberto's first child was born, he created an affirmation, "I trust myself as a parent." This is what occurred when he attempted to use it:

Affirmation	"No" Voice
I trust myself as a parent.	No you don't.
I trust myself as a parent.	You'll mess up, just like your father.
I trust myself as a parent.	You can't handle the stress of parenting.

As you can see, Alberto was engaged in a conversation, perhaps "argument" is the more accurate term, with himself. The dispute pit the affirmation against the critical, shaming voices of negative conditioning from his past. The affirmation said "yes" to his desire to trust himself; the negative beliefs responded, "no!" The next step, therefore, was to change each "no" into a "yes," so that what Alberto *wanted* (the affirmation) and what he *believed he deserved* (the subconscious response) were in total agreement.

This was done by creating a "Second Response" column which provided Alberto with the opportunity to *immediately* respond to the "no" voice and set the record straight. Reviewing each "no" response, he was able to ask himself, "Is there any way I can respond to this negative statement? Are there any misperceptions or falsehoods that I would like to clear up? How do I wish to set the record straight?"

You may find this process useful for yourself. It has two advantages. Since a lie left unchallenged will eventually assume the aura of truth, quickly responding to the "no" diminishes its power and validity. In addition, replacing the "no" voice with a positive statement makes it less likely that the former will return. If you're a person who finds it easy to work with visual images, you can erase the negative picture or scene in your mind's eye and replace it with a positive one.

Let us return to Alberto. As he answered each misperception with the truth about himself, he wrote his reply in the "Second Response" column, directly opposite the statement it is meant to replace. The following dialogue shows how he responded to his limiting beliefs.

Affirmation	"No" Voice	Second Response
I trust myself as a parent.	No, you don't.	Yes, I do.
I trust myself as a parent.	You'll mess up, just like your father.	I don't have to repeat his mistakes.
I trust myself as a parent.	You can't handle the stress.	There are many sources of support I can turn to.

Alberto was clearly empowered by confronting his negative beliefs and replacing them with the truth about himself. As a final step in this process, he took a number of statements from the "Second Response" column and brought them together to create a cohesive declaration of the good he was seeking. Here is his statement:

I trust myself as a parent. Even though I am a first-time parent, I have many resources to draw upon—the first of which is my love for my child. In addition, I can learn from the past and not repeat the mistakes my parents made. Although I won't be perfect, there is much that I will do well. My child is safe in my hands.

Upon reading these words to himself each day, Alberto was able to further reinforce the power of the original affirmation.

When working with this process, let your intuition be your guide. You don't have to refute every statement in the middle column. Just respond where it feels appropriate. Experience how empowering it feels to give yourself the support you deserve. You'll be amazed at how quickly you can release and transmute old beliefs when you answer your negative self-talk with positive affirmations.

To learn more about using affirmations, check out Douglas Bloch's affirmation books, *Words That Heal* and *Listening to Your Inner Voice* (see page 338).

An Important Note

Using affirmations in the manner we have described will help you to become aware of and release any prior negative programming—conditioned ways of thinking—you may have developed. This may not be enough, however, if you came from an especially troubled background. Additional sources of support, such as twelve-step groups, counseling, group therapy, or inner child work may be needed to work out unresolved issues. In addition, many excellent parenting classes are available that teach the communication skills needed for effective parenting. Affirmations are an excellent supplement to any therapy or self-help program.

Positive Self-Talk for Teachers and Counselors

The following section is designed to demonstrate how the affirmation process can support you in your role as a teacher or counselor. As with the previous section for parents, we will focus on the significant issues in which affirmations can be most helpful. At the end of the chapter, we will provide a space for you to write down one or two affirmations which you can work with on a daily basis.

Creating an Optimal Learning Environment

The goal of every dedicated teacher is to create an environment in which students are inspired to learn. The following affirmations list the main conditions that contribute to an optimal learning environment. Pick a few that resonate with you and work with them.

Affirmations for Creating an Optimal Learning Environment
(Said by the adult to herself)

I create an enjoyable and exciting learning environment.

I impart my love of learning to my students.

I have an attractive, organized classroom.

I present information in an enjoyable way.

I involve my students in the learning process.

I find ways to motivate and inspire my students.

I acknowledge students for their good effort and for their work.

I am open to new ways and techniques of teaching.

Patience

Good teachers and counselors exhibit the quality of patience, which means realizing that students learn at different rates and with different styles. Some students are fast learners while others take longer to catch on. If we are patient with those who are slow, they will learn in the time that is right for them. Patience is a way of honoring each student and her process. We can affirm a child for small improvements she makes.

The emotional development of children also occurs at different rates. Behavior change is a slow, painstaking process in which immediate, tangible results are rare. But the seeds we plant will sprout and mature if we have the patience to wait. Here are some affirmations to say to validate the subtle improvements that do occur:

Affirmations for Patience
(Said by the adult to herself)

I am patient with my students/clients.

I am patient when my students have difficulties in learning.

continued———➤

> I am patient when my students/clients seem stuck.

> I am patient with myself.

> It's okay to have days when I feel tired and discouraged.

> It's okay for my students/clients to have their down days.

> I welcome small, incremental changes.

> My students/clients are doing the best they can.

Classroom Management

Although managing a classroom of twenty to thirty children makes balancing the federal budget seem insignificant, students can be motivated by using love and natural consequences rather than fear and intimidation. The following affirmations can be used to support your desire to have a classroom based on mutual respect between students and teacher. Pick one or two and use them to reinforce your current classroom objectives.

Affirmations for Classroom Management
(Said by the adult to herself)

> I am calm and collected in the classroom.

> I make good choices in how I respond to the students when they act out.

> I discipline my students with love.

> I respect my students and they respect me.

> My students know that I am on their side.

> We work together so that everyone wins in my classroom.

> I can ask for help and support when I reach my limits.

> I am constantly improving my classroom management skills.

Accepting Your Limitations

As a counselor or teacher working with children, you are no doubt aware that a variety of forces outside of your control can interfere with how much you can help the child. For example, while you can consult with the parents, there is no guarantee that you will get their cooperation or that they will implement the changes you request.

If you are a counselor working in an organizational or school setting, the extraneous duties of paperwork, meetings, lunch duty, all take time from important counseling work. Teachers also face extra responsibilities such as preparing lessons, grading tests, staying with children after school—as well as the daily stresses of large classrooms, discipline problems, too little time to do the work, and staff and administrative issues. Schools often take responsibility for aspects of childcare that were once assumed by parents and the community.

In the fields of education and human services, there is always a discrepancy between what you *want* to do and what you realistically *can* do. The following affirmations are designed to help you make peace with and accept these limitations:

Affirmations for Accepting Your Limitations
(Said by the adult to herself)

I accept that there are many aspects of this child's life beyond my influence.

I recognize and accept my limitations.

I am doing what I can to serve my students/clients.

I prioritize my time to do the essentials.

I work within the system to produce positive results.

I focus on the good that I have achieved.

Detachment

The ability to detach is an all-important survival skill for education and human service professionals. Detachment means leaving your work at your workplace, not taking your clients' or students' problems home with you, and letting go of disappointing results.

Another aspect of detachment is allowing children to work through their own problems, even if they must experience pain. It is tempting to jump in and "fix" someone. But doing the work for a child takes away her opportunity to become responsible for her own life.

Detachment also means not imposing your value system on a child. A vocational counselor who values a college education must be aware of her bias as she counsels a student set on becoming a car mechanic.

Finally, a counselor needs to be detached from outside criticism. When parents, teachers, or administrators take issue with your evaluation or treatment plan, you can affirm, "I do what is best for the child."

Here are some other ways to affirm your ability to stay detached:

Affirmations for Detachment
(Said by the adult to herself)

I leave work problems behind at the end of the day.

I separate myself from my clients' pain.

I can be detached and still care.

I accept the consequences of my students'/clients' decisions.

I let go of my need to control outcomes.

I release the need to make everyone happy.

As I work on my own issues, I become a better teacher/counselor.

Self-Care

Many teachers and counselors find that working with children can become so consuming that it takes precedence over their own needs. In the emotionally demanding work of teaching and counseling, caring for others must be balanced with caring for oneself.

Self-care lies at the foundation of any helping relationship. The more we give to ourselves, the more we have to give to others. As we take care of our own needs, we avoid projecting those needs onto the client. The following affirmations serve as a reminder that all healing begins at home:

Affirmations for Self-Care
(Said by the adult to herself)

I take good care of myself.

I nurture and support myself.

I do enjoyable activities outside of work.

I have other professionals who I consult when I need to.

Working on myself is the most important work that I do.

I model a well-balanced life for my clients/students.

Acknowledging Yourself for Your Contribution

After the immediate family, teachers are the most influential care-givers in a child's life. Teachers who think they are just teachers don't realize the incredible influence they have on a child's mind. In many cases, teachers spend more time with the child (up to ten hours a day, including after-school activities) than do the actual parents. And because they are responsible for imparting all-important academic and social skills, teachers play a major role in building a child's self-esteem. Many talented and successful people testify that the turning point in their lives occurred when a teacher believed in them and took a positive interest in their future.

Many studies have been done on the Pygmalion effect in the class-room, exploring how teacher expectations influence student perform-ance. In probably the most famous study, eighteen elementary school teachers were told that, based on results of special testing given to all of their students, certain students in their classes had been identified as having great potential for intellectual "blooming." The names of the children given to the teachers were actually chosen randomly by the researchers, not according to their test scores. When tested a year later, the children who teachers had been told would "bloom" showed more than twice the gains in test scores compared to the other children in their classrooms. The teachers' beliefs about their students' aptitude had become a self-fulfilling prophecy.[3]

Despite their importance, many teachers experience themselves as undervalued and underpaid by society. In addition, schools receive the brunt of the criticism when children don't learn, even though families and communities share the major part of the responsibility. In many respects, schools have been made the scapegoats for the untreated problems of society. It is therefore up to teachers to give themselves the recognition and appreciation they deserve.

Counselors also need to remind themselves of the importance of their work. In the educational setting, school counselors are the first line of defense for kids who act out at home or in the classroom. And in cases where the child is totally removed from the family, the counselor or caseworker may become the most important adult in the child's life. Looking back over his career, one counselor remarked, "I have been in this business for sixteen years, and I still get awed by the healing I witness. Every time a child is nurtured and loved, a part of him that was dead comes alive."

Nurturing the minds and emotions of young children is a sacred act, a noble calling. Each day you are called to speak the truth in order to get the job done. Not many professions offer this type of training for developing the qualities of honesty, integrity, dedication, and compassion.

Here are some affirmations that are designed to help you validate yourself and your work:

Affirmations for Self-Acknowledgment
(Said by the adult to herself)

I respect, acknowledge, and honor myself for being a teacher/counselor.

I am making a significant contribution.

I am making a difference in the lives of children.

I am a good role model for my students/clients.

I am planting seeds that will bear fruit in the future.

Even when I can't see it, much good is taking place.

Working with children is a noble calling.

Serving the children is my number one priority.

Working In-Depth with Your Affirmations

Take a moment to look back over the chapter and locate a specific section or sections that specifically speak to a need or challenge you are currently facing. Then select two affirmations from the sections and write them in a journal or on a separate piece of paper.

Over the next week, write and say these affirmations as you feel the need. Allow them to reinforce and strengthen the goal or state of mind you are seeking. Some professionals like to write them on three-by-five-inch cards and keep the affirmations by their desk. Others repeat their affirmations each morning as they drive to work.

As you say or write an affirmation, you may notice a small voice in the back of your head that tries to contradict or refute it. Part of successfully working with affirmations involves addressing and responding to this negative self-talk. The previous section on self-talk for parents contains a simple but powerful process that will help you to become aware of and transform these doubts and concerns. Applying this technique will enhance the effectiveness of whatever affirmations you use.

PART TWO

Positive Talk for Self-Esteem and Emotional Well-Being

> Every waking moment we talk to ourselves
> about the things we experience.
> Our self-talk, the thoughts we communicate to ourselves,
> in turn control the way we feel and act.
>
> *Dr. John M. Lembo, psychology professor*

CHAPTER **5**

Using Positive Talk to Build **Self-Esteem**

> There is no value judgment more important to man—
> no factor more decisive in his psychological development
> and motivation, than the estimate he passes on himself.
>
> Nathaniel Branden, The Psychology of Self-Esteem

Self-esteem can be defined as our basic sense of self-worth that comes from all the thoughts, feelings, and experiences we have accumulated about ourselves in life. These impressions and evaluations add up to our feeling good about ourselves or feeling inadequate.

Characteristics of Children with High Self-Esteem

Children with high self-esteem exhibit the following characteristics:

- They feel they are important, that they matter.
- They are responsible—to themselves and to others.
- They have a strong sense of self; they act independently and are not easily influenced by others.
- They acknowledge their abilities and talents and are proud of what they do.
- They believe in themselves; they are able to risk and to face challenges.
- They express many types of emotions and feelings.
- They have a high tolerance for frustration.
- They exhibit emotional self-control.

- They feel connected to others, have good communication skills, and know how to make friends.

- They care about their appearance and take care of their bodies.

Parents who foster high self-esteem in children exhibit the following characteristics:

- They possess high levels of self-esteem themselves.

- They consistently show respect for their children's rights and opinions.

- They set clearly defined limits on their children's behavior.

Why does one child grow up with high self-esteem and another not? The answer lies in the dynamics of the child's relationship with his adult caregivers. A child who is touched, held, rocked, and loved automatically experiences himself as important and worthy. The child who is neglected, abandoned, or abused comes to believe that he is no good.

In other instances, self-esteem issues arise out of the physical circumstances into which a child is born. For example, a child raised in poverty may feel ashamed of having to wear shabby clothes to his school. A child born with a withered arm will have to overcome feelings of inferiority associated with his physical disability.

The Role of the Witness in Building Self-Esteem in Children

At the beginning of Chapter 4, we identified the adult witness as that person who validates, affirms, and acknowledges the child. The witness builds children's self-esteem in two ways—by giving positive strokes for being and positive strokes for doing.

Strokes for being arise as we provide a child with unconditional positive regard, which the child internalizes as self-love. Through the love and caring of the witness, the child learns that to at least one adult, he matters. Strokes for doing are given by reflecting children's successes back to them and acknowledging the things they are good at. Here are some ways to give that feedback:

- Create small successes. Give kids opportunities to succeed.

- Encourage children to make their own decisions.

- Respect their opinions.

- Support and encourage their creativity.

- Let them explore and take risks.

- Allow children to make mistakes and to learn from them.

- Make a distinction between the child and his behavior. Make the behavior "wrong," not the child.

- Avoid comparing one child to another.

- Acknowledge the child for what he is doing right rather than criticize him for what he is doing wrong.

The Role of Affirmations in Building Self-Esteem

Because they say YES! to a person's inner being, affirmations are ideally suited for building children's self-esteem. The sense of being okay at the core level is beautifully conveyed by the affirmation "I am me, and I am enough."

Other self-esteem affirmations include:

> I like myself.
> I am lovable and huggable.
> I am my own best friend.
> I say nice things to me.
> I am special.
> There is no one exactly like me.
> I treat myself well.
> It's great being me.

Shame: The Enemy of Self-Esteem

One of the great enemies of self-esteem in children is shame. Shame has been identified as a major contributor to emotional distress, low self-esteem, and addictive behavior. In his book, *Healing the Shame That Binds You,* John Bradshaw identifies two types of shame—*healthy shame* and *toxic shame.*

Healthy shame is a natural human emotion that arises when we are exposed, embarrassed, or unexpectedly caught off guard making a mistake or doing something we're not proud of. Toxic shame arises when a child internalizes negative feelings and sees himself as a flawed and defective human being. A guilty child with healthy shame recognizes his error and says, "I *made* a mistake." A child with toxic shame concludes, "I *am* a mistake." Guilt is about *doing* something wrong; toxic shame is about *being* wrong.

Bradshaw also speaks of the shaming voices in our head that reinforce and perpetuate toxic shame: "I'm no good," "What a dunce," "How could I be so stupid?" "I'll never amount to anything." In the perennial TV show *Charlie Brown's Christmas Special*, Charlie Brown repeatedly asks, "Why is it that everything I touch gets ruined?" This type of shaming self-talk is repeated by millions of children around the country every day.

Affirmations provide a simple and effective way for a child to overcome shaming self-talk. Any time he hears himself putting himself down, he can say CANCEL! CANCEL! This statement short circuits the negative self-talk and stops it in its tracks. The child then uses a positive affirmation, replacing the shaming thought with a loving thought. Here are examples taken from a class of fifth graders:

Shaming Self-Talk	Healing Affirmation
You're no good.	I'm okay.
I hate myself.	I like myself.
What a jerk!	I'm a nice person.
You're stupid.	I'm smart.
You're ugly.	I'm attractive.
You're fat.	I like my body.
You're a butthead.	I'm cool.
You're a loser.	I'm a winner.
You're worthless.	I'm awesome.
You can't do anything right.	There are many things I can do.
No one cares what I have to say.	I have important things to share.

You can have your child make his own two lists. A fun way to end this exercise is to give him some colored markers or crayons and say, "Now that you have turned your negative criticisms into positive affirmations, you don't need those negative thoughts anymore. Take your crayons and cross out everything in the left-hand column. Make sure you get to every negative thought." It is inspiring to watch children gleefully cross out the left-hand column.

Just as parental criticism and abuse are often the source of a child's shame, nothing protects a child more against shame than parental love—a love that appreciates and respects the child for who he is and affirms him as a unique and worthy person. By giving children unconditional positive regard and teaching them to use affirmations, the spiral of shame can be stopped. When a child learns to say and feel, "I love and accept myself," he cannot stay feeling shameful for very long. Nor will he desire to alter his mood by taking harmful drugs and chemicals.

IN ACTION

Nine-year-old Tyson was constantly putting himself down. To help him respond to the critical voice, his teacher made up a game. She pointed to Tyson's right shoulder and said, "What does this guy say?" After Tyson had recited some critical comments ("I'm no good," "I'm dumb," etc.), his teacher pointed to the left shoulder and asked, "Now what does he say?" The voice on the left shoulder said positive and affirming things about Tyson.

Tyson named his two voices angel and devil. Experiencing his self-talk as two beings sitting on his shoulder made the affirmation process real for him. With practice, his angel voice grew stronger.

IN ACTION

While taking his four-year-old nephew to the zoo, Carlos was caught off guard when he heard his nephew Felipe say out loud, "I hate myself." When Carlos brought the matter up to Felipe's parents they said, "Oh yes, Felipe often says such things."

Fortunately, Carlos was a school counselor. The next day he sat down with Felipe and asked him, "If you wanted to say something nice to yourself, what would it be?" Carlos then helped Felipe record

continued→

his positive self-talk on a tape which they set to music. He instructed Felipe's parents to play the tape for him every night before bedtime.

Two weeks later, Felipe's shaming self-talk was on the wane. Carlos also recommended a local family therapist since Felipe's low self-esteem was partly caused by his being the scapegoat for his parents' marital problems. Carlos also referred Felipe to a support group at school where he could talk about his feelings and get strokes from his peers.

Affirming Self-Responsibility

What is self-responsibility? It is accepting that you are able to respond to the events in your life and have some sense of control over your destiny—that you are "response-able." As one teacher told her class, "It used to be that everyone made decisions for you and what happened to you was everyone else's fault. But that's not true anymore. Now you have some ability to direct and manage your life."

Being responsible means realizing that one's actions have consequences. We can help children become self-responsible by allowing them to experience and learn from the consequences of those actions. If Saundra forgets to take her lunch to school, she goes hungry or has to borrow lunch money. The next day, the memory of the inconvenience is likely to prompt her to remember that lunch.

Self-esteem is like a beautiful statue. Every time a child acts irresponsibly—skips school, hangs out with friends instead of studying, breaks promises and commitments—he chips away at that statue. But the process can be reversed. When a child resumes taking responsibility for himself—showing up for class, being on time for practice, doing his assignments—he restores the statue to its original grandeur.

A child's transition from being motivated by fear and coercion to being motivated by self-responsibility takes time, patience, and practice. But once that transition is made, he will never return to the old way. Here are some affirmations that can facilitate that transition:

Affirmations for Self-Responsibility
(Said by the child to himself)

I am responsible for how I feel.

I am responsible for what I do.

I am responsible for my day.

I keep my promises.

I admit it when I do something wrong.

IN ACTION

During a weekly social skills support group meeting at his school, Jake, a fifth-grader, reported the following incident:

Jake: I was late for school and I had to stay inside at recess.

Counselor: Why were you late?

Jake: I missed the bus.

Counselor: Why did that happen?

Jake: My mom didn't set my alarm.

Counselor: Whose fault was that?

Jake: My mom's, of course.

Jake's peers shouted out, "Wait a minute. It's not his mom's fault. Jake is responsible for getting up in the morning."

The counselor responded, "It seems like most of you agree that it was Jake's responsibility to make sure he got up in time for school. What are some areas in your own life where you experience yourself as totally responsible?" The group members gave the following responses:

- getting up in the morning
- choosing my clothes
- breakfast
- showing up for school
- doing my homework

continued——➔

Grudgingly, Jake concluded that it was indeed his responsibility to make sure that the alarm was set so he would get to school on time. That night, he remembered to set it.

Defining and Affirming a Child's Strengths

Children with high self-esteem feel capable and competent in the world. One way to help children develop a sense of competence is by encouraging them to do things for themselves. For example, a group of high school juniors was given the opportunity to plan their annual camp-out. They picked out the camping equipment, planned the meals, and bought and prepared the food. When the camp-out happened again the next year, they were able to say, "I can do this. I've done it before."

When children get so wrapped up in what they can't do, they lose sight of their positive qualities. Encourage a child to take inventory of his strengths. One counselor tells his students, "You may not be big enough to play basketball for the Portland Trailblazers, but there are many things you can do. Everyone has special talents and abilities. Think of something you do well that you feel good about."

In taking inventory of his strengths, the child need not restrict himself to the verbal and mathematical competencies that are measured in school. Each child has a passion or talent he can feel good about. A class of third-graders identified the following strengths:

- "I am good with numbers."

- "I can draw and paint."

- "I play ball well."

- "I am a good listener."

- "I can fix things."

- "I am a good friend."

Like a tennis player whose powerful serve wins tournaments, children succeed by "playing to their strengths." Here are some positive self-statements that children can use to identify and celebrate those strengths:

Affirmations for Defining a Child's Strengths

(Said by the child to himself)

I am capable.

I have my own strengths.

I have my own abilities and talents.

I can do things well.

One of my strengths is _____ (fill in the blank).

One of my talents is _____.

One thing I can do well is _____.

I feel good about what I can do.

IN ACTION

Eric is an active, likable teenager. Like many boys his age, he has difficulty adapting to the sedentary atmosphere of the classroom. To give him something positive about himself to focus on, Eric's parents ask him to write a list of statements that affirm his strengths. Here is Eric's list:

Eric's Strengths

I'm a good athlete.

I know how to take care of our yard.

I'm a kind person.

I take care of my younger siblings.

I'm a hard worker.

Eric then kept copies of this list on his bulletin board and in his wallet. A few weeks of saying his affirmations enabled him to release his feelings of inferiority and gave him the confidence to begin improving his concentration at school.

CHAPTER 6

Positive Talk for
Physical Health, Body Image,
and Athletic Performance

> The greatest force in the human body
> is the natural drive of the body to heal itself—
> and that force is influenced by the belief system
> which can translate expectations into physiological change.
>
> *Norman Cousins, author and editor*

The power of words to impact our bodies can be seen in a simple experiment using muscle testing. Ask a person to hold his arm straight out in front of her. Then ask her to resist while you push down on the arm. This will give you a baseline strength. Next, have the participant say out loud three times, "I am a weak and unworthy person." Now, test the arm again and you will find that it has weakened. Have the person repeat, "I am a strong and worthy person," and the arm will return to its original strength.

Positive Self-Talk for Physical Health

In recent years, there has been an explosion of interest in the mind-body connection, helping us recognize that what we think and what we say to ourselves affects our body chemistry. One of the pioneers in this field of study is Herbert Benson. He introduced self-calming techniques that can lead a person to a "relaxation response"—a lowering of blood pressure, heart rate, breathing rate, and metabolic rate that yields many long-term health benefits.[1] In other words, we can talk ourselves into relaxing, and that is good for our health. The emerging field of psychoneuroimmunology is also showing us the effects of our

70

mind and emotions on our nervous and immune systems.[2] Feelings such as depression and despair weaken the immune system, while those of hope, joy, and optimism strengthen it. There is also growing evidence that patients with positive attitudes are more likely to recover from illnesses and experience pain relief than patients with negative attitudes.[3]

We can talk ourselves into healthy behaviors as well. One study showed that students who avoided negative self-talk and used positive self-talk combined with positive feelings and thoughts increased the likelihood they would engage in such healthy practices as vigorous exercise, use of seat belts, and avoidance of alcoholic beverages.[4] Children can employ affirmations to give themselves empowering messages about their health and well-being. Here are some affirmations to share with them:

Affirmations for Health and Fitness
(Said by the child to herself)

I take good care of my body.

I eat nutritious foods.

I get the right amount of sleep.

My body feels good to me.

My body does all the right things.

I am strong and healthy.

I take good care of my body.

I listen to what my body tells me.

Germs run the other way when they see me.

My body heals quickly and readily.

IN ACTION ➤

The body is a self-righting organism that is extremely receptive to positive suggestions. Latisha's mother used this knowledge to help her daughter fight off wintertime sickness. Normally, Latisha was run down for a number of days after catching a cold. After taking a workshop on mind/body health, her mother learned a new strategy.

The next time her daughter caught a cold, she said to her, "Your body sometimes gets sick, but it also heals easily. It heals quickly and readily." Latisha then repeated, "My body heals quickly and readily." Latisha was able to recover in half the normal time.

IN ACTION ➤

Childhood health problems such as wetting and soiling, headaches, stomachaches, ulcers, colitis, and asthma can be affected by a child's emotional and mental state. Bart, a fearful four-year-old, came to preschool complaining about various pains in his body. After a physician determined that the pains had no physical basis, the teacher said to him, "When you don't feel well, relax and repeat, 'I am happy, well, and grateful. I am happy, well, and grateful.' Then see how you feel." Bart fell in love with the affirmation and began to repeat it on a regular basis. Soon his complaints left.

Positive Self-Talk for a Child's Body Image

As well as being affirmed for their health, children need to be affirmed for their physical appearance. A child's body image forms the basis of how she will experience her body as an adult. Unfortunately, many children are growing up with an extremely negative body image. They do not like how they look; they do not like how their body performs; they literally hate their bodies. This self-loathing leads them to eat unhealthy foods that can create various medical problems such as obesity.

In the elementary years, children compare themselves with their peers in order to evaluate their abilities. In the process, they learn about the ways in which their physical appearances differ. All too often these differences are put down and ridiculed by other children or adults. A child will be judged as too fat or too thin; too tall or too short; too pale or too dark. Perhaps she wears glasses ("four-eyes"), has a limp ("gimpy"), or has big ears ("Dumbo"). Even the sound of a child's voice affects how others perceive her. A child who stutters is often ridiculed. The cruelty that children inflict on each other about body image creates wounds that follow a child into adulthood. The ongoing effects of this body shame helps to explain why many Americans are dissatisfied with some aspect of their body image.

Nowhere is positive self-talk more therapeutic than in helping a child form positive images about her body. Positive self-talk can replace attitudes of self-hate with a firm foundation of self-love and self-respect. Even if the child does not like the shape of her body or the sound of her voice, she can find aspects of her body that she appreciates.

If the child has had a long history of body image problems, expect the healing to take some time. The best treatment, of course, is prevention. The earlier a child forms a positive body image, the more immune she will be to the remarks of others.

Body Image Affirmations
(Said by the child to herself)

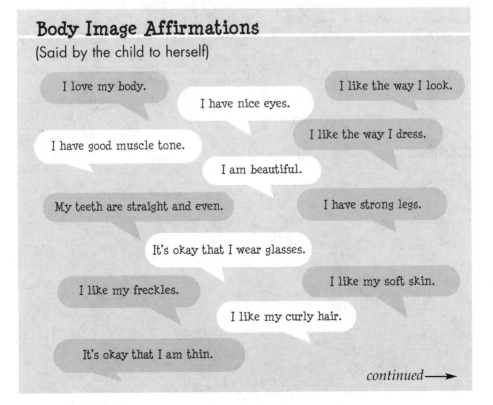

I love my body.

I have nice eyes.

I like the way I look.

I have good muscle tone.

I like the way I dress.

I am beautiful.

My teeth are straight and even.

I have strong legs.

It's okay that I wear glasses.

I like my freckles.

I like my soft skin.

I like my curly hair.

It's okay that I am thin.

continued⟶

I am unique.

I have a beautiful voice.

I am special.

I have a nice smile.

It's okay that I am _____
(fill in a trait).

IN ACTION

Carla, an attractive fifth grader, asked her school counselor for an appointment.

Counselor: What is bothering you, Carla?

Carla: I'm fat. I eat too much.

Counselor: Where did you hear that?

Carla: My mother told me.

Counselor: Carla, I'm surprised your mom said that. You're not over-weight at all. You look just right for a fifth-grade girl.

Carla stared at the counselor with a wide-eyed, "No kidding!" sort of look. She was evidently quite pleased to hear that her weight was normal. Carla's counselor gave her the following positive affir-mations to reassure her about her body image:

Carla's Body Image Affirmations

I love my body.

I feel good in my body.

I am the right weight for my age.

After working with Carla, the school counselor scheduled some appointments with Carla's mom. In their sessions, he gently made her aware of how she was inappropriately labeling her daughter. He also gave Carla's mom some body image affirmations since it was clear that the mother was unconsciously projecting her shame about her own body onto Carla.

IN ACTION ➤

One morning over breakfast, ten-year-old Mariko spontaneously said to her uncle, "I like my body except for my teeth. Boy are they ugly."

"Your teeth look fine to me," her uncle replied. "Those empty spaces will probably be filled in by your second teeth."

"No they are not fine. My teeth are ugly!" Mariko insisted.

Although Mariko could not accept that her teeth were okay, she did agree to use her uncle's affirmation, "My teeth are getting better and better." This allowed her to direct thoughts of self-acceptance to a part of her body that she had previously maligned.

Positive Self-Talk for Athletic Performance

> In basketball, as in all sports,
> the mental is to the physical as 4 is to 1.
>
> Bobby Knight, Texas Tech basketball coach

Bobby Knight is not the only successful sports figure who understands the importance of mental attitude in sports performance. When Olympic decathlon winner Jackie Joyner Kersey was asked to define the secret of her success, she replied, "The three Ds—desire, dedication, and determination." Ask any successful coach or athlete to define the ingredients of a winning performance, and he will stress mental factors—the desire to succeed, keeping one's focus and concentration, "and above all, believing in yourself."

In this chapter, we will explore how positive self-talk can assist a child to (1) enhance athletic performance and (2) maintain her focus and motivation in the face of difficult challenges.

Believing in Yourself

Before Michael Jordan ever heard of basketball, he told his mother that one day he would become an "Olympian." In the 1984 and 1992 Summer Olympics, Jordan led the United States basketball team to victory, and he became the highest scorer in the NBA. At the age of five, Billy Jean King ran into the kitchen and told her mother, "I'm going to do something wonderful." Twenty years later she was the best women's tennis player in the world.

Great athletic performers have a positive expectation of their destiny. From early on, they tell themselves that they are going to be great—and that belief becomes a self-fulfilling prophecy. Without a positive self-image, even the most talented athlete will fail to live up to her potential.

Visual Rehearsal for Athletic Performance

One of the most effective ways to improve athletic performance is to combine affirmations with visual imagery. This technique, known as visual rehearsal, involves imagining the exact outcome you want before it happens, as if you were seeing it as a movie. An Olympic pole vaulter uses visual rehearsal when she imagines herself successfully clearing the bar before the jump.

Visualization works because the brain and nervous system cannot tell the difference between a real event and an imagined one. Perhaps the most well-known demonstration of this principle concerns an experiment in which a basketball team was divided into three groups. The first group practiced their free-throw shooting every day for a month. The second group of players sat in the stands and visualized themselves making the free-throws. The third group neither practiced nor visualized. At the end of the month, the three groups were tested for improvement in shooting percentage. As expected, the third group made no gains. However, the group that simply imagined shooting free-throws improved at virtually the same rate as the practice group.

As you teach visual rehearsal to children, bear in mind that not everyone who visualizes sees actual pictures. Mental imagery can be visual (seeing), auditory (hearing), kinesthetic (touching), and olfactory (smelling). Olympic triple gold medalist Jean-Claude Killy rehearses winning a ski race by hearing the cheers of the crowd, feeling the cold wind on his face, and seeing himself cross the finish line. Each child will find the mode that is right for her when creating her mental movie.

IN ACTION

Theo was becoming increasingly frustrated as he failed to clear the high-jump bar on the first day's tryout for the high school track team. "I'm no good at this. I can't ever get it right," he moaned.

"I can tell you're frustrated," the coach said. "It must be very discouraging to hit the bar so many times in a row."

"You bet it is," Theo replied.

"I've been watching you, and I believe you have the talent to make this team," the coach continued. "Do you mind if I show you how you can change your approach to the bar?"

"Why not?" Theo replied.

After giving Theo a few pointers about his technique, the coach taught Theo to visualize himself clearing the high-jump bar while repeating the affirmation, "I am clearing the bar with grace and ease." By reprogramming his nervous system (through using the affirmation) and changing his jumping style, Theo succeeded in making the team and maximizing his athletic potential in the high jump.

Using Positive Self-Talk to Respond to Frustration and Adversity

"When the going gets tough, the tough get going" may be a cliche, but it describes one of the key ingredients of athletic success. Peak performers have the strength of character and the mental skills to stay positive in the face of distractions and adversity. They focus on the present—not the previous play, the opposing team's comments, or their anxiety about the future. Let's examine how positive self-talk can help any child affirm herself in response to three common adversities—an unfair call, losing a game, and being in a slump.

Affirming Yourself After a Bad Call

No matter what type of sport you are playing, there are times when a call will go against you. Athletes with low self-esteem tend to lose their cool and concentration after a bad call and then use that as an excuse for not performing well. Often they take the role of victim, saying, "The referee made a bad call because he doesn't like me."

A far more empowering strategy is to feel the anger and frustration, let it go, and then get on with the game. After receiving a questionable traveling call, one basketball star turned around and scored six straight baskets. He got his revenge by playing harder and raising the level of his performance. The following affirmations will help a child stay cool after a questionable call:

Affirmations to Say After a Questionable Call
(Said by the athlete to herself)

I keep my cool when things don't go my way.

The referee just made an honest mistake.

I breathe and count to ten.

I keep my focus and concentration on the game.

I come back on the next play.

Affirming Yourself After a Poor Performance

Losing is a fact of sports. Although losing hurts, it does not have to be devastating; in fact, it can be a positive event. Winners use the losing experience as a way to become aware of their weaknesses and make the necessary adjustments. A chess grandmaster once stated, "I learn more through the games I lose than through those I win. A loss exposes flaws in my game and forces me to correct them. The next time I reach the same position, I am well prepared."

Having the right attitude is crucial to turning lemons into lemonade. Without high self-esteem, it is easy to put yourself down, especially when you make a mistake or a bad play. Instead of saying, "Jerk! How could you have blown it!" championship players tell themselves, "I made a poor play. I let it go. I'll get it right the next time." Here are some additional championship affirmations:

Championship Affirmations
(Said by the athlete to herself)

It was a tough loss, but I will come back.

One bad game does not make a season.

I made a bad play, and I'll do better on my next try.

My mistakes help me become a better player.

IN ACTION

Sixth-grader Roger was in his second month of tennis lessons. His forehand stroke was coming along, but he struggled with his backhand. After hitting his seventh straight backhand shot into the net during a crucial game, Roger threw his racket and kicked up a dust storm on the clay court. This explosion weakened his concentration, causing him to double fault. His game rapidly deteriorated.

After the game he and the coach talked things out. Roger realized that if he were to become a competitive tennis player, he would have to control his anger. Together, he and the coach applied the four-step anger management process in Chapter 10 (see page 158) to control his outbursts. When Roger felt an outburst coming on, he was to say "STOP," take three deep breaths, and walk to the sidelines. Then he would repeat the following affirmations:

Roger's Positive Self-Talk

I can stay cool.

I am breathing deeply.

I will do better on the next point.

I will bend down to reach the ball.

My backhand is steadily improving.

After practicing his anger management, Roger learned to maintain his composure and concentration, even after missing shots.

Affirming Yourself During a Slump

Everyone has bad days. When those bad days turn into bad weeks—or bad months—an athlete is in a slump. Examples of slumps include:

- a pitcher not finding the strike zone

- a batter not hitting the ball

- a basketball player missing shots

- a quarterback throwing incomplete passes

- a tennis player netting serves

Slumps are frustrating. A few weeks ago the player had her stuff. Now it's gone and it won't come back, no matter how hard she tries. Although she may feel as if she has little or no control over the situation, the athlete can still decide how she talks to herself.

The low self-esteem player tells herself, "This will never end," and "What is the matter with me?" She gets angry at herself, which further harms her performance. The high self-esteem player, on the other hand, says, "I can handle this downturn," "All slumps must end," or "I'm still a good player." She learns to live one day at a time. Soon the day arrives when her performance improves.

Affirmations to Say During a Slump

(Said by the athlete to herself)

It's only a matter of time before I break out of this.

Soon I will connect with the ball.

I will regain my rhythm.

I believe in myself.

All slumps must come to an end.

I remain calm and relaxed.

CHAPTER 7

Positive Talk for
Learning and Academics

One of the main components of a child's self-esteem revolves around his academic performance. Failure to learn can be catastrophic to the individual and staggering in its costs to society. Not only will the person as an adult typically end up with lower job satisfaction, lower earnings, and thus have limited resources for himself, but society absorbs the costs of lower taxes paid and, in many cases, the costs of welfare, public subsidies for health care and housing, and crime control.

In this chapter, we will explore how children can employ positive self-talk to help see themselves as successful learners.

Overcoming the Belief That "I Can't Learn"

One of the greatest obstacles to learning in the classroom is the belief "I can't learn." The "I can't" attitude usually arises when a child has a bad experience with a subject in elementary school and develops a negative belief about his being able to master the material. Affirmations can assist in removing this learning block by replacing the student's negative self-talk with new beliefs about himself and his ability to learn. The following examples show how fifth-grade students turned their "I can't" beliefs into "I can" self-talk:

"I Can't" Self-Talk	"I Can" Self-Talk
I'm a dummy.	I'm smart.
I can't learn this.	I can learn the material.
This is too hard.	I can get help.
I'll never get it right.	I will figure it out.

continued⟶

"I Can't" Self-Talk	"I Can" Self-Talk
I give up.	I can try again.
I just don't understand long division.	I can learn this.
I messed up that test.	I'll do better next time.

Other affirmations for learning can be found in Chapter 18.

IN ACTION

Amy, a third grader, was having problems keeping up with the rest of the class in reading development. Because reading was often done out loud in a group, she got embarrassed and frustrated.

Amy's Negative Self-Talk

I can't read that.

I'm stupid. I can't do it.

I'll never pass the test.

After hearing Amy's complaints, her teacher approached her and said, "You may feel stupid, but I know you, and I can tell that you are not stupid. I know you can be a good reader. Would you like to try telling yourself you can do it?" Then, she and Amy created the following affirmations for Amy to say to herself:

Amy's Affirmations

I can read—with help.

I will read, in time.

I have confidence in me.

I can improve my reading with practice.

Amy went on to become an excellent reader.

IN ACTION

Darrin, a sophomore, proclaimed on the first day of his algebra class, "I can't do math. I don't understand it. I'll never be able to pass this class."

Fortunately his teacher, Ms. Bennet, worked with affirmations. She began the class by handing out a test and asking Darrin to locate one problem that he could solve. After he showed her the correct answer, she responded, "You see, you *can* do this." On subsequent tests, Darrin wrote "I can do math" at the top of the page.

Over the next few weeks, Ms. Bennet gave Darrin other positive affirmations about his ability in math.

Darrin's Affirmations

I can do math.

I can have fun doing math.

I can accomplish what I set my mind to.

I will work with the teacher until I get it right.

Then, one day while doing story problems, Darrin spontaneously blurted out, "This stuff is fun." He eventually earned a B in the class.

As these two examples demonstrate, the support of an adult ally is critical in helping a discouraged child to open the "I can" door to successful learning.

Learning to "Try On" Success

Most students have at least one subject in which they lack confidence. While some children use their weaknesses as an impetus to try harder, many use a difficulty as an excuse to quit. Maggie, a bright fourth grader, proclaimed to her teacher, Mr. Coles, "I hate reading."

"How do you know you hate reading when you don't read books?" the teacher asked.

"I tried it once and didn't like it," she replied.

"Before you totally give up on yourself," suggested Mr. Coles, "why not try on success?"

"What does that mean?" asked Maggie.

"It means picking someone in the class who you see as successful. Then find out what he or she does, and you do that, too. Do this for two weeks and see how you feel."

With the support of her parents and teacher, Maggie agreed that even though she didn't like to read, she would do a minimum of three hours a week of outside reading, which is what the good readers in the class did. Two months later, she proclaimed that reading was now her favorite subject.

Another subject Maggie "hated" was health. Once again she decided to try on success. With her teacher's help, she learned how to read a textbook, take notes, and pick out the main ideas. Soon, health became a favorite subject, too.

The "good feelings" that come with success are infectious. Through combining positive self-talk and doing what it takes to succeed, a child can transform his self-image from a non-learner to a learner.

Overcoming Test Anxiety

> For many years, I have been asking myself why intelligent kids act unintelligently at school. The simple answer is, "Because they're scared."
>
> John Holt, author and teacher

In school settings, academic performance is often measured by tests. While this presents no problem for those who are naturally good test-takers, many other children feel inhibited and blocked at the thought of taking a test.

Children with high test anxiety engage in negative self-talk such as, "I am going to fail this test." When they sit down at the exam, their minds go blank, even on those questions where they know the answers. This failure experience leads to more anxiety which perpetuates the poor performance.

The first step in reversing this process is to assure the student that failing a test is not the same as being a failure. Self-esteem affirmations such as "I am okay," "I like myself," "I am a smart kid," "I am intelligent," and "I believe in myself" will start the ball rolling.

Next, you and the student can create affirmations that say he is capable of doing well on tests. Such affirmations include, "I can learn to take a test," "I have the ability to succeed on timed tests," and "This is a skill I can learn."

Finally, the child can learn specific skills that lead to success on timed tests. Such skills include:

- staying relaxed during the test

- breathing deeply

- following your first instinct

- answering the easy questions first

- visualizing getting the score you desire (it's amazing how well this technique works)

As a final part of the process, allow the student to take practice timed tests before the real one. This will enable him to put his skills into action in a real-life situation without being subjected to the pressure of the actual test. Having succeeded in this dress rehearsal, he will be prepared for "opening night."

Here are some powerful affirmations that can be incorporated into any test anxiety reduction program:

Affirmations for Overcoming Test Anxiety

(Before the test)

I do well on tests.

I study and learn the material.

I am well-prepared.

I remember all the information I need.

I improve with practice.

(During the test)

I am calm.

I answer one question at a time.

I remember to breathe.

continued⟶

I start with a question I know and save the hard ones until later.

I praise myself for solving each problem.

My intuition guides me to the right answers.

(After the test)

I passed this test!

I knew I could do it.

My hard work paid off.

I'm proud of myself.

I am improving.

I'm reaching my goals.

Visual Rehearsal for Success on a Test

To help her students increase their confidence on an upcoming math fact test, Mrs. Corwin led the students in the following relaxation and affirmation exercise the morning of the test.

Hold your breath for three seconds, exhale and relax. Very good. Now let's do it again. Hold your breath for three seconds, exhale, and relax. Now that you are relaxed, I want you to give yourself a mental pep talk by silently repeating these affirmations. "I can do well. I know the material." In addition, visualize yourself getting the test back from me with the exact score that you want.

When the test begins, scan the page until you find a question to which you know the answer. Then pick another easy one. Leave the hard questions until later. Soon you will be relaxed and confident, knowing that you will go through the entire test with ease, making educated guesses to the questions you are not sure of. When you feel ready, open your eyes and begin the test.

After the students opened their eyes, Mrs. Corwin asked them to write the words, "I always improve on my math fact test," on the top of the first page. When the scores were tallied after the test, every student's score improved from the previous math fact test. Some even got the scores they had visualized. The only student who didn't improve was the one skeptic who didn't write, "I always improve on my math fact test," on his paper. Needless to say, his affirmation appeared in large print on his next test.

Releasing Negative Self-Talk About Test-Taking

Here is a powerful exercise to help students identify and release their fears about an upcoming exam. To begin, ask your students to write down all of the negative thoughts about an upcoming test on the left side of the paper.

Next, ask each student to write a positive affirmation directly opposite each negative thought. Those who have difficulty reframing their negative statements can ask for help. Feedback should be specific and concrete. Focusing on past successes also helps. Thus, a student who was afraid of doing poorly was told, "At the beginning of the year, you read at a lower level, but look how much you have improved."

Here is how Mrs. Corwin's class turned their negative self-talk around:

My Negative Thoughts About This Test	My Positive Thoughts About This Test
I'm afraid I'll fail and won't be able to go to middle school.	This test doesn't affect whether I go to middle school.
I'm afraid I'll do worse than anyone else in the class.	I am well prepared for this test.
I'm afraid I won't show improvement.	I've already improved a lot this year.
I'm a dummy.	I'm smart and capable.
I don't do well on tests.	I've studied very hard for this one.
I'm scared of tests.	I am getting help from my affirmations.
I always do poorly on tests.	I remember times when I have done well on tests.

Finally, ask the students to cut their sheet in half and destroy the negative side. Students find this a cathartic and satisfying experience. The positive affirmations are then placed on each student's desk, where they remain until the time of the test.

IN ACTION

Shelly was so afraid of taking tests that she got sick the night before an exam and missed school. After talking with her about her fears, her teacher and counselor gave her the following meditation for getting out of a panic attack.

The teacher said, "Shelly, if you tense up and your mind goes blank, repeat the following to yourself:

'I acknowledge that I am panicking. I am focusing on my breathing. I watch my breath go in and out. I take a moment to think of something pleasant. Now I am relaxed.

'I slowly focus my eyes on the page. I see a question that I know the answer to, and I answer it. I see another question I know, and I answer that. I feel good about knowing these answers. I am back on track.

'I answer one question at a time at a relaxed pace. I make educated guesses at the questions I don't know. I have all the time I need to do well on this test.'"

The next time Sally felt herself panicking, she tried this technique out. She focused on her breathing, relaxed, and then spotted a question she could answer; then another. Soon her confidence returned and she was able to finish her test without further attacks.

Overidentifying with Grades

Far too often, students equate their personal worth with the grades they receive. This overidentification with grades affects both the poor and excellent student alike.

After doing poorly on his science midterm, John was devastated. "I got a C on the test," he told his teacher. "I guess I must be a 'C person.' How can I go for my dream when I'm just C material?"

Mr. Bartlett replied, "John, I understand you are upset with your test score. But remember, school performance does not necessarily correlate with success in life. Many successful people, like Tom Cruise, Ann Bancroft, and Whoopi Goldberg, had problems in school. You can accomplish great things even if you do poorly in a specific subject."

Overidentification with grades also affects high-achieving students, many of whom play the hero in their family or are driven by the expectations of their parents. Because these students rely on their high grades to define their self-worth, they live in fear and anxiety of getting anything less than an A.

Here are some affirmations that can help students detach their self-worth from their grades:

Affirmations for Detaching Self-Worth from Grades
(Said by the child to himself)

Grades show only a small part of what I can do.

I have specific talents that I can find use for.

I feel good about myself as a person.

I am more than my grades.

I have what it takes to succeed.

IN ACTION

Another self-esteem problem posed by grades occurs when students compare their marks to those of their peers. Such was the case with Carol, a student with a straight-B average who criticized herself because her two best friends got straight A's. When Carol received a C in algebra, she became suicidal. The principal called in the family for counseling.

To begin, Carol and her counselor identified Carol's negative self-talk about her grades:

continued⟶

Carol's Negative Self-Talk About Grades

There must be something wrong with me.

I'm not as smart as my friends.

I'll never do as well as my friends.

I'm a failure.

In a meeting with the school counselor, Carol and her parents talked about Carol's strong desire for success and her need to compare her performance to those of others. Carol realized that she could measure her progress by setting and reaching her own personal goals. Whenever she found herself comparing her performance to those of her friends, she used these affirmations to get back on track:

Carol's Self-Esteem Affirmations

I measure my progress by my own internal standards.

I compete with myself.

Success is doing better than I did last time.

I'm glad when my friends and I meet our personal goals.

I let go of the desire to compare myself to my friends.

Carol did improve and got into the honor society. She also received an award—"humanities student of the year." Then, in her junior year, she took the SAT tests and scored in the upper 10 percent, but her friends scored in the upper 2 percent. Once again, she compared herself to them and felt worse. Consequently, she and her parents created a new set of affirmations to deal with this issue:

continued ⟶

Carol's Self-Esteem Affirmations

I can get into good schools
with these scores.

I have unique abilities
that will bring me success.

I will achieve in
my chosen career.

I'm reaching my goals.

Carol went on to college and pursued a successful career as a filmmaker.

Tips for Parents at Report Card Time

Report card time can be a stressful experience for both parents and children. When a child comes home with his first bad grade, it's easy for a parent to panic and overreact. One parent admitted, "When I was told that my son couldn't tell time in second grade, I was afraid he would grow up to be a bum."

It does little good to scold or punish a child who is having difficulties at school. Here are some guidelines on how to respond when your child brings home a less-than-favorable report card:

- Sit down with your child and look over the report card.

- Praise your child. Find at least one good thing to comment on such as attendance or no tardies.

- Be calm. Let your child tell you about his poor grades.

- Ask for information in nonshaming and nonblaming ways by using the words *what, why,* and *how.* For example, "What can you do next time to improve your grades?" "How do you think this happened?" "Why do you think your grade was low?"

- Empathize with the child. For example, "I'm sorry you got a D. Tell me about it. I bet you're feeling upset."

- Make a plan to work with your child and his teacher.

- Don't take the performance personally or be too invested in the outcome. Remember, it's just a grade. In elementary school, the long-term effect of a poor grade is negligible.

- Most kids take pride in what they do. Upon receiving your support and guidance, they will work to make changes, not because they are being coerced, but because they want to.

Sometimes a parent puts academic pressure on his child because he is unconsciously using the child to satisfy his own unmet needs. For example, one parent enrolled her son in a Japanese class at age five because she hoped that by having a knowledge of the language, the son would become a successful businessperson. The mother, it seems, had always wanted to go into business for herself. Through self-evaluation and counseling, this parent learned to find fulfillment in her own life and released the need to live through her child.

Here are some ways to affirm yourself and your child during report card time:

Affirmations for Report Card Time
(Said by the parent to himself)

I respond calmly to my child's report card.

I ask questions in a nonshaming way.

I avoid critical, judgmental, and angry remarks.

I praise the areas in which my child does well.

I allow my child to take responsibility for his own grades.

I have faith in my child that he will make whatever changes are necessary.

I let go of my need to control my child's academic performance.

My child, his teacher, and I are all learning allies.

continued⟶

(Said by the parent to the child)

We're proud of you for trying.

You don't have to do equally well in all subjects.

You don't have to do the same as everyone else.

We love you whatever your grades are.

IN ACTION

Because of the pressure being put on him by his parents to perform in school, ten-year-old Shariff began to do poorly in his subjects. Mr. Baker, Shariff's fourth-grade teacher, noticed that Shariff's academic performance clearly decreased as the year progressed. He called Shariff's parents and said, "Shariff's a bright kid, but he's just not living up to his potential. I know someone who could definitely help out—Mr. Jensen, the school counselor. Why don't you give him a call?"

Shariff's parents met with Mr. Jensen for a counseling session during which Mr. Jensen discovered that they were high-achieving perfectionists who harassed Shariff with comments such as, "Why can't you get A's like your older brother?" (the family hero) or "We're just so disappointed with you." Not surprisingly, Shariff was demoralized by this constant criticism.

After talking with Shariff about the situation at home, Mr. Jensen set up an appointment to see his father, who Shariff felt pressured him the most to excel.

Counselor: What do you want for your child and his life?

Father: I want him to be happy.

Counselor: How do you want your relationship with him to be when you are sixty and he is thirty?

Father: I want a loving relationship.

Counselor: What does that have to do with his being a straight-A student?

continued⟶

Father: Probably nothing.

Counselor: I understand that your own fears are grounded in a genuine desire to see your son be happy. But what you are doing is creating the opposite effect. You are turning him off to school and to you. If you want Shariff to do better, you have to start by accepting him for who he is. Not all children in a family are equally academically motivated. The more you try to push him, the worse he will feel about himself and the more discouraged he will become.

In further conversations, Mr. Jensen discovered that though Shariff's father was a successful businessman, he had always felt insecure about his lack of education. Thus, he unconsciously hoped that his son's academic achievement would heal his own shame and inadequacy. Once he became aware of this dynamic, the father was able to take the pressure off his son. Here are some affirmations he used in the process:

Shariff's Father's Affirmations for Accepting His Son

I can relax.

My son will be okay.

I release the need to live through my children.

I accept myself the way I am.

I know what's really important for me and my child.

Our relationship is more important than his grades.

I trust my child to use school in a way that best serves his needs.

Over time, Shariff's parents were able to reduce their expectations and become less critical of Shariff's work. As the pressure on Shariff decreased, he could relax, and his work improved.

IN ACTION

Thirteen-year-old Austin is a bright and eager student who performs well in school. One day Austin came home with three Cs on his report card. Instead of overreacting, Austin's mother helped him take responsibility for his grades. Here's how their conversation went:

Mom: Do you know why you got those Cs?

Austin: I didn't turn in all of the required work.

Mom: Do you know what you need to do to improve?

Austin: Yes, I do.

Mom: I encourage you to make those changes—if that's what you want.

Austin made the necessary adjustments and improved his marks in the next semester.

The Problem with Grades

Many people, including the authors of this book, believe that the giving of grades, particularly at the elementary school level, is unnecessary and may be harmful. Here is some of the evidence:

- Grades fail to honor and support each child for his unique talents, abilities, and learning style. Grading puts children all in the same pot and compares them using an arbitrary standard.

- A public television documentary on the nature of creativity listed surveillance, evaluation, reward, and competition as four factors that stifle creativity in young children. The last three of these are a direct consequence of the giving of grades.

- Students equate their grades with who they are. The C student too often sees himself as a C person.

- The grading system encourages children to go for the grade instead of going for the learning. Robert Frost said that all great endeavors are done for their own sake. How can we expect children to pursue a path in life for the love of it, when the grading system teaches them to go for the external reward?

- Grades encourage students to judge themselves based on other students' performances rather than measuring their progress according to their own standards.

- Grades put undue pressure on children. In extreme cases, kids run away, have emotional breakdowns, and even commit suicide over failed academic expectations.

A principal at an elementary school replaced grades with a simple system of evaluation that employed two categories—"Here's what Johnny's good at" and "Here's what he needs to work on." Even the categories "excellent," "satisfactory" and "unsatisfactory" were omitted, as they were just another way of giving A, B, and F. This change was deeply welcomed and appreciated by teachers, parents, and students alike. No one missed the old system.

Affirming a Child's Unique Type of Intelligence

When we talk about intelligence, we do not mean
the ability to get a good score on a certain type of test,
or even the ability to do well in school. . . . By intelligence,
we mean a style of life, a way of behaving in various situations
and particularly in new, strange and perplexing situations.
The true test of intelligence is not how much we know how to do,
but how we behave when we don't know what to do.

John Holt, author and teacher

For a child to have a balanced, positive view of himself, he must see himself as a many-faceted person who is better at some things than others. Take, for example, two acknowledged geniuses, Einstein and Mozart. Each excelled in his own domain, but not in the other's. Mozart's musical intelligence did not make him a great scientist; although Einstein enjoyed playing the violin, his mathematical intelligence did not make him a world-class musician.

When most people are asked to define "intelligence," they think of a general characteristic that you either have a little or a lot of and that manifests equally in all areas. In his book *Frames of Mind*, psychologist

Howard Gardner argues that intelligence is not a single, all-pervasive quality. Gardner has defined eight distinct types of intelligence:

1. mathematical
2. linguistic/verbal
3. visual/spatial
4. musical
5. kinesthetic—body intelligence
6. interpersonal—the ability to understand and get along with others
7. intrapersonal—the ability to understand and know oneself
8. naturalist

Unfortunately, our culture generally does not give equal importance to these intelligences. In many schools, a student's mathematics and verbal intelligences are considered of primary importance. Children with well-developed kinesthetic or interpersonal intelligences may get some recognition for being popular or good in sports. However, children who excel in the musical, visual/spatial, nature-based, or intrapersonal arenas often get minimal acknowledgment.

In *Emotional Intelligence*, Daniel Goleman identifies yet another important area of intelligence concerning emotions. Children who are aware of emotions—their own and others'—and who are able to manage their emotions, motivate themselves, and handle relationships well have a higher degree of emotional intelligence.

Every child needs to be acknowledged and honored for his unique abilities and intelligences. When children are praised for and focus on their strengths, self-esteem is the natural result.

Affirmations for a Child's Unique Type of Intelligence

(Said by the adult to the child)

It's okay to learn things in your own way.

You have your own strengths and talents.

continued⟶

There are things that you do well.

Your particular talent is very important.

It's okay to do well in some subjects and less well in others.

It's Okay to Make a Mistake

We ought also to learn, beginning early,
that we don't always succeed.
Life holds many more defeats than victories for all of us.

John Holt, author and teacher

For too many students, school is a place where it is not okay to make a mistake. They worry about not giving the right answer for fear they will be judged as dumb or stupid by the teacher or their classmates. Some feel so much shame after making a mistake that they never try a second time.

In *How Children Fail,* John Holt recalls asking one of his classes, "What goes on in your mind when the teacher asks you a question and you don't know the answer?" The students replied that they were scared to death—scared of failing, scared of being left back, scared of being called stupid, or worse yet, thinking of themselves as stupid.

We need to teach children that making mistakes is not a sign of stupidity. On the contrary, trial and error are the necessary antecedents to learning and progress. Geniuses, inventors, and entrepreneurs may make hundreds of mistakes before they reach their goal.

One of the greatest gifts we can give our children is to teach them to overcome the fear of being wrong. Children need to be reassured that no one is perfect, that making mistakes is part of the human experience. If a child makes a mistake on a math problem, we can tell him, "I guess that didn't work out. What other ideas do you have?"

Here are some affirmations for overcoming the fear of making a mistake. If you were taught to fear making mistakes in childhood, you can use these affirmations for your own self-healing:

Affirmations for Making Mistakes

(Said by the adult to the child)

It's okay to make mistakes.

Adults make mistakes, too.

You can learn from your mistakes.

You are improving those areas you need to work on.

Smart people learn from their mistakes.

(Said by the child to himself)

It's okay to make mistakes.

I learn from my mistakes.

Mistakes help me to improve myself.

I am doing better each and every day.

IN ACTION

Akio, a fourth grader, was having trouble learning multiplication. After diligently working on an exercise to practice multiplication facts, he proudly showed his answers to his teacher, Mr. Barnes. Unfortunately, most of the answers were wrong. Instead of immediately pointing out the mistakes, Mr. Barnes first complimented Akio on his effort and motivation. "Akio, I can tell you are a hard worker. I really appreciate your effort and concentration. I see you left one simple step out. Let's go over the formula again so you can better understand it."

The message conveyed with these words was, "I appreciate the intent behind what you do. I appreciate your motivation. You did make a mistake but it is no big deal; we can handle it." As a result of hearing these words, Akio emerged with the following self-talk:

continued ⟶

Akio's Positive Self-Talk

I am a hard worker.

My good effort is appreciated.

I will work on my multiplication until I get it right.

I can learn these new multiplication facts.

The essence of life is process, not results. If children are taught to affirm themselves in this way, they will grow into adults who are willing to risk, learn, and grow.

IN ACTION

Julie, a high school junior, walked into her counselor's office and stated, "My teacher hates me!" It seems that Julie received an F on a paper that she had "accidentally" left in her locker. Julie feared the paper wasn't good enough. Rather than risk having it rejected, she decided not to turn it in.

After Julie talked over her fears with her counselor, she decided to hand the paper in. Here are some affirmations she used to make this attitudinal shift:

Julie's Affirmations

I can give the teacher a chance to look at the paper.

If I turn it in, I'll find out how to improve it.

I can learn to write better.

It's okay if I don't have the perfect paper.

To Julie's surprise, she got a C. Using the teacher's suggestions, she rewrote the paper and received a B+. In the future, she was far more willing to risk having her papers evaluated. Here are Julie's new beliefs that emerged from this experience: "I can live through rejection," "I am a better writer than I thought I was," and "I can take a chance."

Self-Talk Activity: It's Okay to Make a Mistake

The following is the transcript of a lesson called "It's Okay to Make a Mistake," presented by an elementary school counselor to a first-grade class. Its purpose is to help children become more aware of how they speak to themselves when they make a mistake and replace critical self-talk with positive and supportive self-talk. The lesson can be presented by a teacher, counselor, or parent to a group of children or to a single child. We encourage you to take this lesson and share it with the children in your life.

The lesson begins with the counselor standing before the class with a puppet in one hand. The counselor says, "I've noticed something we all have in common. When we are not learning as fast as we want and make mistakes, we say certain things to ourselves that are negative. Today you will find out some of the things that you say to yourself when you make a mistake." Then the puppet speaks.

Puppet: I'm perfect. I don't make mistakes.

Counselor: Is that true?

Class: No!

Counselor: Is there anybody in this room who hasn't made a mistake?

Class: No.

Counselor: Do you know who Albert Einstein is?

David: A scientist.

Counselor: Yes, he was one of the smartest people who ever lived. Did he make mistakes?

Class: Yes!

Counselor: So we can all make mistakes, even Albert Einstein. You see, it's important to make mistakes. If you aren't allowed to make mistakes, then you never learn. If I handed your arithmetic papers back and didn't check any wrong, at first you would be happy. Then what would happen?

Michelle: You would think that two plus two equals seven, not four.

Counselor: Mistakes actually help you. Now let's look at how we talk to ourselves when we make a mistake. When you make a mistake, do you say to yourself, "I'm a bad and ugly person"?

Class: No!

Counselor: What do you say?

David: I need to work on it.

Michelle: I'll do better next time.

Counselor: Good. Now let's say that I'm a silly adult and David makes a mistake and I come over to him and say, "How could you be so stupid?" How would David feel?

Class: Bad! Rotten!

Counselor: Would David feel like going back to work and doing it right?

Class: No.

Counselor: What if instead, I told David, "That's just a mistake. You'll do better next time"? Would that help?

Class: Yes. He would want to try again.

Counselor: Good. Now, what I'd like to tell you is that you don't have to wait for an adult to say these things. You are first graders, and first graders can do this for themselves. I want you to think of some nice things you can say to yourself after you make a mistake.

I'm going to give you each a piece of paper with an empty cartoon bubble and a smiling face. Inside the bubble, next to the smiling face, I want you to write some words that make you feel good after you've made a mistake.

After the children complete the cartoon bubbles, the lesson ends.

CHAPTER **8**

What to Say When You Are Scared: Positive Talk for **Childhood Fears**

Children have good reason to be afraid. Small and defenseless, they inhabit a world full of danger and uncertainty. In this chapter, we will explore how to use positive self-talk to manage and master their fears.

The Origins of Fear

An infant is born with two innate fears, the fear of falling and the fear of loud noises. All other fears are learned. These fears develop in the following ways:

- by the **direct experience of a danger.** Mary is stung by a bee and develops a fear of bees.

- by **hearing about a danger.** Joan is told by her older sister how scary the roller coaster ride is.

- by **witnessing another person's fear.** Brian's father is deathly afraid of dogs and transmits that fear to Brian. It is common for anxious parents to unconsciously pass on their anxiety to children.

- by **temperament and family patterns.** Some children are high-strung or overly sensitive. Others do not bond well with their parents. These children feel insecure and unsafe. This type of free-floating anxiety may or may not express itself as a specific fear or phobia.

Once a fear is developed, it is often exaggerated by a child's vivid imagination. Thus, after seeing a scary movie about vampires, a five-year-old may start to imagine that vampires are hiding in her closet, waiting to come out after dark.

The severity of a child's emotional problems stemming from her fear depends on the intensity, frequency, and duration of the fear. For example, it is common for a child to feel scared about going to school on her first day. But if these fears persist over the next few months, the problem is serious and will require special attention.

Types of Fears

Children experience many kinds of fear. Among these fears are losing their parents, getting sick or dying, robbers, drowning, falling, getting lost, hospitalization, fires, airplanes, and global destruction. The type of fear a child experiences is often based on her developmental stage:

- **infancy and toddlerhood:** fear of separation, strangers, loud noises, bright lights, and loss of physical support

- **preschool:** fear of animals (especially dogs) and insects, dark (especially at bedtime), death, illness, doctors and dentists, heights, monsters, imaginary creatures, nightmares, school, deep water, storms, and other natural events

- **middle childhood and adolescence:** fear of physical injury, poor school performance, taking tests, looking different, not being accepted by other kids, making mistakes, being criticized, speaking before a group, and fear of the opposite sex

These and other strongly felt fears can manifest in physical symptoms such as headaches, stomachaches, teeth grinding, asthma, stuttering, anxiety attacks, bedwetting, nail biting, sucking, and nose picking.

Strategies for Reducing Fear

Separating real from imagined fears is a basic fear-reducing strategy. In helping children to deal with their fears, it is important to distinguish between two types of fears they experience. The first kind of fear protects them and helps them stay safe. When we cross the street and spot a car coming toward us, this fear wisely shouts, "Get out of harms way!"

The second kind of fear is more perceived than real. Examples of this are fear of the dark, fear of making a mistake, fear of asking for help, fear of trying something new, and fear of making new friends. Instead of protecting us, this type of fear gets in the way of normal functioning, learning, and growth.

The key to mastering fear is to be able to distinguish between these two types of fear so that we can attend to the protective fears and release the imagined ones. The following technique can help young children to accomplish this:

A school counselor asked a group of first graders to list their fears. Then he picked a specific fear—the fear of tigers.

Counselor: Have you heard of a kid being attacked by a tiger?

Children: No.

Counselor: What are the chances of you being chased by a tiger on the way home?

Children: Not good.

Counselor: You know what's not on the list? Fremont Street (where the school resides). Why should Fremont Street be on the list?

Children: Because cars and trucks can kill you.

Counselor: That's right. The most dangerous thing you do every day is to walk around cars and in and out of them. Every week a thousand people die in car accidents. Have you ever heard of a thousand people dying of tiger bites?

Children: No.

Counselor: So it's important to know the difference between the things that can really hurt you and the things that only seem like they can hurt you.

A second fear-reducing strategy is *systematic desensitization.* This method involves exposing the child to the source of the fear in small, gradual steps that can mastered. For example, a child with a dog phobia would first be shown a picture of a dog, then see a dog on a leash, then touch the dog, and finally hold it. Because this method reverses the original learning of the fear reaction, it is also called *counter-conditioning.*

Modeling is a third fear-reducing strategy. Here, the child watches another person experience the fearful situation in a calm and collected way. For example, a child with a fear of dogs would watch as her best friend pets and hugs his new cocker spaniel. "Look!" the friend says assuringly, "Spotty is really a nice dog. He won't hurt you." After observing her friend engage in this fearless behavior, the first child will feel far less afraid of Spotty. This technique is also known as *observational learning*.

The Role of Positive Self-Talk in Overcoming Childhood Fears

All people, adults and children, have fear. Fear is not the problem; the problem is how we perceive and respond to the fear. Fear always has two components—the actual fearful stimulus and what we bring to it from our state of mind. It is in this second area—in working directly on the cognitive thoughts and self-talk that are reinforcing the fear—that affirmations prove most useful.

Affirming the Ability to Cope

There is only one fear behind all fears—the fear of not being able to cope. If we knew that we could handle anything that came our way, there would be little to fear. Too often, however, children believe that they cannot cope. Affirmations can heal a child's feelings of power-lessness and helplessness by providing messages that she can take care of herself. As Edward Sarafino states in his book *The Fears of Childhood:*

> Children who feel helpless in the face of danger are vulnerable to fears. . . . Children who have confidence in their ability to master and control events and challenges are less vulnerable to fear. . . . This is why one of the most important messages children can learn from their experiences, thinking and fantasies is: *I am not helpless. I am a competent person who can achieve goals and take care of myself. I can master and control happenings in my world if I try* [emphasis added].

Here are some other positive self-statements that reinforce a child's belief in her ability to cope:

Affirmations for Coping

(Said by the child to herself)

I can cope.

I am learning to take care of myself.

I can handle what comes my way.

I can reach out for help if I need to.

I have the power.

I am safe.

I have a guardian angel watching over me (for those who have a spiritual or religious orientation).

IN ACTION

Growing up, Marty was continually told by her concerned parents, "Watch out," "Be careful," "Let me do this for you; you might get hurt." By the time she was a teenager, Marty felt powerless, paralyzed, and helpless. After talking with her school counselor, she identified the following self-talk:

Marty's Fearful Self-Talk

The world is a dangerous place.

I can't take care of myself.

I can't do anything.

I am helpless.

The counselor and Marty created the following affirmations:

continued——>

Marty's Fear-Busting Affirmations

I am a strong and competent person.

I can take care of myself.

I can handle what comes my way.

Other people are here to support me.

The counselor repeated these words to Marty and then asked her to look in the mirror once a day while she repeated them to herself. She also encouraged Marty to deal with her fears by trying a number of small tasks where she was sure to experience success. Finally, the counselor talked with Marty's parents to make them aware of the fearful words they were saying. All of this helped Marty to believe in herself and in her ability to cope.

Affirmations for Courage

When asked if he ever felt afraid in battle, General Patton replied, "Of course I experience fear, but I never take counsel from my fears." This idea is beautifully put in the following affirmations:

I am afraid, and I will act anyway.
I can do things, even when I feel afraid.

The message these affirmations convey are simple but profound. They say that we can be afraid and still act. Fear does not have to lead to paralysis.

Another word for the willingness to move forward in spite of your fears is courage.

IN ACTION

In the book *The Magic Journey* by Ilse Klipper, a king sends his three children on a mission to find a special ring in a dark cave. As the children approach the cave, they begin to feel afraid. The story continues:

> Their knees began to shake and their feet would hardly move. They began to wonder if they really wanted to go by themselves into a big, dark cave. The king, sensing their fear, said, "Remember my children, you can find a great treasure if you will forget your fear. If you really want to find the ring, you can. . . . From now on, repeat these magic words over and over, I AM BRAVE, I AM BRAVE, I AM BRAVE."

By faithfully repeating her affirmation, the child named Sita overcame her fear, found the ring, and became ruler of the land.

IN ACTION

Nolan's fifth-grade class went on a field trip. Nolan, a star football player, was afraid of heights. At first, he wouldn't even consider the trip because part of the hike involved a ten-minute walk over a high bridge. He was afraid that he would fall off the bridge into the river below. Fortunately, Nolan's teacher said, "Nolan, I know you are afraid, but working together I think we can overcome this fear."

When the class arrived at the bridge, the children stood on both sides of Nolan to support him. The bridge was closed to traffic, so Nolan walked down the center of the road while he repeated affirmations which he previously had rehearsed with his teacher:

Nolan's Positive Self-Talk

I am safe.

I have my support group on both sides of me.

This bridge is strong and it will hold me up.

I am feeling fear and I am walking across the bridge.

continued⟶

> I am feeling fear and I am putting one foot in front of the other.

> I am feeling fear and I am focusing my eyes on a spot ten feet in front of me.

After crossing the bridge, Nolan felt empowered. With the support of his teacher, friends, and his own thinking, he faced and overcame a severe phobia. Nolan's final words were, "After this, I can master anything."

The Importance of Acknowledging the Fear

Courage begins with acknowledging that we are afraid. As simple as this sounds, children rarely receive such permission to feel their fear. A child who expresses fear is usually:

- ridiculed and shamed ("Don't be such a baby!")
- scolded ("Stop crying this instant.")
- coerced ("Go to the dentist, or else.")
- overprotected ("I'll take care of this for you.")
- discounted ("There's nothing to be afraid of; stop acting silly.")
- ignored ("You'll grow out of it.")

All of these responses invalidate the child's right to feel her feelings of fear. And if she can't even admit she is afraid, how can she move beyond it?

Here are some affirmations that acknowledge a child's right to feel her fears:

Affirmations for Validating and Acknowledging Fear
(Said by the adult to the child)

It's okay to be scared.

It's okay to be afraid.

Big boys and girls get scared sometimes.

Grown-ups get scared.

I get scared, too.

Together we can help you to feel less afraid.

Now let's take a look at how positive self-talk can be applied to some common childhood fears.

Fear of Bullies

In a nationwide survey of students published by the American Medical Association, nearly one-third of the students reported that they experience bullying, either as a target or as a perpetrator.[1] Bullies taunt, tease, jeer, blackmail, threaten, physically intimidate, spread rumors about, or otherwise seriously torment other children who either cannot or do not defend themselves. Children cannot learn effectively in school if they fear for their safety. In addition, youth who are bullied report being lonelier, having fewer friends, having poorer grades, and being more likely to smoke and drink alcohol.[2]

In the past, it was thought that children became bullies because they lacked self-esteem, but many bullies have high self-esteem and are generally well liked by other children. They may not have developed empathy skills, so they are not necessarily aware of how hurtful their actions are. Whether perpetrated because of low or high self-esteem, bullying is an aggressive act, designed to gain power over another. Children who are victims of bullying can benefit from reassuring affirmations from their parents and other caregivers. Here are some affirmations to use with a child who has been bullied:

Affirmations for Reassurance
After a Child Is Bullied
(Said by the parent to the child)

You deserve to be treated respectfully.

Your worth does not depend on a bully's opinion.

You are wise and courageous.

I am confident you will learn how to protect yourself.

I will back you up if you ever need me to.

Michele Borba, in her book *Building Moral Intelligence: The Seven Essential Virtues that Teach Kids to Do the Right Thing*,[3] encourages parents to listen to the whole story about a bullying experience their child has had. It is important to pay close attention to how the child has responded in order to offer more effective options. Then, she recommends teaching the child some bully-proofing strategies and helping her practice them. Since each child and each situation is different, offering your child a range of options can be helpful. Borba says these six options are the most successful:

- **Assert yourself.** A strong voice and upright posture, along with firm language—"*Stop it*"—can show the bully you won't be intimidated.

- **Question the response.** Answer the insult non-defensively with a question, for example, "Why do you want to hurt my feelings by saying that?"

- **Use "I want."** Say what you want to happen: "I want you to stop saying that."

- **Agree with the teaser.** Humor can help: "So you think I'm a dork? You're right. I win prizes in dork contests all the time."

- **Ignore it.** Bullies like to make people squirm. If you look uninterested or walk away, they don't get what they want.

- **Make fun of the teasing.** A rehearsed response to "You're pathetic" could be "So?"

Have your child practice these strategies, role-playing with her the kind of situations she has experienced with the bully. You can also teach your child affirmations to increase her confidence and remind her what to do:

Affirmations for Fear of Bullies
(Said by the child to herself)

I am worthy of respect.

I like myself as I am.

I can tell someone to stop bullying me.

I am confident within myself.

I can set limits.

I can stay calm and take the actions I practiced.

I am just as worthwhile as other children.

IN ACTION

Kathy Kneitzke teaches her fifth graders to imagine putting up an invisible shield to protect them and give them power when they are subjected to bullying. She has them create drawings of their shields, decorate them, and write affirmations on them such as "I count," "I stand tall," and "I have courage."

IN ACTION

Children who report bullying behavior to parents or teachers are often subject to further harassment for "tattling." Ms. Kneitzke reminds students who are afraid to tell on the other child that "A right's a right; a wrong's a wrong."

continued⟶

Davisha talked to Ms. Kneitzke about the problem she was having with Lakia, who kept "tapping" her in the lunchroom. Fearful of being taunted for tattling, Davisha didn't want her teacher to talk to Lakia about the tapping. Ms. Kneitzke asked Davisha what she had done about it before coming to tell:

Davisha: I told her I didn't like it and that I wanted her to stop.

Ms. Kneitzke: Do you think that was an okay thing for you to say?

Davisha: Yes, I have a right to say that.

Ms. Kneitzke: If you've given her the message clearly that you don't like it and asked her to stop, and she still does it, then was what she was doing right?

Davisha: No.

Ms. Kneitzke: Isn't a right a right and a wrong a wrong?

Davisha: Yes.

Ms. Kneitzke: Then that's how you can know that asking for help from an adult is okay.

After this reassurance from her teacher, Davisha felt more confident. She still didn't want her teacher to talk to Lakia, but she was able to ignore Lakia's behavior and discourage it from continuing.

When bullying persists, despite the best efforts of the child, adult caregivers may need to step in and talk with the bullying child and sometimes the child's parents. Parents can enlist the help of school counselors or administrators if the bullying takes place at school.

Fear of Violence

Children are exposed to a great deal of violence through television shows, movies, and electronic media. In addition, they often overhear conversations by the adults in their lives who are distressed about violence on the news and in the community. Some children become familiar with violence firsthand in their neighborhood or school. All of these influences can instill a sense of niggling fear in a child: *Will someone jump me on the way to school? Will someone start shooting in the lunchroom?*

In reality, most children are not in great danger of a violent attack on a daily basis. In fact, according to the National Center for

Educational Statistics and Bureau of Justice statistics, most schools have no serious violence in a typical year. Despite a public perception that schools are increasingly dangerous, schools are really becoming safer—the crime rate in schools dropped by about a third from 1993 to 1999.[4]

Still, children become fearful, and they rely on their caregivers to help restore their sense of safety and security. If children are in schools and neighborhoods where violence is more common, they need tips on how to keep safe and support in dealing with their fears. Here are some ways parents and teachers can help minimize children's fear of violence:

1. **Develop open communication.** Encourage your children to talk about their fears. It does not help to tell them, "Don't be scared." Instead, validate their feelings and let them know you think their questions and concerns are important.

2. **Provide reassurance.** Let your children know you love them and that they don't have to face their fears alone. Give straight-forward information about events or situations that may be frightening them. If you don't know the answer, be honest. For example, if a child asks, "Why does that sniper want to kill children?" you can reply, "I don't really know why. Maybe he's very angry about something and doesn't know a better way to handle his angry feelings. We can't always know why people do things like that." Then offer reassurance: "I will do everything possible to keep you safe."

3. **Monitor the media.** Set limits for your children on exposure to television shows, movies, and electronic media that display violence. Join with them in watching the news and other shows that discuss current events, and talk about how the violence in the world affects real people like them. If you see them imitating violent actions they've seen on a screen and laugh about them, that is another good occasion to talk about how violence is very painful and real.

4. **Help children find ways to express their feelings.** Making drawings, playing with toys, journaling, or writing poems are ways they can "talk" about their fears. Let them tell you about what they have created.

5. **Help children reach and communicate with others.** Let them know how to write a letter to the President or to a newspaper about their thoughts on any violence that upsets them.

6. **Let children know your own feelings.** Show them that it is a natural reaction to become anxious and fearful when something violent happens. Be sure to offer some reassurances as well—to yourself and your children, which will teach them that fear does not have to be crippling.

Here are some affirmations you and your child can both say to counter fears of violence:

Affirmations for Reducing Fear of Violence

It's okay to be afraid when something violent happens.

I can take precautions to be safe.

I can help make my world a safer place.

There are people who can help me if I don't feel safe.

I can figure out what to do if I have a problem.

I am very safe almost all of the time.

IN ACTION

Ms. Kneitzke reminds her fifth graders that there are very few times when something violent and dangerous actually happens. She asks them to think about this question, "What percent of the day are you directly affected by violence?" Then she encourages them to say to themselves, "Mostly I'm safe. I have friends who can help me, and I can ask my parents and teachers for help."

Fear of Animals

The fear of animals is a universal childhood fear. The most common animal fears are those of dogs and of bugs (bees, wasps, spiders). Other phobias include fear of snakes, rats, mice, lizards, and cats.

Educating the child about various animals is a first step in reducing these fears. For example, you can explain that most insects and animals try to avoid people. Some insects land on kids, but they usually fly away. Bees don't sting unless you accidentally step on them. Dogs bark because that's how they talk. Their loud talk may be annoying, but it won't hurt. In addition, you can help the child distinguish between harmless and harmful animals in your area (for example, poisonous vs. nonpoisonous snakes), and teach them how to protect themselves to avoid being harmed.

If the child is afraid of a pet you want to own, start with gradual exposure. Let the child watch you as you handle the puppy. In extreme cases, use systematic desensitization (see page 105). Once the pet moves in, teach the child to approach and pet it in a way that is respectful and nurturing. A dog is less likely to bite and a cat less likely to scratch when gently handled.

The following affirmations can help a child to distinguish between appropriate and exaggerated fears of animals:

Affirmations for Reducing Fear of Animals and Bugs
(Said by the adult to the child)

I understand your fear of dogs (or any other animal).

Dogs are loud and scary, but a dog behind the fence won't bite you.

Dogs do many nice things for people.

Spiders are icky looking, but most don't bite.

You can tell the difference between animals that can hurt and those that can't.

When you feel scared, you can think about something pleasant.

If something happens that's a problem, you can get help.

IN ACTION

Manny was afraid of dogs. On the way to school, he had to pass by a house with a large German shepherd in the backyard. Even though the dog couldn't jump over the fence, he barked so loud that Manny was petrified. As a result, Manny walked three blocks out of his way going to and from school.

Manny's dad, with the help of the school counselor, set up the following program to help Manny overcome this fear:

- First, the father walked in front of the house where the dog lives. He also went up to the fence and showed Manny that the dog couldn't get out.

- Next, he and Manny walked across the street from the house together. He said to Manny, "It's okay to feel a little nervous right now. This dog is dangerous and it could hurt us if it were out of the fence. But it is behind the fence and he can't get out."

- Next, they walked by the house but on the same side of the street as the dog. While he was walking with his dad, Manny did the following to take his mind off the fear:

  * He breathed deeply.

  * He thought about his favorite song.

  * He imagined that Superman was walking by his side.

  * He practiced saying, "I am safe from this dog. My dad is here to protect me if something happens."

- Finally, Manny walked by the house by himself on the far side of the street, and then on the near side as his dad watched. To celebrate his accomplishment, Manny's family had his favorite meal for dinner. Manny never grew to like barking dogs, but he was able to reduce his fear of them.

Nighttime Fears

Nighttime fears pose a common problem for children and their families. In many respects, fear of the dark is cultural. In Western culture, dark represents the unconscious, the unknown, the irrational—things we are taught to fear.

Along with fear of the dark, children have fears about monsters, shadows, noises, robbers, or anything that disrupts their peace of mind and sleep at night. Here are some strategies to help your child overcome these nighttime fears:

1. **Teach her what is harmful and what isn't.** One mother told her daughter, "Shadows or noises in the dark can be scary, but they don't hurt you."

2. **Show her that there are things she can do to protect herself.** Before sleep, help her check for monsters under the bed, in the closet, behind the curtains, and in the toy box—to demonstrate that they are not present. The child can sleep with her nightlight on and the door open. If the child is still frightened, she can call you and get the reassurance she needs, or turn on the room lights to scare away the monsters. In other words, she can take action to deal with the fears.

3. **Teach her to breathe deeply and imagine a scene in which she is secure and happy.** At the same time, she lies down in her bed and slowly tenses and relaxes each major muscle group in the body. The child may also wish to repeat a soothing affirmation such as "I am safe and well."

4. **Create a game in which you and your child use a flashlight or other light source to project images on the wall of a dark room.** Your child uses her hands, stuffed animals, or other familiar objects to create these shadow images. The child tries to guess which shadows belong to which objects. Then, if she sees shadows during the night, she will experience them as part of the game.

Sleeping time can also be disrupted by nightmares which arise out of fearful events and experiences that took place during the day. If you are aware of such an event, have your child talk it out before bedtime. This will decrease the chance that the trauma will be processed in the dreams. You can also teach your child to give herself a "signal," such as tucking in her stuffed animal next to her or gently massaging her own tummy, that it's time for sleep.

Affirmations for Reducing Nighttime Fears

(Said by the adult to the child)

It's okay to feel afraid of the dark.

I felt scared as a child, too.

Let's look under the bed so we can see there are no monsters there.

There are things that seem scary that probably will never bother you.

(Said by the child to herself)

I can go to bed alone.

When I get in bed, my whole body feels wonderful.

I think of something nice to help me relax.

As soon as I give my body the signal, it starts to go to sleep.

My family and I are safe.

If something bad happens, I know what to do.

I can call 9-1-1 in an emergency.

God is protecting me (for those with a spiritual orientation).

IN ACTION

Two months after her family moved to a new house, Minda, a fifth grader, became afraid to go to sleep in her room for fear that a stranger would break in and hurt her and her parents. Minda's grandmother had been mugged recently, and her new house was burglarized shortly after the family had moved in.

continued ⟶

Minda's Fearful Self-Talk

Something bad will happen to me if I close my eyes.

I can't go to sleep.

Minda went to see her school counselor. The counselor involved Minda in art activities aimed at understanding her fears, taught her how to do whole-body relaxation, and helped her memorize affirmations that she could repeat each evening before bedtime. These affirmations were:

Minda's Affirmations

I am capable of handling anything that happens in the night.

I am intelligent and strong and can figure out what to do.

The chances of someone breaking in during the night are very, very small.

After six weeks of counseling, Minda announced that she was ready to "stop being weird about bedtime." She was consistently going to bed by 9:30 P.M. Minda and her parents celebrated her achievement by going out to dinner.

Fear of the Doctor or Dentist

The idea of getting a shot, having a cavity filled, or being hospitalized can be terrifying thoughts for a young child. As adult caregivers, we can assist the child to cope with fear of medical and dental experiences in a variety of ways:

- **Educate the child** about the upcoming experience. Tell her in your own words, or read a book to her about going to the doctor, dentist, or hospital.

- If the child is going to have a painful procedure done, such as getting a shot or having a cavity filled, it is helpful to **have her first experience the environment in a nonpainful, nonthreatening way,** for example, by playing with the toys in the waiting room or having the doctor show her the stethoscope she's using. Such experiences build trust between the child and the care provider so that when the time arrives for the shot, the child is much less afraid.

- **Tell the truth** about the pain. You can say, "This will hurt a little while, but it probably won't bother you a lot."

- **Role-play.** Pretend you are the dentist and the child is the patient. Then reverse roles.

- **Do a guided visualization** in which your child sees herself having a positive experience at the doctor's.

- When a painful procedure arises, your child can **use specific techniques to lessen the discomfort.** These include:

  * focusing on the breath

  * recalling a happy experience

  * thinking about a favorite place to play or a favorite location in nature

  * humming a favorite song

  * creating her own pain to focus on instead of the pain caused by the medical procedure. Pressing a fingernail to her flesh is one way to accomplish this.

Ultimately, the best way to insure that your child has a positive, trusting, nonfearful relationship with her doctor or dentist is to talk with her openly and honestly about the situation. The following affirmations will start you off in the right direction:

Affirmations for Reducing Fear of the Doctor or Dentist

(Said by the adult to the child)

Going to the dentist/doctor will help you stay strong and healthy.

This shot will be over quickly.

This shot/filling may hurt at first, and then the pain goes away.

Everyone feels the drill differently, but it doesn't usually hurt.

(Said by the child to herself)

The dentist/doctor is gentle and kind.

She is helping my teeth/body stay healthy.

This filling may hurt now, but it will help me so I can chew that apple later.

I can relax and breathe when I am at the dentist/doctor.

This shot may hurt now, but it will keep me from getting the measles.

I can think of a happy image.

I can hear a happy song in my mind.

Affirmations for Going to the Hospital

(Said by the adult to the child)

You are going to the hospital so you can feel better.

It's not your fault you got sick.

You can tell someone how you are feeling if you feel sad, angry, or scared.

continued→

> In the hospital, there are people who will listen to you and answer your questions.

(Said by the child to herself)

> I am going to the hospital to get well.

> It's scary, but I can handle it.

> My mom and dad will be nearby.

> There are nurses I can call if I need help.

> I can bring my favorite stuffed animal to the hospital.

> My friends can visit me.

IN ACTION

Annika was going to the dentist for the first time. When told about the upcoming visit, she cried, "Mommy! I don't want to go." Her parents explained to Annika who the dentist was and how he helps children have strong and healthy teeth. They told Annika, "When your teeth get sick, your whole body feels bad." Finally, they read her several children's books about going to the dentist. On the day of the appointment, her father gave her the affirmation: "The dentist is my friend. He helps my teeth stay healthy." Her mother also said, "I know that going to the dentist is scary. You don't know what will happen. But I will be there in the room to keep you company. You can also bring one of your stuffed animals to keep you company. Would you like to bring Bubba, your stuffed bear, or Precious the rabbit?"

By giving Annika a choice about which animal to take, her parents helped her make an active move toward going to the dentist, and hence gave her power over the fearful situation.

continued——▶

Annika's Positive Self-Talk

The dentist helps me stay well.

I can take my stuffed animal.

Mommy will be there with me.

IN ACTION

Seven-year-old Marshall was visiting the doctor and was about to receive a booster shot. He knew it would hurt. Staring at the needle, he cried out, "I don't want to have a shot!"

Marshall's mother reflects his fear back to him and then offers support: "It sounds like you are afraid of seeing the doctor. I know that the shots hurt last time. But I will stay with you, and you can squeeze my hand.

"Close your eyes and take a deep breath. You've gotten shots before and you made it through okay. I know you can do it again. When this is over, we can find something that will help you feel better."

Marshall's Positive Self-Talk

I need to get this shot.

I can handle getting the shot.

It will only hurt for a little bit.

My mom will be with me.

Supporting the Adult Caregivers

Having a child who is sick or hurt presents a unique challenge for adult caregivers. Aside from the normal worry and concern that parents feel, the crisis can bring up painful memories of childhood illnesses and the fears that accompanied them—specifically the fear of abandonment. Therefore, parents as well as children need to be reassured. The following affirmations will help to provide this much-needed support:

Affirmations for the Adult Caregivers

(Said by the parent to herself)

Sickness is a part of childhood.

I am giving my child the best care I know.

I feel good about the medical care my child is receiving.

I can talk about my feelings with my partner or friends.

I am taking care of myself during this time.

My child and I can both cope with this.

School Phobia

School phobia is defined as an extreme fear of school in which the child avoids school at all costs. Symptoms include crying, pleading, malingering, or faking illness in order to stay home. If made to go to school, the child will feel sick, whine, and ask to call home.

School phobia generally occurs at one of three times during a child's school career: (1) at the onset of formal education, (2) during the shift to middle or junior high school, or (3) at the end of compulsory education.

To help a child overcome school phobia, find out what upsets her about school (for example, problems getting along with other kids, academic difficulties, conflict with the teacher), and then talk to her about it. If the fear is extreme, you can consult the school counselor. In some cases, children are worried about some problem at home, such as domestic violence or the serious illness of a parent, and fear that bad things will happen when they are at school.

In addition to using techniques described earlier such as systematic desensitization (see page 105), the parent, teacher, or school counselor can use affirmations to reassure children that:

- School is safe.

- She is welcomed by the teacher and the children.

- All is well at her home.

If these conditions do not exist, then the adult witness should do what she can to remedy the situation.

Affirmations to Heal School Phobia
(Said by the adult to the child)

It's okay to feel afraid of school.

There are rules at school that will keep you safe.

There are adults who will look after you.

You can learn to read.

You can meet new friends.

I am doing fine at home.

IN ACTION

Haneef, a beginning first grader, is afraid of going to school. Using the technique of systematic desensitization (see page 105), Haneef and his counselor took the following steps over a twenty-day period:

- They sat in a car together in front of the school.
- They approached the school steps.
- They approached the door.
- They entered the building.
- They approached the classroom a certain distance each day down the hall.
- They entered the empty classroom.
- They sat in the classroom with the teacher.
- They sat in the classroom with the teacher and two classmates.
- They sat in the classroom with the teacher and the entire class.

During this time, Haneef also repeated many of the affirmations listed in the previous section, as well as his favorite: "I am safe, I am loved." Haneef gradually overcame his phobia.

IN ACTION ➡

Seven-year-old Andrea and her family moved to a new town in the middle of the school year. The day before she was to begin at the new school, Andrea expressed fears that the kids would not be her friends because she was new.

After Andrea finished speaking, her mother immediately acknowledged and validated her daughter's fear. "It's okay to feel scared," her mother said. "You are starting a new situation in a new town. Here are some things you can say to yourself that will help the fear go away." Then she gave Andrea two affirmations: "I am a likable person" and "I make friends easily." Andrea and her mother practiced the affirmations together.

The next morning, at Andrea's request, her mother accompanied her to school and spent the first two hours of the day sitting in the classroom. This helped Andrea to feel secure in the new setting. When the first recess bell rang, Andrea said to her mom, "I feel fine now. You can go if you want to."

After school Andrea's mother commended her for her courage. "I know that was a scary situation for you. But you felt the fear and went to school anyway." Later that evening, Andrea announced, "You don't have to come to my class tomorrow. I'm okay by myself now. My teacher's really nice, and so are the kids."

Addressing the Parent's Anxious State

From our study of family systems, we know that a child's anxieties never exist in isolation. A child who is anxious about starting school is often expressing the parent's own anxiety about her child separating from her. One mother insisted on walking her child from home to the classroom, taking off the child's coat, and remaining until class started. Clearly it was the mother who was fearful about the separation.

Many teachers find it helpful to explain to the parent that once she leaves, the child usually becomes engrossed with the other kids and activities and forgets that her parent is gone. In the meantime, the following affirmations can help the parent to cope with her anxiety.

Parent's Anxious Self-Talk	Parent's Healing Affirmation
I worry about my child.	My child is in good hands.
She seems so upset right now.	I can always call to check on things.
I'm concerned the staff doesn't know her yet.	The teacher will tell me if there are any problems.
I feel guilty for leaving her.	I am a good parent.
What will I do by myself?	I can be home alone today without my child.
	I can find activities that are meaningful to me.
	I can reach out for support.

In addition to the use of affirmations, you can employ therapies such as "inner child" dialogue to work through the separation anxiety that you have carried over from your own childhood. This involves remembering the feelings you had when you were a child, giving those feelings a "voice" through journaling or other ways, and offering reassurances to that still-frightened "child" within yourself.

The Teacher's Role in Welcoming the Child

Once the anxious child begins school, her teacher can do a great deal to help her feel she belongs. She can begin the day by greeting the child and saying the following affirmation: "It's good to see you. I'm glad you're in my class. I'm glad you're here."

The child who receives this type of personal attention feels acknowledged and validated. A touch, a smile, a "hello" is all it takes. I call this policy "three strokes a day." Try to give each child some type of positive feedback—a comment, a touch, a smile, a kind word—three times a day. This strategy works not only for the first week of school, but during the entire year. When children feel welcomed and appreciated, they blossom and flourish.

Fear of Social Interaction

One of a child's greatest fears is the fear of being excluded by her peers. Children with low self-esteem or a history of being teased feel especially vulnerable to rejection. Rather than risk shame and humiliation, they withdraw and develop a self-imposed isolation. No doubt you remember such a child from your school years; or perhaps you were that child.

The key to healing this fear lies in teaching a child to love herself. This means giving her unconditional acceptance and then helping her to internalize it by using self-esteem affirmations ("I like myself," "Other people like me"). If the child feels there is something specific about her (looks, intelligence, social class) that will cause other children to reject her, you can help her to affirm and accept those aspects of herself.

Once a child feels genuinely appreciated by at least two people (you and herself), she'll be far more likely to risk reaching out to others.

IN ACTION

Some children seem to set themselves up for rejection by pursuing kids who don't want to be with them. The child reasons (unconsciously), "No one could really like me, so I'll go out and prove it."

After Deion repeatedly complained to his counselor because James wouldn't play with him, his counselor replied, "You say you want to play with other kids and you're upset because they say no. Sounds to me like you are picking the wrong people." Then she gave Deion the following affirmations:

Deion's Affirmations

> I can ask the right people to be my friends.

> I choose to be with kids who want to be with me.

Another piece of advice the counselor gave was: "Don't ask to join the group activity. Just go up to the kids and say, 'Hi. I'm joining the game.' You'll be surprised how most of the time they will let you right in." Deion took her advice and got in line to play soccer. When it came to be his turn to go in, no one objected.

What to Say When You Are Sad: Positive Talk for Coping with **Loss, Divorce,** and **Depression**

> Grieving is a normal, healthy activity. Grieving is something that human beings must do in order to survive losses.
>
> *Alla Bozarth-Campbell, author and poet*

Two years ago Tom's father died. Tom, age sixteen, sulks in his room, leaving only to eat meals and attend school. His grades have gone from very good to poor. Recently, he and a friend broke into school and damaged school property.

Nine-year-old Jan's mother died when she was seven. Since then, she has been accident- and illness-prone. She told a counselor, "My friends are still mad at me for crying about my mom. They feel I should be over it by now. I've been getting hurt a lot. I don't know why."

Seven-year-old Susan has been "parenting" her mom and four-year-old brother for fourteen months since her dad died in a train accident. One day, during show and tell, Susan began to sob and said that she wanted her mommy to be a mommy again so that she could be the little girl.

These children are reacting to the trauma of loss of a parent. Other losses include:

- loss of a relative (grandparent, sibling, cousin, aunt or uncle)
- loss of a friend (through a move or death)
- loss of a pet (through death, running away, or having to give the pet away)

- loss through a move
- loss of a love (break up of a significant relationship)
- loss of health
- loss of function of a body part
- loss of parent through divorce

The Effects of Loss

Facing loss is particularly tough on children. In the wake of loss, a child will act out, lose concentration, do poorly in school, break rules, whine, withdraw, exhibit hair-trigger emotions, or become the "hero" child. Children also develop a variety of physiological reactions to loss. These include tiredness, sleep difficulties, appetite disturbances, stomachaches, tightness in the chest, sighing, hiccupping, skin rashes, general debilitation, and loss of muscle strength.

With the proper support, children can work through their feelings about the trauma. On the other hand, when children are not supported in working through their loss, they exhibit psychological problems later in life. One study has linked teenage suicide to unresolved early childhood loss. As Swiss therapist Alice Miller states:

> It is not the trauma itself that is the source of illness but the unconscious, repressed hopeless despair over not having been able to give expression to what one has suffered and the fact that one is not allowed to show and is unable to experience feelings of rage, anger, humiliation, despair, helplessness and sadness.[1]

Dimensions of a Child's Grief

Like adults, children experience many feelings when they grieve. These feelings may occur in any order and may show up repeatedly.

One of the first reactions to loss is shock or denial—either not recognizing the loss or minimizing its impact. Common statements reflecting denial are, "Mom and dad will get back together" and "My mom is not going to die."

Another major feeling that children experience is fear—fear of their future safety and well-being, especially if the loss involves a primary caregiver. The child will then wonder, "What's going to happen to me? Who will take care of me? How will I get my needs met?"

Sadness is a universal feeling connected with loss. The hurt a child feels is a natural consequence of the rupture of a close, bonded relationship.

In addition, a child feels anger at having been left and abandoned. Especially when a parent or other primary caregiver dies, he may think, "How could you leave me? You know my life depends on you. You were supposed to take care of me and now you're gone!"

Children also engage in bargaining. By promising to do something or to be better, they hope to reverse the loss. A child will think, "If I love my daddy enough, he will get well" or "If I'm a good boy, maybe my dog won't have to die."

Children's self-oriented outlook also leads them to feel responsible for the loss. Self-statements include, "If only I were better, maybe my parents would have stayed together," "It's my fault; I must be unlovable," and "I got angry at someone and he died; I guess I caused it."

Factors That Support a Child's Grieving

A number of factors contribute to a child's healthy grieving experience:

- The child has a healthy relationship with the primary family.

- The child gets immediate and accurate information from adults. Children can handle the facts better than we think. What has happened should be clearly addressed. Avoid vague phrases like "lost" or "passed away."

- The child is able to participate in closure or completion such as final rites.

- Above all, children need the support of at least one comforting, reassuring adult who is a stable presence and tells the truth. This is the adult witness we spoke of in Chapter 4 (see page 29).

The Role of the Supportive Adult

Here are some ways you can support a child going through grief:

- Invite the child to ask questions and to talk about his feelings. Don't assume you know how he feels.

- Discuss your own feelings. If you shield the child from your own grief, you are telling him, "These feelings are bad." When you cry, you model healthy grieving for the child.

- Explain that life is a series of "hellos and good-byes." Grieving is a normal, healthy, healing activity that helps us to survive loss and say good-bye to people and things we love.

- Let the child know that he is not unusual for having these feelings; they are normal and to be expected.

- Let the child know that he can take as much time as he needs to move through his grief. Too often kids are hurried in their grieving and told, "Don't feel bad" and "Why are you taking so long to get over it?"

- Because sadness is the "healing feeling," the child's grief will eventually lead to closure if allowed to unfold without interference. While it is tempting to jump in and try to fix the pain, the best thing you can do for a grieving child is just to reassure him that you are there for him.

- Monitor your own anxiety and fears that are triggered by loss. Ask yourself, "In what ways do I feel uncomfortable talking to children about death?" If you feel uneasy, you can say to the child, "I get scared thinking about death, and it's hard for me to talk about it." The child will understand.

- It's okay to admit "I don't know why Daddy died" or "I don't know why your friend died."

- Reassure the child that this pain won't last forever.

If you are the witness to a child in grief, here are some affirmations you can say to yourself to support you in your healing role:

Positive Self-Talk for the Adult Witness

(Said by the adult to himself)

I am a comforting, stable presence in this child's life.

I listen to what the child has to tell me.

continued⟶

> I support the child to go through the grieving process.

> I have faith in the natural healing process.

> I am secure and compassionate enough to let the child feel his pain.

Positive Self-Talk for the Grieving Child

Affirmations can support a child through the grieving process in a number of ways:

- They can give him permission to fully feel his grief.

- They can help him to realize that what he lost will always be a part of him.

- They can remind him that eventually the pain does subside, that "this, too, shall pass."

If the child is grieving over a death, you can tailor the affirmations to match the child's perception of death. From birth to age four, kids are relatively ignorant of the meaning of death. From age four to seven, they see it as reversible and temporary. After age seven, they see it as irreversible and final.

You can also adapt the affirmations to fit with the child's spiritual understanding of death. Most children believe that we come from someplace before life and go somewhere else after death. Thus, an affirmation like "My mom knows that I'm doing okay" would be appropriate.

An Important Reminder

Affirmations are most effective if they are used after the child's initial shock and grief has begun to subside. If used too early in the grieving process, affirmations can talk children out of their feelings and get them stuck in denying or minimizing the pain. Hence, they should be used in the middle and late stages of grieving.

Grieving the Loss of a Pet

The death of a pet is often a child's first encounter with loss. Such was the case for Dorothy, a fifth grader, when her beloved cat Abbey was hit by a car. The following affirmations were used by Dorothy and her parents after the cat's death. Note that the affirmation for getting a new pet is placed at the end of the list, indicating that it is to be used later on in the grieving process.

Affirmations for Grieving the Loss of a Pet
(Said by the adult to the child)

I'm sad Abbey died. I miss her.

Cats are like people; they have to die.

Abbey is in heaven and her pain is gone.

She will always be a part of you.

There will never be a cat like Abbey, but you can learn to love your new cat.

Grieving the Loss of a Friend or Sibling

The ultimate consolation about the loss of a friend or sibling is that once we love someone, that person lives forever in our heart. Our love for another stimulates chemical changes in the body that are imbedded at a cellular level. The experience of that person is literally a part of us.

Many of the affirmations to help a child cope with the loss of a childhood friend can be directly adapted from the previous section. Some of these affirmations listed below were used to help a child grieve for her sister, Sylvia:

Affirmations for Grieving the Loss of a Friend or Sibling
(Said by the child to himself)

I miss Sylvia.

I feel sad about Sylvia dying.

continued———▶

> There are people I can talk to about my feelings.

> I'm glad that Sylvia was in my life.

> Sylvia will always be a part of me.

Grieving the Death of a Parent

A child's survival is directly tied to his parents. How could he not feel utterly abandoned and forsaken at the thought of their death? Although nothing can totally assuage the pain of losing a parent, we can reassure the child that someone will be there to care for him.

When a parent dies, it is important for the surviving parent or other primary caregiver to have a good support system in place. Otherwise, the surviving adult may unconsciously expect the child to take over the role of the deceased parent. Comments such as, "You're the woman (or the man) of the house now; I'm really depending on you," create an inappropriate bonding between the surviving adult and child. While all children can take on extra chores and provide some emotional support for the grieving parent or other caregiver, no child can take on the adult role without serious psychological and emotional consequences taking place.

Another problem occurs when the surviving parent chooses to remarry. Often the children resist accepting the new spouse for fear of being disloyal to the deceased parent. In other instances, they don't want to go through one more change after having been through such a major adjustment. Here are some affirmations that honor the child's feelings of loss while assuring him that loving a new parent does not mean being disloyal to the one who has died:

Affirmations for Grieving the Death of a Parent
(Said by the adult to the child)

> I'm sad your mom (dad) died.

> I miss your mom (dad), too.

> Your family will continue although it will be different.

continued⟶

> Together, we can handle this.

> I am getting the support I need.

> I know that my remarrying reminds you of how much you miss your mom (dad).

> It's okay to continue to miss your mom (dad).

> You can love your new stepparent and still be loyal to your mom (dad) who died.

Please refer to the sections on divorce later in this chapter for more affirmations on learning to accept a stepparent (pages 144–146).

Coping with a Move

A loss that virtually all children face is that of moving. While children vary in their ability to adapt to a change in residence, all feel the loss and abandonment that comes with being removed from their source of security. These feelings may also arise when someone else, such as a good friend, moves and the child feels the grief of being left behind.

After nine-year-old Keith began to act out at school, the school counselor called in his parents for a conference.

"Has anything stressful been happening at home?" she asked.

"Nothing too bad," the father replied. "We just moved, but it was only across town. And Keith's pet cat died, but he was pretty old."

While a move and the death of a pet seemed like minor disruptions to the father, they were traumatic to Keith. Here are some affirmations that Keith's counselor used to help him adapt to these changes:

Affirmations for Coping with a Move
(Said by the child to himself)

> My old house was special, and I'll always remember it.

> I can always write or call my friends.

continued ⟶

I am excited about my new place to live.

I am excited about meeting new people and making new friends.

Grieving the Loss of a Love

Breaking up is hard to do—especially when one is young. Without the life experience to put a breakup in perspective, the loss of a romantic relationship can overwhelm a teenager. Please refer to Chapter 17 for specific affirmations for dealing with the effects of a breakup.

Grieving for the Loss of Health or Loss of a Body Part

As we move through life, there will be times when we experience loss of health through an illness or accident. While major health crises usually arise in the latter stages of life, children also face their share of injuries and sickness, and some have long-term physical disabilities (see Chapter 18).

IN ACTION

Thirteen-year-old Marina was the star athlete of her eighth-grade class. One day she severely injured her knee in a fall. She realized that she would have to discontinue her sports activities—track, tennis, and field hockey. Because her creativity was expressed through her athletic pursuits, Marina experienced an identity crisis. A part of herself died—and with this death came great grief.

Marina and her school counselor created these affirmations:

Marina's Healing Affirmations

(Said by the counselor to Marina)

You can go on with your life.

It makes sense that you miss the presence of sports in your life.

You can find new talents to express.

continued——▶

(Said by Marina to herself)

I am sad that my athletic career is over.

I can learn to develop new talents and interests.

I still have a lot to give.

I have a lot to look forward to.

It is not an easy task for a child to shed her identity and find a brand new way of defining herself. Through counseling and the use of affirmations, Marina learned to accept this loss and redefined her life and purpose.

Dealing with the Loss That Comes with Divorce or Permanent Separation

With the possible exception of the death of a parent, the divorce or permanent separation of a child's parents is the most traumatic event he can face. While parents may choose not to be together, children need both of their parents all of the time. This is why even years after the divorce or separation, children fantasize about their mom and dad getting back together again.

The impact of their parents splitting up varies with the age and emotional makeup of the child. Children whose parents divorced when they were two or three report not remembering much and accepting the fact that mom and dad lived separately. On the other hand, preteens and teenagers usually experience their parents' divorce with great anguish.

As in any loss, the three primary emotions that children feel in response to divorce or permanent separation are (1) fear, (2) sadness, and (3) anger. Let's explore the role of affirmations in helping children cope with these and other difficult emotions they face.

Dealing with Fears About Divorce or Permanent Separation

A child experiences the breakup of a family as a direct threat to his survival. His initial response to this survival threat is fear—specifically the fear of being abandoned. He may think to himself, "Please don't go. I'll do anything if you don't split up. You're all I have. If you leave I won't be able to sleep, I won't be able to eat, I won't be able to think, I won't be able to do anything. There will be nobody to take care of me. I will die if you leave me."

As the supportive adult witness, you can reassure the child that he will survive and will not be abandoned by the adult world. The affirmations listed below are designed to provide this reassurance and comfort:

Affirmations for the Child's Fears About Divorce
(Said by the adult to the child)

I'm sad your mom and dad split up.

You will survive.

People love you and they will take care of you.

You will live with mommy or daddy.

Your dad (mom) loves you even if he only sees you twice a month.

Dealing with Sadness About Divorce or Permanent Separation

Another powerful emotion that a child feels when mom and dad split up is sadness. Because sadness is the healing feeling, we need to give a child permission to experience this natural part of the grieving process. Injunctions such as "Don't cry," "Don't get upset," and "Be a brave boy" only serve to disrupt the grief experience. Please refer to the affirmations earlier in the chapter that give the child permission to feel his sadness (see pages 133–135).

Dealing with Anger About Divorce or Permanent Separation

Part of a child's frustration and helplessness about being left comes out as anger. If that anger were put into words it might say, "How dare you do this to me. Why did you even have me if you didn't know how to get along? Not only are you splitting my world apart, you are fighting in front of me and using me as a Ping-Pong ball. I'm furious at you. I'd like to call the police and the judge and force you to get along and get back together."

By using affirmations to acknowledge and validate this legitimate anger, we can help the child to express his feelings of anger constructively rather than acting them out or turning them in on himself:

Affirmations for a Child's Anger

(Said by the adult to the child)

You must feel very angry about your mom and dad splitting up.

I want to hear about your anger.

I might be angry, too, if I were you.

You can beat a pillow to vent your anger.

You can go outside and run as fast as you can.

(Said by the child to himself)

It's okay to be angry when I feel hurt.

I can be mad at mom and dad.

I can let out my anger without hurting anyone.

It feels good to express how angry I feel.

Dealing with Guilt About Divorce or Permanent Separation

Many children feel responsible for their parents' breakup. They believe it happened because of them ("If only I had been better, they would have stayed together") or that they can bring their parents back together ("If I messed the marriage up, I can correct it").

Sometimes a child will withdraw or get in trouble in order to become the focus that holds the parents' relationship together. Even kids from healthy families take on the responsibility for their parents' emotional state. The following affirmations will help the child see that he is not responsible for his parents' breakup:

Affirmations to Help a Child Release His Guilt
(Said by the adult to the child)

It's not your fault that mom and dad can't get along.

Even before you were born, we had problems.

Moms and dads are responsible for their relationship.

Kids don't cause divorces, parents do.

You are still loved.

Helping Parents Release Their Own Guilt

Parents also feel guilty about the failure of their relationship with their spouse or partner. They know that splitting up is causing their children to suffer. Here are some affirmations to help parents cope with their pain when they see their children in distress:

Affirmations to Help a Parent Release His Own Guilt
(Said by the parent to himself)

I love my children and will continue to love them.

I can work with my ex-partner to meet my children's needs.

I can give my children accurate and compassionate information about the divorce.

I love my children enough to keep them out of disputes with my spouse.

My children will survive this.

Dealing with the Shame About Divorce or Permanent Separation

No child likes to feel different, odd, or strange. Yet despite the realities of single parenthood, our cultural myths still present the two-parent family as the ideal unit. Consequently, a child sees the parents' breakup as a sign that his family is defective and that he is defective. He thinks, "If my family doesn't measure up, then I don't measure up; I am different. I am a misfit. I am damaged goods because my parents broke up."

As a parent, you can affirm to your child that no matter what happens with his family, he is basically okay. Counselors or teachers can also use these affirmations with their clients or students who are undergoing a family transition.

Affirmations to Help a Child Release His Shame About Divorce or Permanent Separation

(Said by the adult to the child)

You are okay, even if your parents are breaking up.

You are still a great kid.

Your family is still fine; it's just going to be set up differently.

Many kids have parents who divorced.

You are not the only one going through this.

Learning to Accept the Stepparents

When one of a child's original parents remarries or has a new permanent partner, he may feel jealous or resentful. Prior to the stepparent's arrival, he received 100 percent of his parent's attention. Now he must share the parent with the new mate.

Even when the child likes the stepparent, he is frequently pulled in two directions. When Tim's mom remarried, Tim said, "I really like my new stepdad, Joe. He does a lot of things—hugging, touching, talking—that Dad didn't do." On the other hand, Tim believed that such feelings showed a disloyalty to his original dad.

To help Tim resolve his dilemma, Tim's dad gave Tim permission to feel close to the new stepparent. He said, "Timmy, I understand your feelings toward Joe. I'm glad you like him as your stepdad."

This type of affirmation can be given by the stepparent as well. Ideally, Joe will feel secure enough to say to Tim, "It's okay with me that your dad is important to you. I understand that he is still 'Dad' to you."

Such divided loyalties can also be experienced by children toward their grandparents. For example, Aaron's grandmother died suddenly. Soon afterwards, his grandfather began to date another woman and eight months later married her. Aaron was confused and angry at his grandfather for "forgetting" his grandmother so soon and marrying someone else. Aaron felt that if he acted nice to his grandfather's new wife, he would be disloyal to his grandmother who he loved very much.

The following affirmations can be used by both sets of parents or grandparents to assure the child that there is enough love to be shared by all:

Affirmations for Learning to Accept the Stepparents
(Said by the adult to the child)

It's okay for you to love your stepparent (said by the original parent).

It's okay that your dad is still "Dad" to you (said by the stepdad).

It's okay that your mom is still "Mom" to you (said by the stepmom).

You can love each of us in a different way (said by either parent).

It's okay to feel uncomfortable about having two dads and two moms.

continued ——▶

(Said by the child to himself)

It's okay for me to get close
to my new stepmom (or stepdad).

If I don't feel like getting close to my
new parent right now, that's okay.

I have a right to my feelings,
whatever they may be.

A Ritual for Divorce

While the wedding ritual celebrates the beginning of a marriage, we do nothing to honor its death. This lack of closure can keep the parents enmeshed and leave their children bewildered.

In response to this need for completion, Barbara Peeks, a child psychologist, created a ritual for divorce. In the presence of a counselor (or a third party), the parents come together and read to their children a list of fifteen statements that clearly describe the nature of their separation. The ritual's clarity and sense of finality allow both children and parents to grieve the loss and move on to the next step. Moreover, the public nature of the ritual makes it more likely that the commitments made by the parents will be honored.

Fifteen Things Parents Need to Say to Their Children About Divorce or Permanent Separation

1. We both love you and we will continue to love you.

2. You were conceived in love, and that will never change.

3. You did nothing to cause our breakup.

4. We will always help and protect you.

5. We cannot get back together as husband and wife.

6. We divorced as husband and wife but not as your mother and father.

7. We will communicate and work together on matters that involve you.

8. We will not say bad things about each other.

9. You will be able to visit all your grandparents, uncles and aunts, and they won't say bad things either.

10. You do not have to choose between us.

11. We will support each other's rules.

12. We want you to do well in school and in life.

13. We do not want you to have problems because we are divorced, and we do not want you to use divorce as an excuse.

14. We do not know all the details about the future, but we will tell you when we know.

15. You have our permission to love and to respect your stepparent.

Helping the Child Who Is Depressed

It wasn't too long ago that psychiatrists and psychologists believed that children did not get depressed. With increased awareness about depression, better diagnosis, and the advent of a new class of anti-depressants, that view has drastically changed. The American Academy of Child and Adolescent Psychiatry estimates that at least 3.4 million children under age eighteen suffer from depression.[2] Depression is a significant risk factor for suicide, and from 1980–1997, the rate of suicide increased by 11 percent among young people age 15–19 years; among children age 10–14 years, it increased by an alarming 109 percent.[3] Suicide is the third leading cause of death for adolescents and young adults.[4]

Children who suffer depression exhibit a wide variety of symptoms, sometimes making it hard to diagnose. Some kids with depression look like unhappy adults; they're sad, despondent, tearful, and have a loss of appetite. Others, however (especially boys), react in an opposite manner; they become aggressive, hyperactive, break rules, get in fights, and use drugs and alcohol. Moreover, depression in children often coexists with other problems such as learning disabilities, eating disorders, anxiety disorders, and substance abuse. In addition, 20 percent of children who have ADHD (attention deficit hyperactivity disorder) also have depression, and it is believed that these disorders may be genetically and neurologically related.[5]

Here is a list of symptoms of depression in children:

- They act badly or are irritable for no apparent reason. They are demanding and difficult to please. Since nothing makes them happy, they complain about everything. Their attitudes and behavior alienate the adults and peers around them.

- They frequently look sad, tired, ill, or tearful. They do not seem to have the usual amount of childhood energy and curiosity, or they lack the sense of humor and fun that most children have.

- They complain of not feeling good or of stomachaches, headaches, or other physical ills.

- They have little tolerance for frustration. They are easily stressed out and overwhelmed and tend to worry a lot or have exaggerated fears.

- They become upset, clingy, and overly dependent when they are separated from their parents.

- They may experience some form of regression, such as sucking their thumbs or wetting their pants.

- They lose interest in activities they used to enjoy, such as sports, hobbies, or attending clubs.

- They are overly shy and have difficulty making friends. They are nervous about interacting with others and may refuse to engage in social situations, or may become increasingly withdrawn.

- Their grades are declining.

- They talk of death and dying.

The problems of boys in our culture also can be focused on. At the turn of the millennium, boys in America drop out of school, are considered emotionally disturbed, and commit suicide four times as often as girls. They get in twice as many fights, commit ten times more murders, and are the victims of violent crime fifteen times more often. They are less likely than girls to go to college (because they haven't done as well in high school), are labeled "slow learners" and assigned to special education classes twice as often, and are far more likely to be labeled as having attention-deficit disorders and placed on powerful prescription drugs.[6]

One reason that boys are so much more at risk lies in the way they are socialized. As therapist Pia Mellody has said, "Boys in our culture are taught that real men are stoic. The ability to not complain, endure pain, and strive in the face of adversity is admired and celebrated in story and in song. The price paid for this isolation is depression."

If you suspect that your child or a child you work with may be depressed, the most important way you can be of support is to get the child into treatment with a qualified mental health professional. Identifying the problem is the first step in treatment, which usually consists of a combination of talk therapy and medications (although the younger the child, the more cautious one will want to be about using drug therapy). In addition, here are some words to say that will show your support for the child, while acknowledging the right to feel his feelings:

Affirmations for Coping with Depression
(Said by the adult to the child)

I love you!

You're not alone in this.

I'm sorry you are in so much pain.

Would you like to hold my hand and talk about it?

I am not going to leave you.

I am going to take care of myself, so you don't need to worry that your pain might hurt me.

You can get better. Help is available.

If you let me show you, I can find the right help for you.

You will not always feel this way.

This, too, shall pass.

You are important to me.

Depression and Teenagers

A cover story in *Newsweek* in 2002 focused national attention on the troubled world of a particular subset of children—teenagers.[7] It pointed out that millions of teens in America suffer from serious, untreated mood disorders, *especially depression.*

Here is a list of some of the classic symptoms of depression in adolescents:

- being ill-tempered, "touchy," overreactive, or difficult to get along with

- aggressive, disruptive, or delinquent behavior

- falling grades

- loss of interest in clubs, athletics, spending time with friends, or other activities they were formally interested in

- compulsive partying, boy or girl chasing, or thrill seeking; or they may be just the opposite—withdrawn, inhibited, and overly serious

- compulsive studying (never taking a break and relaxing) or compulsive exercising

- low self-worth and low self-esteem

- having unrealistic concerns that they are unattractive or are disliked by others

The increase in depression among teens is partially caused by the steady decline in the amount of time parents spend with their children. Two-thirds of school-age children have working parents who are often unavailable during the hours directly after school, leaving 35 percent of twelve-year-olds to fend for themselves. (Researchers call this the "3–6 P.M. teen alone zone."[8]) Of course, some parents have no choice but to leave their teens alone at home for periods of time, and many make good plans with their children to ensure their safety and well-being. But the parents' continual vigilance is important to tend to their children's needs and to be alert to potential problems. A University of Illinois study found that children who are unsupervised after school are more likely to use drugs and alcohol.[9] The FBI reports that during the "teen alone zone," youths are most likely to commit crime or be crime victims. It is also when they are most likely to commit suicide.[10]

Teenage Suicide

Suicide is the third leading cause of death among teenagers (after motor vehicle accidents and homicides).[11] Depression is the major risk factor for suicidal behavior in adolescents, as it is with adults. Children with mood disorders such as depression are more likely to commit suicide than children not affected by such problems. Other risk factors for suicide include:

- substance abuse (drugs and alcohol can exacerbate depression and increase the likelihood of impulsive behavior)

- previous suicide attempts (a person who tries once may try again)

- coexisting psychiatric conditions such as eating disorders

- significant losses and separations

- physical or sexual abuse

- conflict among family members

- family history of suicide

- poor social relationships

- the presence of a firearm in the home

- stressful life events.

Fortunately, clear markers often exist to indicate that a teenager is at risk for suicide. They include the following:

Verbal hints of impending suicide

- I won't be a burden to you much longer.

- Nothing matters. It's no use.

- I feel so alone.

- I wish I were dead.

- That's the last straw.

- I can't take it anymore.

- Nobody cares about me.

Changes in behavior

- accident proneness

- drug and alcohol abuse

- violence toward self, others, and animals

- dangerous or risky behavior

- loss of appetite

- sudden alienation from family and friends

- worsening performance in school

- dramatic highs and lows

- lack of sleep or excessive sleeping

- giving away valued possessions

- letters, notes, poems with suicidal content

Changes in life events

- death of a family member or friend, especially by suicide

- separation or divorce

- loss of an important relationship, including a pet

- public humiliation or failure

- serious physical illness

- getting in trouble with the law

Caring Adults and the Prevention of Suicide

The presence of one or more caring adults in the life of a suicidal adolescent—a person whom the child can turn to for advice—can decrease the likelihood of suicide 50 to 75 percent. Here is what a concerned adult can do when this advice is sought:

Listen

- Stay calm. Don't be outwardly shocked, as this may put distance between you and the child.

- Don't assume the teen is just trying to get attention. Don't try to argue him out of feeling suicidal.

- Show concern. Encourage the child to talk to you or some other trusted person.

- Allow for the full expression of feelings. Don't give advice or feel obligated to find simple solutions.

Share feelings

- Accept the child's feelings, letting him know that he is not alone.

- Discuss how you have felt when you were sad or depressed.

- Be nonjudgmental. Don't debate whether suicide is right or wrong.

- Don't challenge the teen to "go ahead and do it." It is possible that he might take your advice.

- Show interest and support.

Be honest

- Talk openly about suicide.

- If the child's words or actions scare you, tell him. If you're worried or don't know what to do, say so. Simply being a witness to the child's pain can promote healing.

- Offer hope that alternatives are available. Reassure the child that you know how to locate assistance.

Get help

- Don't be sworn to secrecy.

- Professional help is crucial. Assistance may be found from a local mental health clinic, school counselor, suicide prevention center, or family physician.

- Take action. Remove means of self-harm such as guns or pills. Call the National Hopeline Network: 1-800-784-2433.

- Stay close to the person until he is under professional care.

Despite the susceptibility to depression among young people, the good news is that once diagnosed, depression in children and teens is highly treatable. Most depressed children respond quite well to a combination of individual therapy, family therapy, and medication. In more serious cases, day treatment programs, home-based therapy, therapeutic foster care, and/or residential treatment are recommended. In addition, many of the coping strategies and affirmations discussed in this book can help children build their self-esteem and thus decrease their risk for mood disorders.

CHAPTER 10

What to Say When You Are Mad: Positive Talk for
Anger Management

One of the most difficult feelings for children (and most adults) to handle is anger. The difficulty reflects our cultural bias about anger—that it is a bad and undesirable emotion. This belief is passed on to children at an early age. Toddlerhood is called "the terrible twos" largely because of the child's anger. If a preschool child says to her parent in anger, "I hate you," she is severely chastised. In many religions, anger is frowned upon as "unspiritual" or "one of the seven deadly sins." Consequently, healthy anger is rarely encouraged or modeled for children.

When a child does express anger,s he will usually be invalidated in one of the following ways:

- "You shouldn't feel that way." (The anger is discounted.)

- "You're not really mad at your brother." (The anger is denied.)

- "Richard is a nice boy and he doesn't get mad." (He is compared to others.)

- "Don't be such a problem." (The anger is put down.)

Much of the vilification of anger arises out of a basic misunderstanding about its function and purpose. Anger is a basic human emotion we use to get our needs met. Anger enables us to say no and thus separate ourselves from others and become an autonomous being. If you hurt me and I get angry at you, that's my way of telling you not to repeat that behavior.

A child who cannot express her anger has no boundaries. People walk all over her, and she is less likely to say no to peer pressure as she gets older. Bottling up anger has other negative consequences. A counselor once asked a group of children what happens when anger is not allowed to be expressed:

Counselor: Does it go into outer space?

Children: No!

Counselor: Does it go into the ocean?

Children: No!

Counselor: Then where does it go?

Children: It goes inside you.

Counselor: And what happens if you don't express anger when you feel it?

Children: You will do something stupid later, or you will just feel bad.

As the children wisely noted, when anger is not felt and expressed in a healthy way, it gets inappropriately directed toward others (in words or with fists) or is turned inward. Here are some affirmations that children can use to validate their anger:

Affirmations for Validating Anger

(Said by the adult to the child)

You can be angry with me, and I will still love you.

It's okay to express your anger.

We can disagree and still be friends.

We can fight and make up.

(Said by the child to herself)

It's okay for me to feel angry.

My angry feelings are important.

I can get mad at mom and dad, and they will still be there for me.

Situations That Trigger Children's Anger

Three important feelings trigger anger in children—the feeling of being provoked, the feeling of frustration, and the feeling of being treated unfairly. Let's look at some examples of each.

Provocation

- Someone steals my ball.

- Someone cuts in front of me in line.

- My sister uses my toys without asking.

- Someone teases me about my weight.

- A friend breaks a promise.

Frustration

- I can't figure out that math formula.

- I can't get any help from the teacher.

- I strike out with the bases loaded.

- I want to be someone's friend and they don't want to be mine.

Unfairness

- I get passed over when the team is chosen.

- My parents won't let me stay up as late as I want.

- I am accused of cheating when I wasn't.

- The test is too hard.

- The ball was hit fair, but it's called foul.

Let's now look at these anger-producing situations in depth and see how children can handle their anger in a healthy and constructive way.

Responding to Provocation by Being Assertive

There are three ways that a child can respond to being provoked:

1. **Passive.** The child allows herself to be pushed around and taken advantage of. Underneath the compliant behavior she feels rageful and helpless. The anger she feels is turned inward.

2. **Aggressive.** The child responds in kind to the provoker. Aggressive behaviors include physical violence, hitting, and name-calling. The aggressive child is still a victim in that she allows herself to be provoked and thereby gives her power away. A second disadvantage to this stance is that when the child attacks, the provoker frequently retaliates.

3. **Assertive.** The child states her feelings, thoughts, and wishes and stands up for her rights without losing her cool, stuffing her anger, or violating the rights of others. She does this by using "I think," "I feel," and "I want" statements.

Being assertive not only allows a child to respond to provocations in a constructive way, it can prevent them from happening in the first place. Children who are seen as assertive by their peers are less likely to be picked on or harassed.

Assertive Self-Talk
(Said by the child to herself)

I can protect myself by being assertive.

I can stand up for myself.

I use "I" messages to tell others how I feel.

I can have angry feelings and not harm others.

I can feel anger and stay in control.

IN ACTION

One morning, Billy went to his normal position on the safety patrol. Instead of the supervising teacher, there were two bullies who told him, "You're not on safety patrol today. You're a nerd." Billy withdrew, feeling humiliated and angry.

Afterwards, Billy and his counselor talked it over. Together, they identified Billy's passive self-talk and rehearsed how he could respond differently next time.

continued ⟶

Billy's Passive Self-Talk	Billy's Assertive Self-Talk
I can't handle these kids.	I can stand up for myself.
I don't know what to do.	I will tell them how I am feeling.

The next day, Billy was confronted by the bullies. He responded, "That's not your decision to make. That's Miss Zampino's (the teacher). She said I'm on safety patrol, and that's what I'm doing."

A Four-Step Anger Management Process for Dealing with Provocation

Instead of reacting and regretting it later, there is a better way to cope with angry feelings. In between the stimulus (the provoking situation) and the response, a child can evaluate her options and make choices. This anger management process consists of four simple steps:

1. **Stop.** Stop what you are doing. Freeze in your tracks. Give yourself a time out. Some kids like to imagine a red stoplight.

2. **Breathe.** Take a few deep breaths and count to ten. Deep breathing brings oxygen into the bloodstream, which counteracts the adrenaline that is triggered by the anger. Breathing and counting also help to slow down the racing thoughts and angry feelings so that the situation can be evaluated from a calmer perspective.

3. **Think.** Ask yourself, "What would a smart kid do now? If I consider striking back, what are the consequences I will have to face?" This is the time to use affirmations such as "I choose to stay in control" or "I can overcome my fear and stand up for myself."

4. **Act.** After affirming your ability to stay calm, it is time to take action. The best options are to talk or walk—tell the other person how you feel, or simply leave the situation or get help.

Tell children that, if they choose the talk option, they can say, "I don't like it when you call me names. Stop that right now. Cut it out."

Explain that, if they choose to walk away and the other children make fun of them, they can say to themselves, "I don't have to pay attention to them," "I can keep my cool," or "When I don't name-call back, I'm in charge; I'm in control."

Please note that this process works best for children seven and older who have the cognitive skills to apply it. They will need to practice the technique a number of times before it becomes internalized. Initially, it is much more natural for children to react angrily than to think the situation through and choose to remain in control. Here are some affirmations that will help children to maintain their cool when they are provoked:

Affirmations for Responding to Provocation

(Before the provocation)

I can notice when I am becoming angry.

I can remember to count to ten and take deep breaths.

I can feel my anger and still stay in control.

I can talk things out with other people.

(During the provocation)

I notice that I am becoming angry.

I am counting to ten.

I am remembering to breathe deeply.

I am handling this well.

I am doing it!

(After the provocation)

I was able to be angry without exploding.

I remembered to use my affirmations.

It feels great to handle my anger.

I'm proud of myself.

Congratulating oneself after the incident is especially helpful. When children evaluate their behavior and give themselves praise, they are likely to repeat their successes.

Getting It Right the Second Time

It is scary for a child to be out of control. She feels bad that she acted incompetently and feels helpless about not being able to control herself. To support the child who has lost control, first ask her to describe what happened. After she has expressed her feelings and has calmed down, encourage her to tell herself that the next time she will do better. You can offer her these affirmations to say:

Affirmations for Staying in Control the Second Time
(Said by the child to herself)

I lost control and I am sorry.

Next time, I will notice that I am getting angry sooner.

I will choose a different way to respond.

I will remember to stop, relax, and think before I act.

I am responsible for my anger.

IN ACTION

Diego was sent to the school counselor after repeated incidents of hitting a boy who teased him. Diego's counselor began the session by asking him, "Who won? You or Charles?"

Diego: He did.

Counselor: Did you do what you wanted or what he wanted?

Diego: I did what he wanted.

Counselor: Do you enjoy giving up your power to someone you don't like?

Diego: No.

Counselor: What can you do in the future so that you are the one in control?

Diego: I can think before I act.

continued———>

His counselor then went back and reviewed the situation with Diego as follows:

Counselor: Think back to how you were feeling at the time. What were you saying to yourself? What were you feeling in your body?

Diego: My self-talk went something like this: That jerk! I'll show him he can't mess with me.

Counselor: You can choose a different way to talk to yourself. What could you have said differently to yourself?

Diego came up with three positive ways to express his feelings:

I can say, "I don't like it when you do that. I feel mad."

I can say, "Stop or I will go for help."

I can simply walk away.

Diego and his counselor then did a behavioral rehearsal for the new outcome. Diego visualized the anger-provoking situation and practiced responding with the use of his new self-talk and actions. During the week, whenever he thought about Charles and the incident, he repeated, "I let go of getting even, I can use my new anger management skills, and I will stay in control next time."

The next time Diego was provoked, he was able to stay in control and avoid retaliating.

Affirmations for Frustration

It's easy for children to feel frustrated. Not being able to master long division, dropping a fly ball, and feeling powerless in the face of adult authority are just a few of the many frustrating experiences for children.

IN ACTION

Leena, a diligent seventh grader, became furious with herself when she misunderstood a simple algebra formula and consequently got a C on a math test. Her initial angry self-talk went as follows:

continued——➤

Leena's Critical Talk

What a dunce. I hate myself.

I can't believe I missed those questions.

I'll never get into a good college.

I feel like an idiot.

Fortunately, Leena was able to talk out her angry feelings with her teacher. After their conversation, Leena created affirmations to forgive herself for making a careless mistake.

Leena's Healing Affirmations

It's okay to make mistakes.

I'll know what to do next time.

I learn from my mistakes.

Please refer to the section on athletic performance in Chapter 6 (pages 77–80) for another example of handling the anger associated with frustration.

When Life Is Unfair

A third situation that evokes anger in children is the fairness issue. Children have an innate sense of justice. Luis makes sure that he gets an equal scoop when the ice cream is divided between him and his brother. If his brother takes a larger amount, Luis immediately objects.

The fairness question arises when the child and adult have different views on what fair is. While her dad may see a bedtime of 8:30 P.M. as being reasonable, Patricia thinks that 10 P.M. is by far the better choice. In situations such as these, explain to the child as clearly as possible the reasons for your decision. This will help the child to release her anger.

Eight-year-old Danny was in a department store with his mother when suddenly he saw the same pair of hi-tech sneakers that his best friend got for his birthday. Danny's birthday was coming up soon.

Danny: Mom! Can I have those sneakers for my birthday?

Mother: No. That's a little out of our price range.

Danny: But Ritchie got those. Dad makes as much money as his dad.

Mother: I don't care. I just don't want to spend that kind of money on sneakers right now.

Danny: It's not fair!

Later that evening, when Danny had calmed down, his mom sat with him and said, "I know you feel frustrated and hurt that you are not getting those sneakers. I know it is hard. Are there any other shoes you might like?"

After experiencing his mother's genuine support, Danny's self-talk changed from condemning his mother to the following: "There are other sneakers I can get, I can still have a neat birthday, and my mom still loves me."

Anger Management for Adults

Children learn how to handle their anger from observing how their parents and other adults deal with their anger. Therefore, the best way to teach children to use the tools and affirmations in this chapter is to model the expression of healthy anger for them. This means (1) getting in touch with your own angry feelings, (2) being comfortable with your anger, and (3) expressing your anger constructively through such means as vigorous exercise, punching a pillow, yelling in private, talking with friends, taking a shower, or meditating.

Most verbal and physical abuse occurs when adults get angry and lose control. If you observe that your own anger is being inappropriately expressed toward your children, this book contains a number of sections that can teach you to better manage anger. Please refer to the anger management sections in Chapter 4 and Chapter 20 as well as to the material in this chapter.

In addition, organizations such as Parents Anonymous®, The National Council on Child Abuse and Family Violence, and local parenting support groups are ready to lend their assistance. Their phone numbers and addresses are located in the resource section at the back of the book (see pages 342–343).

What to Say When You Are Teased: Positive Talk for Responding to Put-Downs

In Chapter 4, we examined the issue of verbal abuse as it is communicated from adult to child. In this chapter, we will explore ways in which children can defend themselves from harmful words—whether they come from adults or from their peers. Verbal abuse is particularly problematic in the upper elementary grades when children's greater command of language allows them to engage in put-downs, name-calling, teasing, insults, and other forms of verbal harassment.

School-age children are not usually aware of the devastating impact their words can have on others. They don't realize that "words can hurt." In one instance, children harassed a classmate who had a large nose by calling her "ski slope," "witch lady," and "eagle beak." The child was so upset she burst out in tears. Later, the children voiced their surprise that their words had such a negative effect.

There are few things as painful to a child as being put down or criticized. Nonetheless, with the help of an adult witness, children can learn to defend themselves against verbal attacks. Here is a simple five-step process that any child can use to counter the effects of negative words. This process can be applied whether the harsh statements come from another child or from an adult.

Step 1. Identify the put-down.
It's hard to defend yourself from verbal abuse if you don't know you are being abused. Because so many children are subjected to this kind of abuse on a daily occurrence, they experience it as normal. To help children defend themselves against put-downs, we can teach them the concept of *good word, bad word* (modeled after the *good touch, bad touch* strategy used in educating children about sexual abuse).

A fifth-grade student asked her teacher, "Linda said my clothes clash. Is that a put-down?"

"How do you feel?" replied the teacher.

"Put down!"

"Then a put-down is what it is," the teacher replied.

The teacher further clarified the issue for the class: "If you want to know whether you are being put down, say to yourself, 'How did I feel when the other person said that?' Good words make you feel good. Bad words make you feel uncomfortable."

Step 2. Decide that you are not going to accept the abuse.

There is a famous story about the Buddha in which he was severely insulted by an angry man. After the man finished his tirade, the Buddha asked, "If a man offers another person a gift and that person does not accept it, to whom does the gift belong—the giver or the receiver?"

"To the giver," the man replied.

"You are correct," said the Buddha. "Because I do not accept your words, they belong to you."

In a similar fashion, when a child receives a put-down, it is his choice to accept or reject the abusive statement. For example, Gerald went to his mother and complained he was being teased by his older brother.

Gerald: Jimmy said I was stupid.

Mother: Do you really believe that?

Gerald: No. I don't believe that.

Mother: If you don't believe what he says, why listen to him?

After Gerald had this conversation two or three times, he realized he could ignore the teasing.

Step 3. Counteract the put-down by saying positive things to yourself.

Once a child decides that he will not accept a put-down, he can choose to counter its effect by saying a positive affirmation. Here are some positive self-statements that do the trick:

Positive Affirmations to Counteract Teasing

(Said by the adult to the child)

No one has the right to put you down
or to say bad things about you.

You can tell a safe adult how you
feel when someone puts you down.

You can know when you
are being put down.

You don't have to believe
what someone says about you.

No matter what anybody says or does,
you are still a worthwhile person.

(Said by the child to himself)

I don't have to let this
put-down affect me.

This person doesn't know how _____
(smart, talented, handsome) I am.

My best friend thinks I'm totally neat.

I can get help when someone
says bad things to me.

I can find someone to talk to
about my feelings.

I can take action
to help myself.

No matter what anyone says or
does, I'm still a worthwhile person.

Along with positive self-talk, children can defend themselves against put-downs through the following visualization techniques:

- **Think of negative thoughts as being arrows.** What do you do when arrows come at you? You step back out of the way and let them go by.

- **Imagine you are carrying a shield or wearing a suit of armor.** When the arrows of negative words come at you, they bounce off the shield or armor and fall to the ground.

- **Imagine the put-downs are drops of water falling from the sky.** You open your magic umbrella, and they harmlessly roll off.

- **Use the technique of visual rehearsal.** Imagine that you are being put down and then see yourself responding by using your favorite mental image or affirmation. You can draw a picture of what you visualize.

Step 4. Respond to the put-down by using "I" statements.

Saying nasty things back to a teaser means that you lower yourself to his level. Hitting also escalates the conflict. Instead of reacting aggressively, you can be assertive and say, "I didn't appreciate that remark" or "I don't like being spoken to this way." Refer to the anger management process in Chapter 10 (pages 156–159) for more on the subject of responding assertively.

Step 5. Practice feeling good about yourself.

Abusers pick on people who appear weak or defenseless. A child with high self-esteem radiates a power and self-assurance that shields him from potential abuse. As one teacher put it, "If you like yourself, other people can, too. But if you feel bad about yourself, other people will notice it and will want to tease you."

Whether the put-downs come from adults or other kids, most young children do not have the ego strength to resist them alone. Often an adult ally is needed to:

- provide validation and strokes to offset the abuse

- help the child give himself his own strokes through positive self-talk

- help him be assertive and stand up for himself

- provide direct protection and intervention when appropriate

For example, a family gathering was taking place. In the living room were nine-year-old Jackson, his aunt Darcy, and his stepfather Max. In the course of the conversation, Jackson complained that his stepfather favored Jackson's sister Laura. At first, Max got defensive and denied it. Then he said, "You're right. I favor Laura because she is easier to deal with than you." As soon as Max left, Jackson broke down and cried.

Aunt Darcy acted as Jackson's witness. She immediately hugged him and reassured him that he was loved. Then she said, "I heard what Max said and I didn't like it. You have good reason to be upset. Just because you are independent and strong-willed does not make you a bad child. If Max doesn't like to be around children who stand up for themselves, that's his problem."

After feeling his aunt's support, Jackson revealed other instances of his stepfather's verbal and even physical abuse. He also complained that he didn't feel protected by his mother. (All too often the spouse of the abuser acts as a "silent conspirator" by allowing it to happen.) As Darcy prepared to conclude her visit, she assured Jackson, "You can call me whenever you want. I will listen to you and support you."

In this example, the witness helped a child who was being put down by an adult. The same protection can be given to a child who is being verbally abused by his peers.

Replacing Put-Downs with Positive Self-Statements

Even though children cannot control what other kids say to them, they can control what they will say to themselves. In Chapter 5 (pages 63–66), we introduced an exercise that showed children how to turn negative, shaming self-talk into positive self-talk. This same process can be used to replace external put-downs with positive statements.

IN ACTION

Jill was having difficulty feeling socially accepted because of her embarrassing problem of having head lice. Trina, a girl who was an expert at exploiting weaknesses, made fun of this problem. At first, Jill responded by calling names back, but it didn't feel good.

"Are you going to play the mean name game?" the teacher asked.

"No, I am tired of it," Jill said.

"Why don't you examine your self-talk and see if you can tell yourself something else?" the teacher suggested.

When Jill examined her self-talk, this is what she found:

continued ⟶

Jill's Negative Self-Talk

I will get even.

I can't stand this.

This is always happening to me.

I'm always being picked on.

Then, the teacher continued, "I suggest that you find some new words to tell yourself, ones that will make you feel better about yourself."

Jill's Replacement Self-Talk

I am strong and smart enough to stand up for myself in a healthy way.

I can keep my cool when people call me names.

If I am teased, I can respond without hitting or running away.

If Trina doesn't like my hair, that's her problem.

I will use my humor to respond to Trina.

Jill also imagined the situation happening in the future and visualized herself responding with her new patterns. The next time she was teased, she acted assertively and stayed in control.

IN ACTION

Joe was a gentle twelve-year-old boy who lacked confidence in himself. He was also much bigger than the other kids who called him "fatso," "green giant," and "lardo."

Because he didn't have high self-esteem, Joe responded by withdrawing and sulking. As the depression increased, Joe was referred to the school's child development specialist who helped him to identify his existing beliefs.

continued➡

Joe's Negative Self-Talk

The kids don't like me.

I feel defective.

I feel helpless and powerless.

I wish I could disappear.

Fortunately, Joe's parents used affirmations on a regular basis. Joe, his parents, and his counselor put together a treatment plan using these positive self-statements.

Joe's Replacement Affirmations

It's okay that I am bigger.

I am developing at my own pace.

People will like me for who I am.

I like myself for who I am.

At first, the new beliefs didn't take hold because the peer influence was so great. Still, Joe was willing to work with his affirmations because of the support he received from home. After six months of work, he began to feel better. His depression lessened as he started to like and value himself just as he was. Because his oppressors couldn't evoke the normal "poor me" reaction, they lost interest in teasing Joe.

The Psychology of the Teaser

Sometimes children who are cruel to others do so because they do not feel good about themselves. Their behavior is an unsuccessful attempt to feel better by making others feel worse. In addition, they may be:

- trying to get attention
- trying to act cool or become part of the crowd

- trying to get the other child to lose his cool
- feeling jealous of the other child
- attacking in others what they most dislike in themselves
- feeling uncomfortable around someone who is different
- acting out the verbal abuse that they have received
- having nothing else better to do

If a child experiences self-love, he will not abuse or harm another person. When the teaser learns to feel good about himself, his need to put others down diminishes. Moreover, when he experiences how uncomfortable it feels to be teased, he develops empathy. The following affirmations are designed to create this shift in awareness:

Affirmations for the Teaser
(Said by the child to himself)

I can feel good about myself without teasing others.

I'm okay without putting others down.

I feel good when I speak kindly to others.

I am sensitive to other people's feelings.

If I hurt someone's feelings, it is up to me to apologize.

I know what it's like to feel put down.

I treat others the way I want to be treated.

IN ACTION

One of the most painful forms of abuse occurs when a group of children gang up on another. Six fourth-grade girls bonded together to form a "Hate Heidi" club after they and Heidi had a series of misunderstandings and hurts. After being excluded and taunted by the girls, Heidi became so upset that she began to avoid school. Heidi's

continued —→

parents contacted the school counselor who set up a series of meetings with all of the girls.

In the first meeting, the girls were able to tell Heidi in a respectful way what parts of her behavior upset them. They also told Heidi how they wanted to be treated in the future. As they verbalized their feelings and their needs, their resentment lessened.

The girls role-played how they would respond in the future when provoked or angry. They practiced positive self-talk such as, "I can ignore her" and "I can handle this in a mature way," and rehearsed walking away instead of retaliating. Finally, all the children received instruction in an approach called "Fighting Fair," which teaches children about fouls (blaming, name-calling, threatening, etc.) and uses a five-step process to solve problems.[1]

Creating a Put-Down-Free Zone

The first day of the term was not a pretty one for fifth-grade teacher Mrs. Hayden. By the time the 2:35 P.M. bell rang, every conceivable insult, racial slur, and put-down had been uttered by her students. The next day she asked the students to find a way to eliminate the verbal abuse and create a sense of community in the classroom. The students proposed an innovative solution—turn the class into a "put-down-free zone," modeled on the idea of the "nuclear-free zone."

This meant that no child was to put down, insult, criticize, or denigrate a fellow student during class time. To declare the seriousness of their intent, the children wrote and signed a contract that said the following:

PUT-DOWN-FREE ZONE

WE, the undersigned, wish to learn in an accepting and supportive environment, where we are free to:

- voice our opinions and feelings
- take risks—daring to try new ways of learning
- make mistakes as we learn

WE WANT A CLASSROOM ATMOSPHERE THAT IS FREE FROM PUT-DOWNS AND TEASING!

BY signing our names below, we agree to:

- accept one another's strengths and weaknesses
- be supportive and helpful to one another
- encourage each other to learn as much as possible
- participate well in discussions and group work
- recognize each other's progress and to point it out to one another
- use positive self-talk and eliminate negative self-talk

WE CARE FOR ONE ANOTHER AND PUT EACH OTHER UP!!!

WE hereby agree to the conditions listed above:

After signing the contract, the children held each other to the agreement. If one of them would hear an abusive remark, he would say, "This is a put-down-free zone. No insults here, please." Consequently, teasing and name-calling virtually disappeared in this classroom.

One of the beneficiaries of the put-down-free zone was a usually shy Vietnamese child who began to talk about his past and to speak Vietnamese as well as English in the classroom.

"What made you decide to open up?" his classmates asked.

"Since this is a put-down-free zone, I knew that no one would make fun of me," he replied. "I knew I was safe."

Additional information on how children can defend and protect themselves from verbal and other types of abuse can be found in Chapter 20.

PART THREE

Positive Talk for Specific Developmental Stages

> The purpose of our lives is to give birth
> to the best which is within us.
>
> *Marianne Williamson, author and lecturer*

CHAPTER 12

Prenatal Positive Talk

The fetus *in utero* is continually absorbing and learning from its environment, both within the womb and external to it. The fetus can see, hear, experience, taste, and, to some extent, feel rudimentary emotions coming from the mother. This connection is not at all surprising when we realize that the mother's blood, oxygen, and hormones are filtered by the placenta and received by the fetus. When the mother experiences an emotion, chemicals released by her central nervous system act directly upon the unborn child. Thus, affirmations, when combined with a parental love, can play a powerful role in welcoming the newborn into the world. When spoken by the mother or father, affirmations communicate positive messages to the unborn child about herself, the pregnancy, the birth process, and her connection with both parents.

Readers may wonder, "How can affirmations work during pregnancy with a fetus who can't understand the words?" Because the fetus is emotionally bound to the mother through their shared hormones, she can feel the emotional content and love behind the words. Moreover, as documented in books such as *The Secret Life of the Unborn Child*[1] and *The Mind of the Newborn Baby*,[2] an infant can recognize her mother's voice at birth and may even be sensitive to her language. In one case study, a pregnant French woman who worked at a business where English was the spoken language gave birth to a child who showed a remarkable ability to understand English.

Getting Started in the Use of Affirmations with Your Unborn Child

As you read through the affirmations in this chapter, pick one or two and begin to use them on a regular basis. Since the prenatal child can recognize your voice, saying the words out loud will help to strengthen the parent-child bond. If you have named your child early, you may want to call the child by her name while you say the affirmations. This strengthens the baby's sense of identity and helps her feel more connected to the outside world.

The earlier in the pregnancy you begin to use your affirmations, the more effective their positive messages will be. Any time during the day is a good time to say your affirmations. Say them slowly and from your heart. In addition, you may want to play soothing music in the background. Fetuses have been shown to respond positively to music, especially classical music (Vivaldi, Bach, and Mozart are favorites).[3] Finally, singing lullabies is a perfect way to combine music and words. To a child, there is no more soothing and reassuring sound than the lyrical sound of a parent's voice.

Affirmations for Welcoming

Pregnancy is a time of preparing yourself and your partner for the entrance of a new being into your life. This process begins with welcoming the child. If the pregnancy is planned, the welcoming begins before conception. One creative couple placed the following "want ad" on their refrigerator:

"Have body, will birth. Loving and enlivened couple will provide home for soul. Call or come by for an opportunity of a lifetime. Jesse and Ann, Portland, Oregon, USA, Planet Earth."

Two months later they conceived.

Welcoming begins with a simple acknowledgment of the baby's existence, followed by the desire to connect with the new being. Most parents experience feelings of joy and anticipation over the prospect of bonding with their unborn child. Often, however, they may have worries and concerns—about finances, labor and delivery, the state of the world, and so on.

If you have such anxieties about the pregnancy, allow yourself to experience your feelings. Talk them out with others and get some support. If you attempt to repress or ignore your discomfort, the baby will still feel it.

The following affirmations can be used to reinforce and strengthen your desire to welcome and bond with your unborn child:

Affirmations for Welcoming the Unborn Child

(Said by the parent to the unborn child)

Welcome to my womb.

I have been waiting for you.

I'm looking forward to this pregnancy.

We are so glad you are here.

I love you so much.

I'm glad you are here.

I'm glad you're a boy (if you know).

I'm glad you're a girl (if you know).

Affirming the Baby's Physical Well-Being

During pregnancy, the expectant parents want to do all they can to support the growth and development of a healthy fetus. Along with following the basics of good nutrition, exercise, and rest, parents can employ affirmations to communicate to the fetus on a subconscious level that she is physically vibrant and robust. These affirmations can also help to allay a common fear of many parents—that the baby may be ill or have physical problems:

Affirmations for Physical Well-Being

(Said by the parent to the unborn child)

I am creating a healthy environment for you.

I feed myself and you with wholesome, healthy foods.

I am taking good care of us.

You are well rooted and well planted in the uterus.

It's nice to feel you move around.

Because I love you, I am taking care of myself.

Affirmations for Labor and Delivery

Labor and delivery mark the culmination of pregnancy. In the same way that patients who are given positive suggestions before their operations recover faster and experience less complications, women who have positive expectations for the birth process are more likely to have a smooth labor and delivery.

In the pages that follow, we list many ways in which affirmations can support a positive labor and delivery experience. Because the birth process involves a partnership between the mother and child, the pronoun "we" as well as "I" is used to describe this joint endeavor.

Affirmations for Specific Fears About Labor

Many women anticipate labor with great fear and trepidation. The term *birth trauma* was coined in order to describe the discomfort of labor as well as its inherent difficulty (until this century, many women died in childbirth). Admittedly, the fetus's transition from floating in a protected environment to being squeezed out into the world is strenuous for mother and child. But birth is a natural process, and "trauma" can be accompanied by feelings of joy and excitement. Since any of the mother's fears about labor will also be felt by the fetus, addressing these fears is important for all concerned.

A common fear of many first-time mothers is that the pain of birth will be more than they can handle. In addition, their labor may stimulate old memories of emotional or physical pain from their own birth. Here are some affirmations that can diminish the expectation and therefore the experience of pain:

Affirmations for the Fear of Pain During Labor
(Said by the mother to herself)

I am able to cope with the pain of birth.

I surrender and breathe into the pain.

I relax and know that my labor will flow.

After each contraction peaks, there is a rest.

The pain is a necessary part of a wonderful process.

Labor is a labor of love.

Affirming Stamina and Endurance

Birth is a very physical process. It is common for a woman to fear that she will run out of energy and won't be able to push the baby out herself and thus require a cesarean or some other medical intervention.

If the mother is afraid of tiring out, she can start a physical regimen, advised by her doctor, which will build her endurance, stamina, and confidence. In addition, she can follow the lead of Olympic athletes and integrate affirmations and visually rehearse a successful birth. The following affirmations are designed to create the positive mental attitude which will help an expectant mother go the distance:

Affirmations for Stamina and Endurance
(Said by the mother to herself)

I have the energy and endurance to complete the birth of this baby.

I have the strength to push this baby through.

I can finish this labor.

I am preparing myself well for the birth experience.

I trust in and accept the support of friends, family, and medical staff.

Affirming a Safe Delivery

Safety is another consideration for the mother and child. Here are some affirmations that can be used to lessen the fear of complications or delay in the delivery:

Affirmations for a Safe Delivery
(Said by the mother to herself)

My pregnancy is proceeding safely.

We are working together to create a safe, smooth, and easy delivery.

continued⟶

My child is healthy, whole, and well during the delivery.

Birth is a natural process.

(Said by the mother to the child)

It is safe to leave the womb.

Feel free to emerge at a time that is right for you.

Our connection will continue after birth.

You are ready to live outside the womb.

A Birth Meditation and Visualization

In addition to affirmations, the process of creative visualization can be especially helpful in facilitating the birth process. What follows is a guided birth visualization, which is designed to help a woman visually rehearse a safe labor and delivery for herself and her baby. Many Olympic athletes employ a similar process to program their minds and bodies for the successful completion of their chosen events.

Because this mediation is meant to be heard, we advise that you have someone else read it to you, or better yet, make a tape or CD recording, which you can listen to over and over again.

The visualization begins by having the woman attain a state of deep relaxation. This can be accomplished by deep breathing, progressive relaxation, or any other relaxation technique.

Go forward in time to just before labor is ready to begin. Appreciate that the baby is in a well-protected space where everything it needs is supplied. Allow your body to give you a signal that the labor is about to begin. That could be from contractions or from your water breaking. When that happens, it's good to know that you have access to your support team. At any time you will be able to communicate with them and follow their instructions. And as the labor begins, there is a sense of

continued⟶

trust and knowing that all the details will be taken care of. So it's easy now to settle down and begin to notice your body and the changes it experiences as the contractions begin to build.

Now you can feel the contractions as they roll over you. You can breathe and relax as the contractions continue to build. Just allow yourself to relax as they wash over you like a wave. The long and round muscles of your womb move in perfect harmony. You can relax your shoulders, your hands, and your jaw during the contraction. Allow a wave of relaxation to flow over you.

And along with your head and jaw and shoulders, your cervix begins to relax now, as it opens and dilates, opens and dilates, opens and dilates so that the baby's head comes down and pushes gently on your cervix as it begins to open even more. The baby's head drops down into the opening, tucking in to just the right position to make it through the birth canal in a smooth and easy way. The bond between you and your baby is in full expression now as you tune into her sense of well-being. With each contraction the baby drops and pushes a little bit more and the cervix opens and dilates, opens and dilates. Just as a flower opens naturally, this opening of the cervix happens naturally and freely, and the baby continues to move down into the birth canal.

Every now and then a thought might come that "I can't do this" or "This is too hard." That's okay. You can let go of that thought of fear or doubt and come back to the thought that birth is a natural occurrence. The intelligence that produced your baby is guiding it down the birth canal. Your body and your uterus know exactly what to do to get your baby delivered. Your body knows exactly what to do. You can trust and let go. You can trust and let go.

The birth is now proceeding naturally, and you are alert to your baby's needs at each step along the way.

continued——→

You are in contact with your child and all is well. And now the contractions get stronger and stronger. And on the next contraction you notice the urge to push. It's a feeling of bearing down, and there's a pressure on your rectum. And as you breathe you feel like you have to push. Push, push, push. You hold your breathe and then push and feel the baby pressing down and working its way through the birth canal. On the next contraction you once again take a deep breath, tuck your chin in, and push, push, push, and there's a sense that the baby's head is sliding down to the perineum and stretching those tissues so that they burn a little. You can feel the baby slipping down. As you push, the baby's head continues to move toward crowning.

Now the head is crowned. The birth attendant gives it the necessary support, and on the next push the head is birthed. You can see your baby's head as it comes through the opening. You breathe a deep sigh of relief that the head is out. You look around and see the reassurance in the eyes of the birth team as they encourage you to go on and finish. And so you give it one last push and first the shoulders and then the rest of the baby slides right out into the loving hands of the birth attendant.

Now you can take a deep breath and say, "I did it!" and listen for the sound of your baby's first cry. And you reach down and pull your baby onto your chest and smile at him or her and you welcome your baby, saying, "Welcome to this world. I'm so glad you're here. I'm glad you're a boy/girl. Welcome to your loving family."

Affirming Babies Delivered Prematurely

A problematic aspect of pregnancy is the birth of a premature baby. The consequences of premature birth are many—the medical cost, the threat to the baby's life, the pain to the parents, and the disruption of the family system caused by the parents' daily visits to the hospital.

One of the most powerful therapies available to a premature infant is human touch. In one study, premature babies who were massaged and sung to experienced quicker weight gain and shorter hospital stays than a control group.[4] As a clinician or parent, you can combine affirmations with therapeutic touch to give the baby life-affirming messages about her wellness, vitality, and future growth. The affirmations that follow can be said to the premature infant by the parents, nurse, or other adult caregiver:

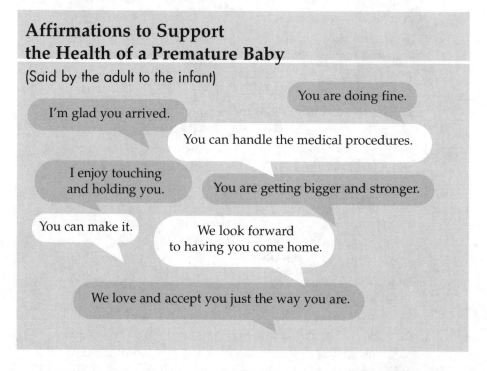

Affirmations to Support the Health of a Premature Baby
(Said by the adult to the infant)

You are doing fine.

I'm glad you arrived.

You can handle the medical procedures.

I enjoy touching and holding you.

You are getting bigger and stronger.

You can make it.

We look forward to having you come home.

We love and accept you just the way you are.

The Transition from Womanhood to Motherhood

Pregnancy can be defined as a nine-month transition period from womanhood to motherhood. Some women make the mental shift to motherhood as soon as they become pregnant. Others make the shift when the baby begins to show. Others make it during labor. And some still haven't accepted their new role when the baby is born.

Motherhood demands a brand new set of skills and attitudes. The woman's sleeping schedule, eating schedule, and many other daily routines are drastically changed. It seems that nothing about her life is the same once the child is born. Although she can return to familiar patterns in time, a newborn requires total dedication.

Because the psyches of mother and child are so closely inter-
twined, anything that supports the mother in her new role will positively impact the infant. The following affirmations can help a new
mother to embrace this all-important transition.

Affirmations for Entering Motherhood
(Said by the mother to herself)

I look forward to motherhood.

I am excited about
being a mother.

I welcome this new
phase into my life.

I have much love
to give to my child.

I can be a mother
and still get my needs met.

I am getting the support I need
from the outside world.

Affirmations for Post-Partum Depression
(Said by the mother to herself)

My body is going through
some normal changes.

My body has just
created a miracle.

I'm basically still okay.

I can get support from my
physician, family, and friends.

This is a phase that will pass.

Affirming the Father's Role During the Pregnancy

Fathers have traditionally had to face the problem of ownership during pregnancy. Once the conception has taken place, the man's physical role in the birth process is over. In times past, the father has been
relegated to the role of observer—standing back and watching from a
distance, feeling uninvolved and left out.

A father can become an important part of pregnancy and labor in a variety of ways. He can accompany the mother on prenatal visits to the doctor and attend childbirth classes. He can be an active participant and "coach" during the labor. In some hospitals, he can "catch the baby," cut the umbilical cord, or carry the child to the nursery. Perhaps most important, he can lend emotional and moral support to the mother, whose feelings of reassurance and safety will be directly transmitted to the fetus.

Bonding to and raising a child is a two-parent job. The father has a different type of participation from that of the mother, but it is equally important and essential if the family unit is to work. The following affirmations are designed to help the father realize his special role in the prenatal experience. If you are an expectant dad, the process of saying these affirmations will increase feelings of connectedness with your child, your partner, and the birth experience:.

Affirmations for the Father's Role During the Pregnancy
(Said by the father to himself)

I am bonded to my child.

I am an important part of this family system.

I am supporting my partner so that she can support our child.

I am fully participating in this birth in love and in consciousness.

I am bonding to my child in many ways.

My spiritual presence is important to her well-being.

Responding to Outside Advice

During pregnancy, parents are open and vulnerable to unsolicited comments and advice from well-meaning friends and relatives: "You shouldn't exercise so hard, the baby will be hurt," "You definitely need an amniocentesis," "One glass of wine won't be bad," and so on. Comments like these, while well-intended, can cause you to question your inner knowing. Please refer to the section "Trusting Yourself" in Chapter 4 (pages 30–31) for words that will affirm your ability to make good decisions about you and your child.

Summary

Good prenatal care, parental love, and the use of affirmations can support a newborn to begin her life on a positive note. Although the newborn won't be consciously aware of it, she will have already developed certain beliefs about herself and the world by the time she emerges from the womb. If the newborn could consciously state these beliefs as affirmations, this is how they would appear:

Positive Beliefs for the Fetus to Develop

I am wanted by my parents.
I am loved by my parents.
My family is ready for me.
Mommy and daddy know how to take care of me.
I am physically and emotionally secure.
I am healthy and vital.
I feel ready to go forward.
I am looking forward to my new life.

Using the affirmations in this chapter will help the fetus to develop these core beliefs that will provide a positive foundation of self-love as she makes her entry into the world.

CHAPTER **13**

Affirming the Infant
(Age 0 to 9 Months)

Developmental Overview

While infants are born with the basic abilities needed for extrauterine survival—such as respiration and digestion—they cannot survive without a caregiver to provide for their basic needs of food, warmth, and security. As a result, the infant is concerned with acquiring a sense of trust—that someone will be there to meet those needs and make the world safe and dependable.

The crucial element for the development of this trust lies in the quality of the caregiver-child relationship. When the child experiences this relationship as loving, stable, consistent, and dependable, he learns that the world is safe and that he can get his needs met. Developing this trust in the world helps him to experience new and unfamiliar situations with a minimum of fear.

The caregiver-child relationship also forms the infant's self-image in that the infant sees himself reflected in eyes of the caregiver. If the infant looks in his mother's or father's eyes and sees love and admiration, he senses that he is basically good. If he looks into those same eyes and sees anger or disapproval, he concludes that something is wrong with him.

A baby is pure feeling. Parent-child bonding occurs at the nonverbal level—through the gazing or mirroring process described above, as well as through nursing, touching, rocking, and movement. In addition, evidence from one study shows that the crying patterns ("cryprints") of newborn infants match their parents' speech patterns.[1] The words of the mother and father literally register in the infant's body. This is one reason why the use of affirmations can augment the parent-child bonding process.

Since infants can't repeat affirmations to themselves, it is the job of parents and other caregivers to voice these positive statements to

188

them. You can say affirmations while feeding, nursing, gazing, or putting the child to sleep. You can also repeat them silently to yourself. As you speak these healing words, their supportive content will register with the infant's subconscious mind and produce results accordingly.

Affirmations for Welcoming

Imagine that a beloved friend whom you hadn't seen in years was coming to visit you for a few weeks. How would you prepare your home for him? What would you say when he arrived? Your newborn, like your friend, needs to welcomed into your home.

Welcoming begins by recognizing that the child is a conscious being and treating him with the respect you would give any person. This comes naturally for most parents who stare at their infant in awe, telling the child over and over how much they love him.

To understand how important the welcoming process is, think back to the times when you did not feel welcomed. Now, imagine what it must be like for a newborn who senses that he is not wanted. Feeling unwanted at birth is a primary wound which leads to a host of problems later in life.

The following affirmations will provide a starting point for you to welcome your newborn into the world:

Affirmations for Welcoming the Infant
(Said by the parent to the infant)

Welcome to this world.

We are so glad you are here.

I'm glad you're a boy.

I'm glad you're a girl.

We have a wonderful home waiting for you.

I look forward to having you in my life.

You deserve to be alive.

Affirming the Infant's Dependency Needs

The newborn arrives into the world totally dependent on the adult caregiver for his survival. In order for him to move beyond that dependence, he must first get those dependency needs met. If the parent affirms the infant's right to be needy and to have his needs met promptly and lovingly, the child's cup will quickly fill up, and he can move toward independence in the toddler stage.

To meet the infant's dependency needs, the parents must respond to the infant's schedule of waking, sleeping, and feeding. Because infants have their own slow and relaxed rhythm, it is a challenge for the faster-paced adult not to try to hurry or rush the child.

Some parents are concerned that by doing all they can to meet their baby's needs they will spoil them. Yet, there is no such thing as a spoiled infant. Babies who are attended to quickly and lovingly need less attention and holding, not more.

Here are some affirmations that give the infant permission to get his needs met:

Affirmations for Meeting the Infant's Dependency Needs

(Said by the adult to the infant)

Your needs are okay with me.

I trust you to let us know what you need.

I will work with you to get your needs met.

Take all the time you need to get your needs met.

We will do our best to adapt to your schedule.

Physical Well-Being and Comfort

Another area of primary importance to the infant is his physical comfort. Above all, infants crave touch. Tactile stimulation is a physical nutrient, like air, food, and water. It is a crucial part of the bonding process between parent and child.

In many parts of the world, babies are carried by the mother throughout the day, benefiting from the continual warmth, sound, and movement as well as the contact. In addition to being touched, infants also need to be warm, dry, and well-fed, just like adults. Below are some affirmations that support the infant's desire for touch and comfort.

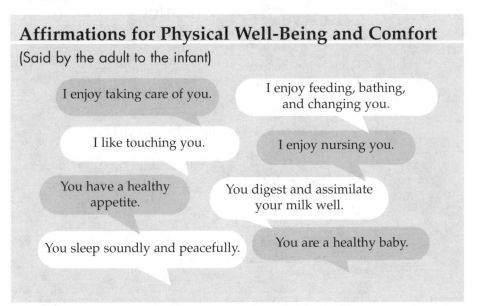

Affirmations for Physical Well-Being and Comfort
(Said by the adult to the infant)

I enjoy taking care of you.

I enjoy feeding, bathing, and changing you.

I like touching you.

I enjoy nursing you.

You have a healthy appetite.

You digest and assimilate your milk well.

You sleep soundly and peacefully.

You are a healthy baby.

Coping with Crying

Infants cry for any number of reasons. They cry when they are hungry, thirsty, sleepy, upset, lonely, bored, frustrated, or scared. Crying is designed to get your attention—without it, the baby cannot survive. Crying is an all-important communication signal from the baby to you. As you accept and affirm this fact, it will become easier for you to interpret what those signals mean. Is the baby hungry, sleepy, or in need of changing? Most parents find the answer by using a process of elimination.

A baby's crying brings up a variety of different responses in parents. Initially, there is the pain of seeing someone who you love in distress. Second, there is irritation over the harshness of the sound. Third, crying can create self-doubts about your skills as a parent. You may think, "What's wrong with me? Why can't I make this stop? I must be doing something wrong." When such concerns arise, it is helpful to remember that infants, like the rest of us, have their crabby days. On these days, you can simply "be there" for your child in empathy and compassion.

Affirmations for Coping with Crying

(Said by the adult to himself)

Crying is my baby's way of communicating to me.

I can figure out what my baby is trying to tell me.

Crying helps me to get my child's needs met.

My child is entitled to his feelings.

I have permission to feel frustrated when my child cries.

It's okay that I sometimes feel helpless when my child cries.

I accept all of my feelings about the crying.

I'm a good parent through the difficult and easy times.

(Said by the adult to the infant)

It's okay with me that you cry.

Crying tells you when you need me.

Crying is your way of communicating with me.

I am doing my best to find out what you want.

IN ACTION

Janice's three-month-old infant was crying continuously. Nothing she did seemed to help. Janice began to feel guilty. "What am I doing wrong?" she pondered. "Maybe it's my fault my baby is so distraught."

To answer these critical voices, Janice created the affirmation, "I love my baby, and I'm doing the best I can with what I know. This will pass." Janice repeated the affirmation to herself as she rocked her baby. Soon mother and child drifted off to sleep.

Summary

Through good parenting and the use of affirmations, parents can support their infant to develop trust. Although he won't be consciously aware of it, the infant will have already developed certain beliefs about himself and the world by the time he is nine months old. If the infant could consciously state these beliefs as affirmations, this is how they would appear:

Positive Beliefs for the Infant to Develop

I am wanted.
I belong.
I am loved.
I am bonded to Mom and Dad.
The world is safe and secure.
My needs are being met.
I can trust the world.
I can trust myself.

Using the affirmations in this chapter will help the infant to develop these core beliefs that will prepare him for the next developmental stage—toddlerhood.

CHAPTER 14

Affirming the **Toddler**
Age 9 to 18 Months (Exploratory Stage)
Age 18 Months to 2½ Years (Separation Stage)

Developmental Overview

During infancy, mother and child participated in a unified, symbiotic relationship. For all practical purposes, mother and child were one. So strong was the connection that the child could hardly tell where it ended and the mother began. In the toddler stage of development, the baby begins to experience herself as a separate entity from the mother. While the infant's motto was "I am you," the toddler says, "I'm gonna be me." Having been physically born as an infant, the toddler is ready to undergo a psychological birth.

This movement from dependency toward autonomy manifests in a number of ways. The toddler starts eating solid foods and becomes less dependent on breast-feeding. She doesn't sleep so much and has an increasingly longer attention span, which focuses on the outside world—objects, toys, and people. Her speech gives her another way to interact with this newfound world. As she learns to manage and control her body, her mobility expands as she crawls, walks, and finally runs.

The toddler also learns about boundaries. She discovers what is permissible as well as how far she can go in actions and words before she is stopped. Setting rules and limits is an art. Parents must walk a fine line between letting the toddler run rampant and crushing her independence. Either extreme blocks the toddler's healthy development of willpower.

Affirming the Toddler's Need to Explore

A toddler's separation begins through exploration. In infancy she learned to trust the world. Now she wants to test the limits of that world. Her body language moves from "I want to be held" to "I want down." And when she is put down, she begins to crawl.

The movement toward exploration happens gradually and perceptibly. Most of the child's early learning took place through looking and listening. Now, she wants to join in the activities around her, grabbing and investigating anything she can get her hands on. She realizes that "out of sight" does not mean out of reach; she opens doors and drawers to find objects to handle and to put in her mouth.

During her exploring, the toddler still needs the comfort of her mother's presence. She will crawl and explore, but will always look back to make sure her mom is within sight. This reassurance gives her the security to explore further. The pattern is to explore, return for connection, and then go out and explore again.

Because of the potential danger involved in exploration, parents must strike a balance between fostering the toddler's exploratory urges and creating a sense of safety. Phrases such as "That's not safe," "This isn't for little people," and "This will hurt you" can be said in a calm yet authoritative fashion. The parent who anxiously yells, "Look out! Watch yourself. Be careful!" communicates a message of fear to the child. If she hears these messages enough, the toddler may soon believe that "the world is a dangerous place," and will curtail future exploratory urges.

The following affirmations are designed to be said to your toddler to validate her need to explore. These affirmations can also be used internally by the adult. If you didn't have permission to explore when you were a toddler, you can speak these words to that child who still lives within you.

Affirmations for Exploration
(Said by the adult to the child)

It's okay to explore.

It's okay to be curious, to touch, and to taste.

I like you when you are active and when you are quiet.

You can always come back and connect.

You can count on my being here for you.

Affirming the Toddler's Need to Separate

The bonding of mother and child was all-important in the infancy stage. In toddlerhood, the developmental lesson is separation. The toddler needs to separate in order to develop a sense of self. She needs to define her own boundaries so that she can know where she ends and where others and the world begin.

Just as the failure to bond leads to developmental problems, so does the failure to separate. Prolonged dependency creates a child who never gets to know who she is, what she feels, and what she wants. Adult caregivers with a strong sense of self don't need to control the toddler or make the toddler dependent on them. The more that parents can find fulfillment in their own lives, the less they will feel compelled to live through their children.

Being made to separate too early can also be traumatic for the toddler. A toddler who hears the message, "Hurry up and separate so I don't have to take care of you," feels abandoned and neglected.

The following affirmations are designed to support and encourage a healthy separation process in the toddler. If, as a toddler, you were not supported in your desire to separate, you can use the affirmations to give the child who lives within you permission to do so now.

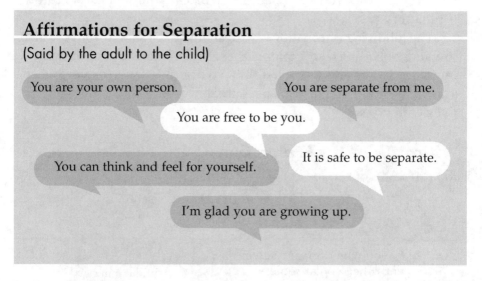

Affirmations for Separation
(Said by the adult to the child)

You are your own person.

You are separate from me.

You are free to be you.

You can think and feel for yourself.

It is safe to be separate.

I'm glad you are growing up.

Affirming the Toddler's Need to Say No

The toddler's need to separate is evident in her need to push against and move away from Mom, Dad, or any other authority figure. This need for "oppositional bonding" causes the toddler to act contrary to everything around her. Often the main words in her vocabulary are "no" and "me."

Saying no allows the toddler to develop a sense of autonomy and power—a necessary part of creating a healthy ego. Instead of complying with whatever is asked, she now gets to decide what she wants. Saying no is also a way to test the limits, to find out how far she can go.

Allowing your child to express her will does not mean letting her walk all over you. Clearly defined limits need to be set in a firm and loving way. Unfortunately, it is easy for parents to lapse into punitive forms of discipline. This is why child abuse often begins at the toddler stage.

The following affirmations are designed to validate your child's right to say no. If you weren't able to say no as a toddler, you can say the affirmations to that child who still lives within you.

Affirmations for Saying No
(Said by the adult to the child)

It's okay to say no.

If you say no, I will still be here.

It's okay to test your limits as much as you need to.

It's good to see you developing your will.

It is safe to feel your power.

I'm glad you are being you.

IN ACTION

Two-and-a-half-year-old Jessica and her mom were late for an appointment with the doctor. Her mom said, "Jessica, you need your shoes before we can go." Jessica defiantly stayed where she was and shouted, "No!"

continued→

After using her favorite anger management affirmations to calm herself, Jessica's mom took the following steps:

- She put Jessica's feelings into words. "It looks to me that you don't want your shoes on. You want to do it your own way."

- Mom then expressed her own needs and feelings. "I understand that you want to do it your way, and Mommy needs to get going. I need you to be my helper."

- When Jessica still resisted, her mom gave Jessica some choices. "Either bring your shoes so we can put them on, or I'll put them in the bag and carry you."

The latter is not a pleasant option for the two-year-old who values her independence.

Dealing with the Anger of the "Terrible Twos"

Along with saying no, toddlers get angry. One source of this anger is the toddler's frustration about not having total mastery over the environment. For example, if a structure that the child has been building with blocks comes crashing down, she may throw a tantrum.

Toddlers also get angry when they have to delay gratification. They want their cookie *now*, not five minutes later. Because toddlers experience rapid mood swings, their anger often comes on suddenly. One minute a child may be playing peacefully. Then, without warning, she becomes furious because she cannot manipulate an object or open a door.

While the temper tantrums of the "terrible twos" test the patience of the most loving parents, the toddler's anger is basically a healthy emotion. Like saying no, anger is a way of defining and maintaining her boundaries so she can become separate and autonomous. Anger helps the toddler to develop her willpower, the major goal of this developmental stage.

A toddler needs to know that it's okay to express her anger. She needs to know that she can be angry and the adult will still be there for her. Otherwise, she will feel emotionally abandoned when expressing her anger. In addition, the toddler needs to know that she and the adult can resolve their conflicts, that they can fight and make up. Those who did not learn how to resolve conflict as toddlers have difficulty doing so as adults. A typical example is someone who gets in a dispute with a friend or relative and then doesn't speak to the person for months or years.

The following affirmations are designed to validate your child's right to be angry and to have her feelings. If you didn't have your own anger validated as a toddler, you can use the affirmations to acknowledge the anger of that child who still lives within you.

Affirmations for the Anger of the "Terrible Twos"
(Said by the adult to the child)

It's okay to be angry.

You can be angry and I will be here for you.

It's okay for us to have fights and make up.

It's okay to be frustrated when things don't work out for you.

It's okay to have your tears.

I'm here to help you deal with these feelings.

Staying in Control
When Your Child Is Out of Control

The angry outbursts of the toddler test a parent's love for the child. As she throws her tantrums, defies your will, and begins to exhaust you, your own anger and frustration will begin to mount. Opposing the child head-on will only get you in a power struggle you don't want to be in. Reacting to the toddler at her own level—by yelling, screaming, hitting, biting, trying to force her to comply, giving an ultimatum, proposing bribery, or leaving the scene in disgust—is counterproductive.

When a dispute begins, you may already be on the edge, either from other incidents with your child or from stresses in your personal life. This may bring on the following self-talk: "I'm losing it. This is the last straw. This is too much to handle." When you hear yourself saying these words, repeat the phrase "CANCEL! CANCEL!" and immediately state a positive affirmation to replace the negative self-talk. You will notice an immediate shift in your attitude about being able to handle the situation. As you stay centered in your nurturing adult, you will provide the toddler with new options and help her to make choices.

Using affirmations to respond to your child's anger is a two-step process. Begin by saying them during times when you and your child are at peace. Think of this as a type of mental rehearsal or practice session for the upcoming event. Then, when a conflict arises, you will automatically retrieve the affirmation or affirmations that will enable you to stay calm and take the appropriate action.

The following are some positive self-statements you can use to support both you and your toddler in the midst of outbursts:

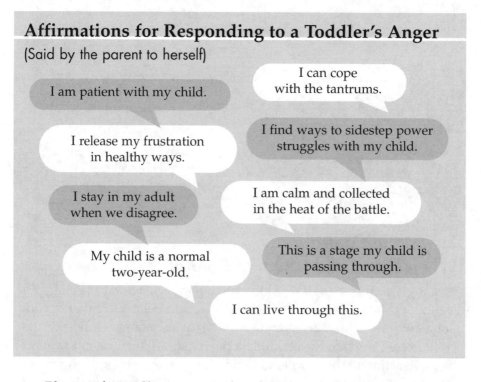

Affirmations for Responding to a Toddler's Anger
(Said by the parent to herself)

I am patient with my child.

I can cope with the tantrums.

I release my frustration in healthy ways.

I find ways to sidestep power struggles with my child.

I stay in my adult when we disagree.

I am calm and collected in the heat of the battle.

My child is a normal two-year-old.

This is a stage my child is passing through.

I can live through this.

Please refer to Chapters 4 and 10 for helpful strategies on how to handle your anger.

IN ACTION

Before breakfast, Sally asked for her orange juice. Her mother replied, "You can have it when we eat in ten minutes." "But I want it now," Sally screamed. After using her anger management affirmations, her

continued ⟶

mother calmly replied, "I know that you want your juice now. But you can wait. I know you can hold on. I'm sorry you feel upset, but I know you can wait."

IN ACTION

The grocery store is one of the most vulnerable environments for parents and toddlers. The child's actions can be seen and heard by all of the shoppers—and what's worse, she seems to know this. She's got the power and the audience and may use this opportunity to behave in a way that brings unwanted attention to you both.

Here's a typical example. Elijah and his mom were shopping when Elijah grabbed a cereal box. When his mom put it back on the shelf, he started screaming. The other shoppers silently stared at Elijah's mother as if to say, "Your kid is out of control. What are you going to do about it?"

After centering herself with her affirmations, his mom did the following:

- **Acknowledged Elijah's feelings.** "I see that you are angry because you can't hold that cereal box."

- **Expressed what was inappropriate about the behavior.** "The reason you can't yell is it disturbs other people in the store, and it's not okay to disturb other people."

- **Provided another option.** "Here is a box of crackers you can hold until we get to the check-out counter. Thanks for being Mom's helper."

Notice that this approach does not shame the child or make him bad for being angry. It simply lets him know in a nonjudging way that his behavior is not appropriate.

If Elijah had persisted, his mom could have said, "I'll have to take you to the car if you continue to scream. Or we can stay and finish shopping quietly." Then, it's important that she follow through. If sitting with Elijah in the car until he calms down doesn't work, it's time to call it a day. The groceries will just have to wait.

Sibling Rivalry

Although they may not always show it, toddlers are universally jealous of new babies. Until the birth of a second child, the toddler was number one in her parents' eyes. Now the love that was exclusively hers is being shared with the newborn. The toddler feels like a spouse who is told by her mate, "I love you so much that I want another mate like you, so I am bringing her home."

The toddler's jealousy toward this usurper is a natural result of every human being's need to see herself as an object of primary value in the universe. As philosopher Ernest Becker stated:

> When you combine [a child's] natural narcissism with the basic need for self-esteem, you create a creature who has to feel himself an object of primary value: first in the universe, representing himself and all life. This is the reason for the daily and usually excruciating struggle with siblings: the child cannot allow himself to be second-best or devalued, much less left out.[1]

The way out of this quandary comes from showing the toddler that love and care are not finite, that your love for the new baby does not threaten or interfere with your love for the toddler. Here are some strategies you can use with the toddler or any older child who is jealous of a sibling:

- **Provide some quality one-on-one time with your older child.** If she gets positive attention, she'll be less likely to ask for negative attention.

- **Give the older child new privileges**—later bedtime or new responsibilities—to show that being the oldest has desirable consequences.

- **Don't try to make the child feel guilty for being jealous.** She has a right to her feelings. Acknowledge them by saying, "I see you are upset about the baby. I hear that you want more of my attention."

- **Show the older child pictures of you taking care of her when she was a baby.** Explain that now you need to do the same things with the baby.

- **Let the child overhear you telling another adult how good she is with the baby.** This is often more convincing than direct praise.

Besides demonstrating this affection through your daily actions, you can also affirm in words that your older child still is, and will always be, a very special person in your life.

Affirmations for Sibling Rivalry

(Said by the adult to the child)

We are a family, and there is enough love for everybody.

I love you and I love your brother/sister.

You are an important member of this family.

I understand if you feel hurt or jealous.

I love you no matter how you feel.

(Said by the parent to herself)

I have enough love in me to give to both my children.

I can love my children in different ways.

I understand that no child really wants to share my affection with her sibling.

I will continue to do my best to affirm both children as they need it.

Affirmations for Toilet Training

Just as the infant learned how to grasp and bite, the toddler experiments with her newfound capacity to hold on and let go. This function is expressed with the use of the hands, mouth, eyes, and eventually the sphincter muscle in toilet training. During toilet training, the toddler must learn to recognize the urge to let go, and then hold on long enough to communicate this sensation to the parent. Her desire to please her parents will be the motivating force behind learning this new skill.

The following affirmations are designed to reinforce the toddler's desire to successfully complete the toilet training period:

Affirmations for Holding On and Letting Go

(Said by the adult to the child)

You can learn to wait when you have to go to the potty.

You can let me know when it is time.

It's okay to have accidents.

You will remember next time.

I still love you.

IN ACTION

Daytime accidents are common, especially during periods of intense play activity. During the warm weather, Cady played outside with her friend for hours at a time. When she came in, her mother noticed that her pants were always wet.

If we analyze what happened, we see that Cady was so involved in her play, that she forgot to pay attention to her internal body cues. If Cady's mom had scolded her, here's what would have happened:

Mom's statement: "Bad girl Cady! I told you to let me know. You'll never be able to get it right. I'm ashamed of you!"

Negative message received by the child: "I'm a bad person. I make mommy angry. I don't know how to control myself."

Rather than scold the child, Cady's mom decided to bring Cady into the house every hour and show her the potty. In addition, she would use the following affirmative statements with Cady:

continued——➤

"It's okay to have accidents. Let's wipe you up so we can feel dry and clean. I know that when you are having fun with your friends, you sometimes forget to tell mom when you need to go potty. That's why I am bringing you inside to help you remember. I appreciate you for working together with me. I know you will remember next time. Mommy still loves you."

When you affirm your child in this fashion, she is not shamed for her mistakes during potty training. The statement "I know you will remember next time" is an especially powerful suggestion to give the subconscious mind.

Letting the Child Develop at Her Own Rate

Like all children, toddlers develop at strikingly different rates, even within the same family. While Jennifer developed an extensive vocabulary at fifteen months, her brother Bruce didn't utter his first word until the age of two. Paul was potty trained at eighteen months, but his brother Ted took until the age of four. Examples such as these indicate that each child unfolds on her own schedule.

It's important to validate your child's unique rate of development. Here are some affirmations to help you do so. If your progress as a toddler was unfavorably compared to that of other children, use these affirmations to tell your inner child that her timing is just fine.

Affirmations for Letting the Child Develop at Her Own Rate

(Said by the adult to the child)

Take whatever time you need to grow and develop.

You can crawl whenever you are ready.

You can walk whenever you are ready.

You can talk whenever you are ready.

You can potty train whenever you are ready.

I love you just the way you are.

Summary

Through good parenting and the use of affirmations, caregivers can support the toddler to successfully meet the challenge of developing autonomy and willpower. Although she won't be consciously aware of it, the toddler will have already developed certain beliefs about herself and the world by the time she is three years old. If the toddler could consciously state these beliefs as affirmations, this is how they would appear:

Positive Beliefs for the Toddler to Develop

It's safe to explore and to investigate.
It's okay to separate from Mom and Dad.
I can be me.
I am my own person.
I can say no.
I can be angry and have my feelings.
I can be angry at Mom and Dad, and they will still love me.
I can control my urges to hold on and let go.

Using the affirmations in this chapter will help the toddler develop these core beliefs that will prepare her for the next developmental stage.

CHAPTER 15

Affirming the **Preschooler**
(Age 2½ to 6 Years)

Developmental Overview

The transitional development from the third to fifth year of life is striking and profound. As in adolescence, the child who emerges from this period is quite different from the one who entered. His struggle for autonomy was initiated during the toddler stage where "no" was his favorite word. Now he is becoming a person who can think for himself and who is his own person.

The preschooler's thinking is described as magical, nonlogical, and egocentric (seeing oneself as the center of all things). Imagination and fantasy take precedence over logic and reason. Part of the child's natural egocentrism causes him to believe that his thoughts are all powerful. Thus, if a person with whom he is angry becomes hurt, the preschool child may feel guilty, thinking that he caused the injury.

Emotions are primary in the life of preschoolers. What they feel is who they are. A preschooler does not express anger—he *is* his anger.

This is also a time of learning cooperation as the preschooler moves from solo play to playing with others. He begins to learn that his behavior can affect another child either positively or negatively. Children also learn the difference between what is right and wrong. Through reward and punishment given out by the parents or other authority figures, they become aware of what is acceptable and unacceptable behavior in social interactions.

Security issues still exist as the child wants to be sure that his mom and dad will continue to be there. Toilet training for most children is completed, although bedwetting may still be problematic. In addition, sleep patterns continue to change as the number of hours spent both napping and sleeping decrease. Nightmares and night fears commonly arise and can disrupt sleep (see Chapter 8 for affirmations for nighttime fears).

Using Affirmations with the Preschooler

In earlier stages of development, all of the affirmations were said by the adult—either to himself or to the child. In this and subsequent chapters, we will introduce affirmations that a child can say to himself.

Although preschoolers have the language to say affirmations, they will not use affirmations unless guided to. Under your guidance, the preschooler can learn to say very simple affirmations such as "I like myself." Review Chapter 3, "Introducing Positive Talk to Children," for techniques to accomplish this.

Affirming the Preschooler's Autonomy and Curiosity

During the preschool years, many things lead to the child's learning to explore and develop his sense of mastery of the world. His range of movement is widened by his capacity to walk rather than crawl. He begins to dress, eat, and learn to ride a bike. His use of language is more precise to the point where he understands and starts to ask, "Why?" This is the time when "kids say the darnedest things."

The following affirmations are designed to be said to your preschooler to support his developing autonomy. If you didn't have permission to explore when you were a preschooler, you can now speak these words to the child who still lives within you.

Affirmations for Autonomy
(Said by the adult to the child)

It's okay to be curious.

It's okay to ask questions.

You can learn what is make-believe and what is real.

It's okay to explore your body.

It's okay to think for yourself.

You can become separate from me and I will still love you.

Starting preschool or day care is a time when a preschooler's desire for autonomy may conflict with his security needs. Please refer to the section on school phobia in Chapter 8 (pages 126–128) for affirmations that address the preschooler's anxiety about the first day of school.

Affirming the Preschooler's Sexual Exploration

The preschool stage is also a time of sexual exploration. Boys and girls begin to pay attention to and learn about their bodies. Boys discover that they have penises and girls learn that they have vaginas. Sex typing occurs as the preschooler develops the attitudes and behavior associated with his gender. It is during this stage that kids are often made to feel guilty or ashamed of their healthy interest in sexuality.

For example, let's say a child is sitting on the seat in the grocery cart when he suddenly starts to play with his privates.

Parent's shaming words: "Stop that! It's filthy and disgusting. Don't you ever do that here again!"

Negative message received by the child: "My body is bad, especially these parts."

A more affirming response would be to casually say: "Honey, it's not okay to play with your penis in the grocery store. We don't touch our private parts in public places."

Here are some statements that affirm the child's right to explore and learn about his sexual identity:

Affirmations for Sexual Exploration
(Said by the adult to the child)

Your body is good.

It's okay to explore your body.

You can be curious about your body.

I'm glad you're a boy (girl).

I accept every part of you.

Affirming Competence and Mastery

One of the main ways that preschool children develop self-esteem is through gross motor competency. Experiences in dressing himself, riding a bike, or learning to use silverware give the child greater mastery over mind and body.

The premier affirmation for competency consists of two words— "I can," as in "I can do it," "I can run," "I can jump," and "I can learn this." The affirmation "I can" tells the preschooler that he can accomplish whatever he sets his mind to.

When we see that a child is struggling to gain competence, the first impulse is often to do the task for the child. Unfortunately, this takes away from the child's self-esteem and feelings of self-worth. Instead, we can break things down into steps so that the child can participate.

IN ACTION

At school, Tiarra was having trouble putting a certain puzzle back together. In frustration, she began to cry.

Here is how Tiarra's teacher responded to the child's frustration: "You know, Tiarra, there is a secret to doing puzzles; you have to look at the edges of the puzzle. If you look at this piece, it has a zigzag at the bottom. Let's find another piece with a zigzag."

The Positive Use of Words

During the preschool years, language becomes a major mode of communication and social interaction. Vocabulary typically increases from about 300 words at the age of two to over 2,100 words by the age of five. With a rich vocabulary, a child can more accurately convey the varied feelings he is experiencing. He can use words to make his needs known and to exert his power in the world.

Through the use of words the child can:

- learn about the world through asking questions

- ask for help

- ask for permission

- solve problems
- let others know how he feels.

Here are some affirmations that can be shared by the teacher or adult caregiver if a child is having difficulty using his words. If you had problems expressing yourself verbally when you were a preschooler, you can also say these affirmations to that child within you.

Affirmations for the Positive Use of Words
(Said by the adult to the child)

You can use your words to tell others how you feel.

You can tell Johnny to stop bothering you.

You can ask where the bathroom is.

You can ask permission to leave the room.

IN ACTION

At school, Greg was pushed by another child. He came crying to his teacher about the incident. Greg's teacher encouraged him to use words to express his dismay: "You can tell Jimmy you don't like to be pushed. You can tell him how you feel." If the child is too young to articulate these words, then the adult can take him to the offending child and say, "Jimmy, you know Greg doesn't like to be pushed."

Affirmations for Bedwetting

Bedwetting is a problem that many preschoolers face, especially during times of stress and trauma such as moving to a new home or the parents' divorce. In other instances, a child may go into such a deep sleep that he doesn't receive the signals from his bladder. When a child does wet his bed, the best strategy is to treat it as any other minor accident. Empathize with the child and reassure him that the problem will stop. If you sense that he is feeling horrible about what occurred you can say, "I know you feel bad right now. But lots of kids wet their beds. You're not the only one. One day the problem will stop and until then, I will be there for you."

IN ACTION

Five-year-old Maureen wet her bed at night. She was just starting kindergarten and so it was a stressful time for her. Nevertheless, she thought something must be wrong with her for having this problem.

Maureen's mom responded by treating the bedwetting as another accident (spilling the milk, dropping the crayons) so that it didn't take on more significance than necessary. Her mom would say, "You know, Maureen, even when we are five, we forget sometimes, and that's all right. Let's clean this up together."

If this had become a recurring problem, Maureen's mom should have consulted the pediatrician to make sure that there was nothing physically wrong. Then she could have said to Maureen, "It seems like you are having a hard time. What can you do so you remember to get up to go to the bathroom?" She could also have gathered more information by asking questions such as "Is it hard for you to get up? Would you like a night light?" and reassured Maureen, "If you call me, I'll come to you."

Affirmations for Bedwetting
(Said by the adult to the child)

It's okay if you wet your bed.

You can ask Mom or Dad to help you at night.

We are proud of you for doing your best.

We love you.

Everyone wets the bed once in a while.

All kids stop wetting. Just be as patient as you can.

You'll get over this pretty soon. Just hang in there.

continued——▶

(Said by the child to himself)

I'm okay even if I wet my bed.

I can ask Mom or Dad to help me at night.

Mom and Dad still love me.

Aside from wetting their beds, many preschoolers experience difficulties falling or staying asleep at night. Please refer to the section "Nighttime Fears" in Chapter 8 (pages 118–121) for information on how to respond to this problem.

Summary

Through good parenting and the use of affirmations, parents and teachers can support the preschooler in mastering the challenges of this developmental stage. Although he won't be consciously aware of it, the preschooler will have developed certain beliefs about himself and the world. If he could consciously state these beliefs as affirmations, this is how they would appear:

Positive Beliefs for the Preschooler to Develop

I can explore and know what is okay for me to do.
I like to ask questions.
I can think many different thoughts.
I can figure things out for myself.
I use my words to ask for what I want.
I can have fun with other children.
I feel good about my body.
All my feelings and sensations are okay.

Using the affirmations in this chapter will help the preschooler to develop these core beliefs which will prepare him for the next developmental stage.

CHAPTER 16

Affirming the School-Age Child
(Age 6 to Puberty)

Developmental Overview

Around the age of five or six, a number of signs indicate a child's transition from the preschool to elementary school stage of development. While earlier she was happy to parallel play and briefly interact in small groups, now she seeks to make friends with specific children and to contribute to the larger community. She may wish to volunteer to help clean the classroom or enjoy having her work displayed for all to see. These and other social behaviors are signs that she is moving away from her earlier egocentrism and learning to get along with others.

In addition to her social development, the task of the school-age child is to develop a sense of competence by acquiring a set of cognitive, physical, and social skills and by learning to carry through tasks to completion. The child is judged by a new set of standards that measure the skills she is supposed to master. If she succeeds in acquiring those skills, she receives praise from the world and thinks of herself as worthwhile and valuable. On the other hand, if she does not succeed, she comes to feel that she is inferior. Hence, psychologist Erik Erikson, who identified life stages of humans, named the challenge of this stage, "industry versus inferiority."

As a final task, the school-age child must learn to adapt to the laws of conduct in the world outside of the family. Whether it is school, scouts, or a sports team, the child is required to function within a social organization and to follow and obey specific rules and guidelines.

Using Affirmations with the School-Age Child

At about the age of seven, certain developmental changes take place within a child's thinking which make it possible for her to create her own affirmations. While the preschooler's thinking is egocentric and nonlogical, the school-age child is able to think logically and sequentially. A seven- to twelve-year-old is capable of a basic form of "thinking before acting." Applying the law of cause and effect, she can reason, "If I say this affirmation, I will feel and do better. Therefore, it is better to say the affirmation than not to say it." For this reason, school-age children are ready to apply affirmations in their daily lives.

Now, let's explore a variety of situations where the school-age child can use positive self-talk to improve her life.

Adjusting to Elementary School

The beginning of elementary school marks a major transition for the six- to seven-year-old. Although she may have already left the security of home by going to preschool, starting grade school means entering another brand new society.

As the school-age child leaves her familiar world and enters a new world, she is understandably apprehensive. Some of her concerns are:

- "I'll miss my mommy; I won't get to eat lunch with her."

- "My baby brother gets to stay home and will get all the attention."

- "No one at school will like me."

- "I'll be the dumbest kid in the class."

- "My teacher won't like me."

Other stresses include worrying about what is going on at home (especially if there are domestic problems) as well as concerns for personal safety—being picked on by bullies, being hurt, getting lost, or being abandoned. To add to these concerns, the first grader must often adapt to a long day that contains a great deal of sitting and talking and often not enough activity.

As a parent or teacher, you can affirm a child's ability to cope with this transition. For example, after the first day is over, you can say, "You were able to do it. This shows you are becoming more independent. Tomorrow it will be even easier." In a similar fashion, you can teach the nervous first grader some simple self-statements that will change her self-talk from fearful to hopeful. Please refer to the section on childhood fears in Chapter 8 (pages 126–128) for a full description of how children can overcome school phobia.

Learning Friendship and Cooperation

A large and important aspect of the school-age child's experience involves learning to get along with others. This skill includes learning to cooperate, play competitive games, and form friendships.

Friendships are particularly problematical. It takes time for a child to learn how to make friends and how to behave in a way that maintains friends. When she does make a friend, the relationship is often transitory. Two children can be friends today, enemies tomorrow, and best friends the next day.

Here are some affirmations that are designed to help the school-age child to gain confidence in her ability to form and sustain friendships:

Affirmations for Forming Friendships
(Said by the child to herself)

I can make friends.

Other kids like me.

Other kids want to be my friend.

I can reach out.

I can let others know that I am fun to be with.

IN ACTION

Making friends is especially difficult for the shy and withdrawn child. Often she feels as if she doesn't fit in and sees herself as an outcast. Having been turned down before, she is afraid of experiencing rejection again.

Seven-year-old Peter was an introverted, quiet child. He liked Liz but was afraid to ask Liz to spend time with him. His teacher, Mrs. Warren, took Peter aside and said, "I'll bet it feels scary when

continued⟶

you think about talking to Liz." After validating Peter's feelings she continued, "Would you like some positive things to tell yourself that will help you to feel less scared?" After Peter said yes, Mrs. Warren gave him the following affirmations:

Peter's Affirmations

I can let Liz know I like to read stories with her.

I like Liz and she likes me.

I can ask Liz to play with me, even if I feel scared.

Peter and Liz had a good time playing that day.

IN ACTION

Ten-year-old Justin fashioned his identity around negative social behavior. He was known for being weird and obnoxious. With the help of his school counselor, a friendship group was formed around Justin to give him information about how he related to other kids and how they perceived him.

Through the weekly sharing, Justin learned that when he did certain things (grabbed, shoved, and said mean words), his peers became upset and didn't want to be around him. On the other hand, when he was polite, the other children would seek him out for his good nature and other positive qualities.

Here are some affirmations that helped Justin to develop more appropriate social behavior:

Justin's Affirmations for Developing Good Social Skills
(Said by the adult to Justin)

Justin, you can learn to get along with other kids.

You can learn to control yourself.

continued➝

> You can get attention in positive ways.

> You can ask before you take what is not yours.

(Said by Justin to himself)

> People like me for my positive qualities.

> I get attention in positive ways.

> I can ask before I borrow somebody's crayons.

> I can say excuse me if I have to pass in front of somebody.

The other significant component in Justin's healing was the unconditional acceptance he received from his counselor. Once Justin realized that he could be loved for who he was, he no longer had to act out to gain attention.

Responding to Exclusion

In forming friendships, children often exclude one another. This exclusion is often unintended and unconscious. For example, Jessica may be having so much fun with Jane that she doesn't want to let Joyce join in. At other times, children exclude each other on purpose.

IN ACTION

Nine-year-old Ian feels hurt because his friends Phil and Ron didn't want to play ball with him. First his teacher used active listening to help Ian state his feelings. When Ian said, "Nobody likes me. Nobody cares about me," the teacher validated his feelings and then suggested the following replacement affirmations for him to say:

Ian's Healing Affirmations

> I can find other people who will play with me.

> I am likable.

continued ⟶

> I can make good friends.

> Phil and Ron may feel differently tomorrow.

After saying his affirmations, Ian found other children to play with. The next day, his original companions invited him back in the game.

IN ACTION

D'Lee's mom took D'Lee and eight other children on a school cook-out. Since her mother needed to give equal attention to the other children, D'Lee felt excluded and rejected. Later, D'Lee's mom said to her, "It seems like you felt ignored today." "Yes I did," replied D'Lee, glad to have her feelings acknowledged. D'Lee and her mom then composed the following affirmations for D'Lee:

D'Lee's Affirmations

> I like to spend time with my mom when I get home.

> My mom still loves me.

> I can share my mom with my friends.

Letting Kids Work It Out

Affirming cooperation in children means giving them the opportunity to work out conflicts in their own way. When a dispute arises, instead of jumping in to fix it, a teacher or parent can ask: "What happened?" "How do you feel?" "What do you think should be done?" This encourages the children to find their own solution.

Here are some affirmative statements a parent or teacher can say to children when they are having a dispute. They can help promote the children's confidence in their own ability to resolve their differences without adult intervention:

Affirmations for Working Out Differences
(Said by the adult to the child)

You can work it out.

You two can work out your differences.

I trust you can solve this problem.

I have faith in you to do it.

You are smart enough to figure this out.

IN ACTION

Tim and Jerry came in from the playground with their faces angry and flushed. Each gave their teacher, Mrs. Garrett, his own story about the cause of the argument. Mrs. Garrett replied, "I'm getting two stories that don't match. It looks like you two need time to think about what happened and get calmer. You can stay in the hall while I go inside and start class. I'll be back in a few minutes to see if you have worked out a solution."

Five minutes later, she checked back to find that the boys had settled their differences.

Stranger-Danger, Bullies, and Sexual Abuse

As the school-age child ventures out of her home into the world, she needs to be aware of the potential dangers from strangers, bullies, or others who wish to take advantage of her. Because of the increase in reported child abuse, many children are now taught how to respond if a stranger approaches them in public or if a relative touches them inappropriately at home. Chapter 20 provides a host of affirmations for the child who is being or has been sexually or physically molested. Here are some affirmations that can help a child to define her boundaries and defend herself from potential abusers:

Affirmations for Personal Safety

(Said by the child to herself)

> I know the safety rules and I know how to use them.

> I don't talk to strangers.

> I know what to do if anyone approaches me.

> I know what touching feels good and doesn't feel good.

> I can tell someone if I am being hurt.

IN ACTION

A universal concern of the school-age child is the playground bully. Nine-year-old Isaac was frequently picked on by Mark, a classmate. Mark periodically called Isaac "Fatso," took the ball from him on the playground, and knocked him down. Isaac was not aware of the power he had to affirm himself and to stop Mark's behavior.

After hearing repeated complaints from Isaac, Isaac's teacher had an "empowering chat" with him. He told Isaac:

- that bullies pick on kids who appear weak because they want to appear more powerful than they are
- that Isaac has the physical and mental abilities to cope with Mark
- that by next week Isaac will have solved his bully problem

To help make this prediction become reality, Mr. Greco gave Isaac the following affirmations:

Isaac's "Anti-Bully" Affirmations

> Bullies are just seeking power they wish they had.

> I can handle Mark.

continued⟶

I can easily say, "Leave me alone," in a firm voice.

I know how to get help if I need to.

The next time Mark approached him, Isaac confidently told Mark not to mess with him. Mark got the message.

Learning to Resist Peer Pressure

As school-age children advance in age, the influence of their peers begins to supercede the influence of the family. Although peer pressure reaches its strongest point during adolescence, it begins during the upper elementary grades. This peer pressure can tempt young children to engage in dangerous activities such as taking illegal drugs or doing a reckless dare. This is why it is important to introduce "refusal skills" to elementary kids and to teach them how to say no to activities that are dangerous or illegal.

Here are some affirmations that can be combined with any refusal skills training program:

Affirmations for Resisting Peer Pressure
(Said by the child to herself)

I say no to things that are bad for me.

I make good choices.

I say no to things that will put me in danger.

I can make different choices than my friends.

I can say, "You're my friend, but I don't care to do that."

Look in Chapter 17, "Affirming the Adolescent," for additional affirmations for responding to peer pressure.

Other Applications of Positive Self-Talk

Responding to Put-Downs and Teasing

Few things are as painful to a school-age child as being put down or shamed by her peers. Although teasing is especially prevalent during the elementary school years, it is an issue faced by children of all ages. For this reason we have devoted an entire chapter to this issue. Please refer to Chapter 11, "What to Say When You Are Teased: Positive Talk for Responding to Put-Downs," to find affirmations that will empower a child to defend herself against teasing and name-calling.

Affirmations for Learning and Academics

The classroom is one of the main arenas in which a school-age child learns to develop a sense of competence. By supporting the child's self-image and self-esteem, positive affirmations can predispose her to mastering academic skills with confidence and ease. Because issues around academics affect children of all ages, we have created a separate chapter on learning and academic performance. Please refer to Chapter 7, "Positive Talk for Learning and Academics," for affirmations that will support the school-age child's mental development.

Affirming a Child's Physical Skills

In addition to academics and social life, the third area in which school-age children develop competence and self-esteem is through perfecting their physical skills. Although not all kids are going to be athletic, they can still feel good about their ability to master their physical environment. Chapter 6, "Positive Talk for Physical Health, Body Image, and Athletic Performance," contains a number of effective affirmations for improving body image and athletic skills.

Summary

Through good parenting and the use of affirmations, parents, teachers, and counselors can support the school-age child to master the challenges of this developmental stage. Although she won't be consciously aware of it, the school-age child will have developed certain beliefs about herself and the world by the time she enters puberty. If she could consciously state these beliefs as affirmations, this is how they would appear:

Positive Beliefs for the School-Age Child to Develop

I make friends easily.
I follow the rules that help me to live with others.
I make good choices about the things that I do.
I say no to things that are bad for me.
I can read and write and spell.
I am learning the things I need to learn.
I can play ball (or some other physical skill).
I have many strengths.

Using the affirmations in this chapter will help the school-age child to develop these core beliefs which will prepare her for the next developmental stage—puberty.

CHAPTER 17

Affirming the Adolescent

Developmental Overview

The major issue of adolescence is that of identity. Until puberty, the child's main frame of reference has been the family and its values. Now, these values are all called into question, as the adolescent seeks to form his own beliefs. He asks questions such as: "Who am I—apart from my parents?" "What is my future?" "Where and how do I find my place in society?" "How do I fit in with my peers and still be myself?" Out of this "identity crisis," his authentic self begins to emerge.

This ending of childhood and birth of adulthood is first evidenced by the physical changes of adolescence. The teen's body enters a major growth spurt with the accompanying hormone changes. It proclaims to the teen, "You will never be a child again. The process you are going through is irreversible."

Because the adolescent is a traveler caught between two worlds, he experiences contradictory wants and desires. A teen's two worst fears are "being like my parents" and "not being like my parents." He wants to emancipate himself from his mom and dad yet still feels dependent on them. He wants to leave home yet fears his freedom. Like the toddler, the teen walks away while simultaneously looking over his shoulder to make sure someone is looking back.

In this state of transition, the teen feels insecure and unsure of himself. Historically, most cultures have had rites of passage in which elders initiate the adolescent into the society of adults. The scarcity of these rituals in contemporary society makes the transition to adulthood additionally confusing for today's teenagers. Without clear guidance from society or from their families, teens become prone to alcoholism, drug abuse, out-of-wedlock pregnancies, depression, and suicide.

The inherently unstable nature of this stage also accounts for the touchiness and classic mood swings displayed by adolescents. One day a thirteen-year-old is insulting and obnoxious; the next day he mows the lawn and fixes dinner for the family. A sixteen-year-old may start the week acting as a mature adult, but by the week's end, he behaves like an irrational, out of control two-year-old. Clearly, it is a time of emotional upheaval.

Guidelines for Using Affirmations with Teenagers

Since a teen defines his identity by opposing an adult's authority, directly presenting affirmations to your teen may be met with skepticism and resistance. Hence, you may initially want to state your affirmations in an offhand or nonchalant way. This can be done through embedding the affirmations in conversations or through spontaneous compliments. For example, the adult can say:

"I know what I would do in this case . . ."

"I know what I would be saying to myself . . ."

"Would you like to hear what Tom did about this?"

IN ACTION

Cindy was an attractive fourteen-year-old. One evening she complained to her father about some recent teasing.

Cindy: Dad, they are making fun of my nose again, just like they did in fourth grade.

Dad: Would you rather have a pointy one like mine?

Cindy: No way.

Dad: There are always people who will tease you. Your nose looks good to me.

Cindy: Really?

Dad: Would you like to know what I did when I was in a similar situation?

Cindy: Sure.

Dad: When I was in school and kids teased me about my weight, I said to myself, "That's just his opinion. I like the way my body looks and feels. If he doesn't, that's his problem, not mine."

Now let's explore the various issues in a teenager's life to which affirmations can be applied.

Affirmations for Achieving Peer Acceptance

The transition from elementary to middle school and then high school represents a major change for the developing child. Instead of being with the same children and teacher throughout the day, he attends six or seven different classes, each with a different teacher. Many children grieve the loss of the sense of community that the elementary class-room provided.

What replaces that lost community is the teen's peer group. The teen looks to his peer group to gain a sense of community, identity, and belonging. At one typical middle and high school, students formed the following peer groups:

- **preppies**—kids who have money, wear nice clothes, are popular, and put on parties

- **jocks**—kids who participate on school sports teams

- **rockers**—those into heavy metal and hard rock

- **nerds/geeks**—kids who are academically oriented

- **stoners**—kids who are into cigarettes, drugs, and alcohol (cigarettes in middle school, drugs and alcohol in high school)

- **skaters**—kids who ride skate boards

- **loners**—those who choose not to be in any group

- **troublemakers**—the kids who act out, get into trouble with teachers, receive detentions, and end up in the principal's office

- **thespians**—theater people

At this point in his life, the most important decision a teenager will make is to decide, "Who will be my friend?" Teen peer groups form a clearly defined social hierarchy, with "preppies" and "jocks" on top looking down on the other groups. Still, the most important task is to be accepted by one's own group. If you are an academic type who fits in with his peers, then being called a "nerd" by a jock is not so bad.

Nonetheless, kids in the *out* groups often feel shamed by the neg-ative judgment from students. Roger, a bright "stoner" who made the honor roll told me, "A stoner or skater is not expected to get on the honor roll. How could he do it? He smokes cigarettes. He's not a person. He's not supposed to make it." To transcend these labels, the teen must affirm his own self-esteem in spite of the external judgments, an admittedly difficult task for most adolescents.

Not being accepted by one's peers is experienced as a deep rejection. Kids who have low self-esteem will do almost anything to be accepted, even if it means making unwise decisions (see affirmations for peer pressure on pages 229–232). Here are some affirmations to help a teen develop a sense of belonging in his new social environment:

Affirmations for Peer Acceptance
(Said by the teen to himself)

I can adapt to this new school.

I can find friends.

There is a group that I can belong to.

I can find a group that shares my values.

IN ACTION

Koco was having difficulty in adapting to his new middle school. Like all children facing new situations in the prepubescent years, he was impatient and anxious. He was desperately trying to fit in and make a place for himself at school, but found making new friends extremely difficult.

Koco's counselor first encouraged him to express his feelings about being left out. Then he gave Koco a new affirmative message to replace his negative self-talk: "It is easy for me to make friends." As Koco began to change his expectations, he started to reach out and make contact with others.

Koco's Negative Self-Talk

I'll never like it here.

Nobody wants to talk to me.

I can't fit in.

continued——→

Koco's Replacement Affirmations

I can get used to this school.

I can make new friends.

I can find a group to belong to.

In addition to the affirmations, Koco's counselor also gave him the following task: "Each day in one of your classes, approach at least one kid and say, 'Hello.' Do this each day for two weeks." Koco took his counselor's advice and reached out. To his surprise, he found a number of students just as lonely as he was who were happy to respond to his overture and start a conversation.

Responding to Peer Pressure

Every teenager faces the tension of maintaining his own identity while being a part of a peer group. The teen has not yet developed a stable internal compass that says, "I know who I am apart from the group." No wonder it is hard for him to stay in touch with himself during this time.

All day long kids are exposed to the following voices of peer pressure:

"Just try it, it's cool."

"Everybody does it."

"This will make you feel good."

"If you want to be popular, just do this."

"If you want to belong in the group, you have to do what they do."

"Come on, we won't get caught."

"You'll get used to it."

Peer pressure causes teens to make unwise choices. For example, kids who steal know their behavior is wrong; they just don't apply that moral judgment to their circumstances. They think, "If I don't go along with the crowd, I'm nobody." Other poor choices include using alcohol and drugs, smoking, engaging in unsafe sex, stealing, and joining gangs.

Here are some questions that teenagers can ask themselves to see if they are being unduly influenced by peer pressure:

- Do I always do what my friends want me to do?

- Do I call to see what everyone else is wearing before I go out?

- Have I ever gone along with something I knew wasn't right—shoplifting or cutting classes—just to be with friends?

- Do I feel I might be giving in to friends and not making my own choices in life?

- Do I drink alcohol or use drugs just because everyone else is doing it?

If a teenager answers yes to one or more of these questions, he is being negatively influenced by his peers. The best antidote to unhealthy peer pressure is healthy self-esteem. A child with a strong sense of self is less likely to be coerced from the outside. That's why it is so important to teach children self-esteem affirmations and refusal skills in the early grades. The following affirmations can also create a foundation of self-love and self-trust that will help a teen to resist peer pressure:

Affirmations for Responding to Peer Pressure
(Said by the teen to himself)

I can be me and still be part of a group.

I can say no to things that I feel are scary and dangerous.

I can say no when people ask me to do something illegal, dishonest, or against my beliefs.

I make up my own mind regardless of what my friends think.

I make my own choices.

I do what is best for me.

IN ACTION

Elena was a popular high school freshman whose best friends were pressuring her to smoke cigarettes. Even though she didn't want to smoke, especially after seeing her uncle die of lung cancer, she was thinking of trying it. Elena consulted her friend Steffan who she admired for being his own person. Steffan asked her to consider, "Are you thinking about smoking because you want to or someone else wants you to?"

After thinking it over, Elena realized that she cared enough about her health not to jeopardize it by giving into her friends' wishes. Then she created the following affirmations:

Elena's Affirmations for Not Smoking

I choose not to smoke.

I am doing what is best for me.

I care about my health.

My health is more important than my popularity.

IN ACTION

Trever, a high school senior, was approached by his buddy Tom during lunch period.

Tom: How about taking the afternoon off and playing pool with us? We need you to drive.

Trever: I'd like to, but I have a test to take this afternoon.

Tom: You're a senior! What do you care about a crummy little test? If you go out with us, I'll buy you a beer.

Here is how Trever's dilemma expressed itself in his thinking:

The Voices of Peer Pressure	Trever's Replacement Affirmations
These guys need me.	I need to pass this class.
The guys will be disappointed.	They will get over it.

continued ⟶

Tom will be angry at me.	I can handle his anger.
The guys will give me a hard time.	I can hang tough.

By focusing on his affirmations, Trever was able to reply, "Sorry, I would really like to go with you. But not today." The next day Tom and the boys did give Trever a hard time, but still saw him as a friend. That Friday evening they got together to shoot some pool.

Affirming a Teen's Looks and Body Image

Appearance and body image form an important aspect of a teenager's self-esteem. Teenagers want to look good in order to be accepted by their peer group and the opposite sex. Even those who don't seem to care about the way they dress are sensitive to criticism. A teen who is told, "Oh, God; where did you get those pants?" or "You look like a nerd" will quickly adjust his wardrobe to gain peer support.

Due to their rapid and often embarrassing physical changes, teens feel extremely self-conscious and insecure about how they look. Their struggle with acne is only the tip of the iceberg. Discomfort with their appearance creates self-talk put-downs such as, "I'm too short (or tall)," "My hair is too thin," "My nose is too big," "My breasts are too small (or large)," "My hips are too small (or large)," "I look funny," and "I've got braces on."

Affirmations provide a welcome antidote to these feelings of shame and self-criticism. The teen can remind himself that his peers do not judge him by the same high standards he uses to judge himself. In fact, many teens are so preoccupied with their own pimples and imperfections that they hardly have time to notice these in their friends and classmates.

Affirmations for Appearance and Body Image
(Said by the teen to himself)

My body is going through many changes which will pass in time.

I can handle the pimples.
My skin is only a part of me.

continued ——➤

I can handle the cracking voice.

I can do the necessary things to look good (styled hair, good clothes, a new pair of glasses).

I will grow when it's time.

Bigger is not always better (for short boys and for girls with small breasts).

I can do things with my size that other people can't.

Everyone develops at a different rate.

I am developing at the pace that is right for me.

IN ACTION

Janet is an attractive eighth grader who is also the tallest person in the class. Initially she saw this as a hindrance to being accepted by boys. Her negative self-talk went as follows:

Janet's Negative Self-Talk

I'm too tall for the boys.

I won't be popular.

I don't fit in.

Who would want me as a girlfriend?

Because Janet had a healthy self-image and outgoing personality, she easily modified these beliefs. In her discussions with the school counselor, she realized that kids would like her for who she was on the inside. Here are some affirmations that she used to attract her first date:

continued⟶

Janet's Positive Affirmations

I'm attractive just the way I am.

Tall girls are cool.

I feel beautiful.

I like the boys and they like me.

Please refer to Chapter 6, "Positive Talk for Physical Health, Body Image, and Athletic Performance," for more body image affirmations.

Dating

During adolescence, sexual and romantic interests which lay dormant come rushing to the foreground. In addition to dressing right, giving the car a shine, and being on his best behavior, positive self-talk can help a teen to date more successfully. Or, the teen can affirm himself for not dating if that is the option he chooses socially

For those who choose to date, affirmations are especially helpful in bolstering the teen's fragile ego after an unsuccessful encounter. The disappointed teen may tell himself: "What's wrong with me? Maybe I don't have the touch. Maybe I'm a loser with girls (boys)." By affirming himself even after being turned down, the insecure teenager develops the confidence to keep trying until he finds a compatible partner.

IN ACTION

Sixteen-year-old LaShawn is attracted to Andrea. He wants to ask her to the junior prom but is nervous about being turned down. LaShawn is good looking and intelligent but also shy and lacks confidence.

LaShawn decides to talk to his soccer coach, Mr. Jones, who has been using affirmations with his players. The coach begins by giving LaShawn a reality check—reminding him that he is smart, intelligent, and good looking. He continues, "You remember, LaShawn, what we do at the beginning of a game. We sit down and say things to ourselves that will help us focus on winning and doing our best. You can do the same thing in this situation."

continued——→

Together, LaShawn and Mr. Jones created a series of affirmations to help LaShawn get over the fear of rejection:

LaShawn's Affirmations

I am likable and attractive.

I can handle it if Andrea turns me down.

There are other attractive girls in the school.

I can ask for what I want.

Andrea can't say yes unless I ask.

To succeed, we sometimes have to take risks.

LaShawn asked Andrea and was turned down. Returning to his affirmations, he got up the courage to ask Carol who accepted and later became his girlfriend.

Coping with a Breakup

The hallmark of a teenager's life can be summed up by the word experimentation. This experimentation can cause a teen's social and sexual life to resemble a game of musical chairs. For example, Nancy is broken-hearted when Joe says he doesn't want to see her anymore. Ten days later Joe changes his mind and calls her back. By then she, too, has changed her mind and is off dating another person. Such are the fickle ways of teen daters.

One reason teenagers fall in and out of love with great rapidity is that they fall in love with the ideal of the other, which has little to do with the reality. By the time they reach seventeen or eighteen, they become more realistic about the kind of person they need and can get along with. Some form more stable relationships, while others remain uncommitted. Here are some affirmations that can help a teenager cope when a relationship is in transition:

Affirmations for Coping with Breaking Up

(Said by the teen to himself)

If my partner doesn't want me, I can find someone who does.

I have the strength to handle this.

It's okay when I change my mind about my partner.

It's okay when my partner changes her mind about me.

It's okay to be single for a while.

IN ACTION

Karin is in a dying relationship. She and her boyfriend break up, come back together, only to fight and break up again. The problem centers around Ricardo's jealousy about Karin's other male friends.

Karin feels devastated about the breakup. Fortunately, she has an understanding relationship with her dad with whom she shares her feelings. Her dad says, "I can see you are in a lot of pain, Karin. Nobody enjoys breaking up. It is very difficult. But there are things you can say to yourself that will help you get through this. Would you like to find out what they are?"

After talking over her feelings with her father, Karin was able to create positive affirmations that gave her the courage to move through her grief:

Karin's Affirmations for Coping with a Breakup

I'm doing the right thing.

It's for the best even though it's hard and scary.

I hurt now, but I know I will get over it.

It's better to be single than to be in a destructive relationship.

There are other wonderful experiences for me to have.

I will love again.

Affirmations for Safe Sex

According to the National Campaign to Prevent Teen Pregnancy, the numbers of youth engaging in sexual experiences has been declining in recent years. Still, about half of all high school students report having had intercourse.[1] With the dangers of AIDS and the prevalence of other sexually transmitted infections, making smart decisions about sex has become critically important for a teen's lifelong health.

Pregnancy is also a major concern. Nearly four in ten young women become pregnant at least once before they reach the age of twenty—nearly one million a year.[2] According to the Children's Defense Fund report on America's children and teens for 1999,[3] every minute a teenage mother gives birth. Aside from the fact that a higher than normal percentage of teen babies are born with birth defects, the young mother is often forced to leave high school and begin a life of economic struggle and public assistance.

A number of factors contribute to accidental pregnancies and unsafe sex:

- For teenagers who don't have other outlets for intimate relating, such as deep friendships or goal-directed group activities, sex becomes the major avenue for attaining intimacy and emotional closeness.

- Many kids think, "It will never happen to me." Part of the reason for this denial is that teens are in a double bind about sex. Society glorifies sex and at the same time preaches chastity. Rather than try to resolve the paradox, kids choose not to think about it.

- Because teens have a pressing need to be accepted, they will often use sex as a way of gaining approval. A boy may say to his girlfriend, "If you have sex with me, then I will love you." Even if she doesn't want to be that intimate, she may accommodate rather than risk losing that love.

- Other teens do not consider themselves sexually active unless they have a steady partner. Therefore, a one-night affair will catch them unprepared when it comes to birth control. Ideally, the teen should ask himself, "Do I intend to become sexually active? If so, then I need to go about it in a responsible manner." Affirmations for self-responsibility (see pages 66–68 in Chapter 5) are beneficial in preparing a teen for this decision.

- Finally, some teen mothers get pregnant on purpose. Some do it to force marriage (not a wise strategy since most teen marriages end in divorce). Others wish to have a baby so that "somebody will love me." Asking a helpless child to meet the needs of an adult is a form of emotional abuse. Counseling and self-esteem affirmations can help the teens in your life to love and nurture themselves so that they no longer seek to get their needs met through having children.

Affirmations for Smart and Safe Sex
(Said by the teen to himself)

I can have sex when I am ready for it.

I can hold off if I want to.

I can choose to get involved or not involved.

If I choose to be sexual, I engage in safe sex.

I take responsibility for birth control.

I like myself enough to have safe sex.

It's always my choice.

IN ACTION

Linda had just met Rick, another sophomore. On their second date he expressed his desire to have sex. Linda liked Rick, but didn't feel ready to become that intimate, especially since he didn't want to use condoms. Nonetheless, she was afraid that he would leave her for someone else if she said no.

Like many girls her age, Linda wanted to be liked and accepted. This desire for approval was in conflict with her need to take care of herself by making responsible choices about sex. Not knowing what to do, Linda decided to have a talk with her school counselor, Mrs.

continued——➤

Colby. In her discussion, Linda realized that if Rick truly cared for her, he would respect her wishes. In addition, Mrs. Colby reminded her that many girls agree to have sex and still get left by their lovers. To encourage Linda to stick by her decision, Mrs. Colby helped her formulate the following affirmations:

Linda's Affirmations for Safe Sex

My life's more important than the approval of any boy.

I choose not to risk getting pregnant.

I deserve to be with someone who cares about what I think.

I will do what is best for me.

I can choose how, when, and with whom I have sex.

I expect Rick and other boys to respect that choice.

Drugs and Alcohol

In forming their new identity, teenagers are motivated to experiment and try out new ways of being. One area in which this need to experiment manifests is through drug and alcohol use. According to the National Center on Addiction and Substance Abuse, 79 percent of teens will try alcohol before they graduate from high school, and a quarter report frequent drug use.[4] They are motivated by peer pressure, availability, and curiosity.

Besides satisfying their curiosity, teens drink and smoke at parties to alleviate self-consciousness so that they can more easily communicate. Teens say that drinking helps them to feel more confident and less awkward and inhibited, especially when relating to the opposite sex. Being high creates the illusion of good communication. Hence drugs and alcohol function as a "lubricant" for sexuality.

Other kids drink socially because they are bored and don't know what else to do. More severe problems arise when kids mix drinking or drugging with driving, or use alcohol and drugs as a means of escape. The latter is common for children raised in addictive or abusive families.

Family can also play a role in helping children say no to alcohol and drugs. The number one reason kids give for not doing drugs is, "It would hurt my family. It would hurt my mom or dad." Groups such as stoners, loners, and gangs, whose primary bond and loyalty is to the peer group, don't experience the same family cohesion and are thus more prone to drug use.

Many excellent drug education programs are now available that teach refusal skills, coping with peer pressure, developing a positive self-image, making good decisions, and communication skills. The following affirmations can be employed as an adjunct to these programs:

Affirmations for Not Smoking
(Said by the teen to himself)

I am a nonsmoker.

I love myself enough to keep myself healthy.

I like breathing fresh, clean air.

My physical health is more important than pleasing other people.

It's always my choice.

Affirmations for Drug and Alcohol Control
(Said by the teen to himself)

I love myself enough not to drink or do drugs.

My physical health is more important than pleasing other people.

I fit in without getting drunk.

I take care of myself when I refuse drugs.

I communicate confidently and effectively without alcohol and drugs.

I am high on life.

I feel good without doing drugs.

It is always my choice.

IN ACTION

The students at Monroe High School had a longstanding tradition of having an all-night kegger for the seniors on the last day of school. One year, a group of seniors announced they were going to have an alternative party without alcohol. Although the plan was ridiculed at first, the party was attended by more than three-quarters of the senior class. The next year, the alternate party permanently replaced the kegger.

The reason for this shift is clear. The alternative party provided something to do—dancing, hot tubbing, listening to good music, and eating good food. On a night when many seniors would see each other for the last time, they chose to get closer to their classmates instead of drinking themselves into a stupor.

Affirming the Teenager's Future

From the age of twelve onward, adolescents develop the capacity to think abstractly. As their thinking moves from the concrete to the abstract, they construct theories, play with ideas, and fantasize about things that have not yet happened. For the first time in a child's life, the future becomes a concern.

Concern about the future is clearly justified by the time they graduate from high school. To begin, the teen is usually leaving home, most likely for the first time to make his way in the world. Whether he is attending college or entering the labor force, finding his place in the larger society is now the burning issue of the day.

Unfortunately, this process is often complicated by pressure from home. Many a teenager complains that parents or relatives are anxiously waiting for him to announce what he will be when he grows up. But discovering one's purpose is not an overnight decision. The average college student changes his major three to five times before graduating.[5] Most people spend their twenties finding out who they are and don't really come into their own until they are about thirty years old.

Often the teen is encouraged to do what is practical (major in business) instead of pursuing a calling that he truly loves such as playing music, teaching English, joining the Peace Corps. Affirmations help take the pressure off by reminding the teen that he is the best judge of what will bring him fulfillment and satisfaction in his work and personal life.

Concerns about the future can lead some teens to avoid graduating from high school because they don't have the confidence in themselves to handle what lies ahead. Others experience despair about the state of the world and the unclear fate of the human race. Here are some affirmations that can empower a teenager to embrace his future with hope, optimism and faith:

Affirmations for Creating a Positive Future
(Said by the teen to himself)

It's okay to be nervous about leaving home.

I am off on an exciting adventure.

I will make new friends in college.

I will make new friends on the job.

I can experiment and try different paths.

I am aware of my special talents and abilities.

I can choose a different career from that of my parents.

I have faith in my future.

I have faith in the world's future.

IN ACTION

Eighteen-year-old Harvey was about to complete high school. Two weeks before graduation his parents strongly suggested he get a business degree at college. They said, "Although this is what we want you to do, we also want you to be happy. So if what we suggest isn't going to make you happy, then don't do it."

After graduation, Harvey told his friends, "I really appreciate my parents for letting me decide how to live my life."

Affirmations for the Parents of Teenagers

In an interview, a woman executive who had risen to the top of a major corporation shared the secret of her success: "I learned not to take things personally." This same piece of wisdom can be passed on to any parent of teenagers—"Don't take their actions personally."

In order to find out who they are, teenagers question the value system they learned from their mom and dad. Knowing that they must leave home, adolescents purposefully create conflict with their parents in order to create distance from them. In a sense, they are experiencing a second toddlerhood. Hence, the first thing that you as a parent can do to preserve your sanity is to realize that your teenager's rebellion is normal behavior.

The degree to which teenagers go from partial to outright rebellion is based on how much their parents try to control them. As a parent, imagine yourself being a well-padded brick wall. You can let the kids bounce off you, but don't try to push back. When you try to impose your will on a child, he thinks, "I'm just trying to find out who I am. Why won't my parents leave me alone?" Paradoxically, when you stop fighting him, the adolescent is thrown back on his own insecurity and often requests your help.

What teenagers are saying to you is, "This is the time of my life when I desperately need to learn to make choices for myself. It's too scary to be turned loose on the adult playing field. So I need you, the adult, to tell me what my playing field is and what the boundaries are. Then turn me loose and let me make my own mistakes and have my own experiences."

A wise parent will help the adolescent make his choices and experience the natural consequences of those choices. He can say to the teen, "You know what you need to live your life. I am here to offer you information and a little bit of awareness. Consider me a guide and a resource. I don't know what your agenda is, but you do. It's your life. You are in charge. Live it."

Affirmations for Letting Go of Control

(Said by the parent to himself)

My teenager's behavior is normal
and to be expected.

It's natural for my kid
to be intensely emotional.

Although I want to hold on, I give
my child the freedom he needs.

I affirm my teenager's desire
to separate from me.

I set limits but keep
them flexible.

I can tolerate what I may
not always like.

I accept both my positive and
negative feelings about my child.

This is a stage he is going
through.

Please refer to Chapter 4, "Positive Talk for the Adult Caregiver," for other affirmations on this subject.

A Final Note

Seeing your child go through puberty offers you the opportunity to reexperience and heal the pain of your own adolescence. If you still have trouble with authority, can't seem to "grow up," are confused about who you really are, see yourself as a conformist, or are having trouble finding your niche in life, you may have unresolved issues from this period.

The more you can heal your unfinished business from these teenage years, the more at peace you will be when your own children go through the trials of adolescence. Instead of getting your buttons pushed by their behavior, you can remain calm, rational—and even helpful.

Summary

Through good parenting and the use of affirmations, parents, teachers, and counselors can support the teenager to master the challenges of this developmental stage. Although he may not be consciously aware of it, the teenage child will have developed certain beliefs about himself and the world by the time he enters adulthood. If he could consciously state these beliefs as affirmations, this is how they would appear:

Positive Beliefs for the Adolescent to Develop

I can be my own person.

I can separate from Mom and Dad.

I am a part of a group, yet still maintain my independence.

I make good choices about the things that I do.

I say no to things that are not good for me.

My body is going through changes and that's okay.

I feel good about my relationships.

I take responsibility for my sexuality.

I am making plans to pursue a fulfilling career.

I take my time in deciding on my future.

I look forward to the opportunities that lie ahead.

Using the affirmations in this chapter will help the teenager develop these core beliefs as he prepares for his new life in the adult world.

PART FOUR

Positive Talk

for Children with Special Needs

> People couldn't understand why my mama would have
> this blind kid out doing things like cutting wood for the fire.
> But she had the foresight to go against the grain. . . .
> Her thing was: "He may be blind, but he ain't stupid."
>
> *Ray Charles, musician*

CHAPTER **18**

Positive Talk for the Child with a Physical, Learning, or Emotional Disability

Each of us is a unique individual with different capabilities and ways of doing things. In this chapter, we will focus on affirmations for children whose physical, cognitive, and emotional/behavioral differences create limits that may be problematic for them and their caregivers. These differences, commonly referred to as "disabilities," fall into three major categories:

- **physical disabilities**—includes children with physical or health problems such as cerebral palsy, cleft palate, muscular dystrophy, spinal bifida, heart disease, leukemia, hemophilia, fetal alcohol and drug syndrome, and visual and hearing impairments

- **cognitive disabilities**—includes children who are learning disabled, language-impaired, and developmentally disabled

- **emotional and behavioral disabilities**—includes children who are severely emotionally disturbed or exhibit extreme behavior problems

It's important that children with these types of differences also recognize their *abilities*, including the special strengths they have that result from these differences. For example, while a child with attention hyperactivity deficit disorder (ADHD) may be highly distractible, when she does zero in on a task, she may have an extraordinary ability to concentrate for long periods.

It's also helpful for children with these differences to recognize that everyone requires assistance in some ways. Some people are short and need help reaching a high shelf; others are tall and can't fit into small spaces. Some wear glasses (adaptive equipment) and can't

247

see without them. Positive self-talk can help children with disabilities live their lives at full capacity, draw upon their strengths, and recognize the ways in which they are just like other children.

Overcoming the Stigma of Being Labeled

The first challenge that any child with a disability must overcome concerns the way she sees herself in relation to the disability. Is she a person who *has* a disability, or is she a disabled *person*—a person who is inherently defective?

Our culture has traditionally supported the latter view—that a person with a disability is somehow flawed at the core. Children with disabilities internalize this prejudice to create the belief that there is something inherently wrong with them. To transform this and other negative beliefs listed above, a child can begin to see herself as separate from her disability, as someone who *has*, not *is*, a disability. She also can recognize that her differences are not necessarily deficits. In some cases, they give her abilities beyond what other children have, such as extra strengths within certain learning styles.

On the first day of school, a well-meaning teacher brought Henry before the class and said, "This is Henry. He has a withered arm, so I want you to be nice to him." Without realizing it, the teacher had conveyed the message: Henry is weak and requires special treatment; he is different from everyone else and needs your sympathy. Fortunately, the school counselor was able to talk to the teacher and the class and explain that Henry was a normal, healthy boy who could be treated just like everyone else. Over the nine-month term, the class learned to value Henry a whole person.

Here are some affirmations for children with disabilities:

Affirmations for Self-Acceptance for the Child with a Disability

(Said by the adult to the child)

You are a special person with your own unique strengths.

You are wonderful and I enjoy being with you.

continued⟶

> Life is not fair but we can focus on the good parts.

> You are a strong person learning to deal with a difficult situation.

> I love you just the way you are.

Releasing Shaming Self-Talk

The following "reprogramming" exercise can be done one-on-one or in a group. Ask each child to write down any negative beliefs or self-talk that she is aware of having about her disability. Once she has formed her list, she can write an affirmation to replace each of the negative self-statements, as shown in the following example:

Child's Shaming Self-Talk	Child's Healing Affirmation
There is something wrong with me.	I am a terrific person.
I'm not normal.	I'm okay just as I am.
I am defective.	Everyone is different. I like being unique.
I am weird.	I like being me.
It's my fault I am like this.	I didn't choose to be the way I am, but I can choose how to live my life.
I'm deformed.	I love my body.
I can't do things well.	I can do many things well.
I give up.	I can try and I can succeed.
I'm helpless.	I can learn to help myself.
I'm different (in a negative way).	I love being me.

IN ACTION ➡

A disability in itself cannot make a child feel ashamed. It is how the child and her family respond to the disability that determines the level of the child's self-esteem and happiness.

Isaiah was a child born without legs. When he was old enough to understand, his mother told him, "I'm sorry Isaiah, that you were born without legs; there's nothing we can do about it. You'll just have to apply yourself a little more than the other kids." Isaiah did just that. He became proficient in wheelchair racing and set a number of world records.

IN ACTION ➡

Like all human beings, children have an inborn need to be accepted and to belong. A child with a disability often feels left out and isolated because she is "different" and doesn't fit in with the other kids. The following letter, written to the high school paper by a student with cerebral palsy, points out that no matter how different we may appear on the outside, we are the same on the inside.

To the Editor,

I am writing this to bring about an understanding of people with disabilities at Madison . . . or anywhere else. This is from my own point of view as a person with cerebral palsy.

I am aware that people often view us as less capable and less valuable than people without physical disabilities. Also, many people are just plain uncomfortable with anyone who is different from themselves. I speak from experience when I say that people with disabilities have a hard time making close friendships with "regular" people.

Most people seem to have a hard time looking past the physical and seeing us for who we really are. People have to know that we are looking for friends

continued ➡

who aren't afraid to take a risk and get to know us on a personal level. People who are willing to share themselves in the same way they do with other friends will find us no different than anyone else.

Cheryl Thompson, Senior

Overcoming Learned Helplessness

> Success implies overcoming an obstacle,
> including perhaps the thought in our minds
> that we might not succeed. It is turning "I can't"
> into "I can" and "I did."
>
> *John Holt, author and teacher*

For many children with disabilities, the words "handicapped," "special need," and "disabled" are synonymous with "helpless." This negative belief is too often reinforced by a world that focuses on what the child can't do. As one teenager complained, "People treat me as if I were made of glass. When they ask, 'Do you need help?' they are subconsciously saying, 'You can't do that.'"

Children are deeply influenced by the expectations of their adult caregivers. When a child hears "you can't," she internalizes it as "I can't."

The student with a learning disability thinks, "I can't read this," or "I can't do this math problem."

The child with a language impairment concludes, "I can't write this sentence."

The child with a physical handicap decides, "I can't play this sport," "I can't do this dance." "I'm a klutz." "I'm not going to try in gym class."

The best way to reverse the "I can't" syndrome is to provide a child with a small success experience. This involves setting up a simple activity that the child can do, and then affirming her ability to do it before, during, and after the activity. In this way, the affirmation and the success experience work together to restore the child's lost confidence.

Once children have a success experience, they are more likely to try the next time—which leads to the likelihood of another success. As one teacher said, "The more you try, the more you are likely to succeed; and the more you succeed, the more you are willing to try again. Nothing succeeds like success."

Another way to overcome the "I can't" syndrome is to give children role models of successful people who have disabilities. One special education teacher recounted the story of a well-known children's author who didn't learn to read until he was twenty-two. Another teacher passed out a list of fifty celebrities with learning disabilities. Christopher Reeves, the actor who played Superman and appeared in other movies, is an excellent role model because of his determination to walk again after being paralyzed from an accident. He is now walking with assistance and doing many other things that his doctors told him he would never be able to do.

Transforming "I can't" into "I can" is a life-long task that begins with a child telling herself that she is capable. Fortunately there is a drive within every child for autonomy, self-sufficiency, and self-reliance. This desire for independence will grow and blossom wherever it is supported.

Affirmations for Overcoming the "I Can't" Syndrome
(Said by the adult to the child)

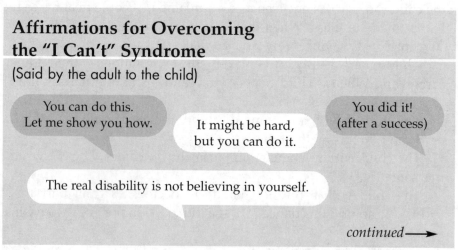

You can do this.
Let me show you how.

It might be hard, but you can do it.

You did it!
(after a success)

The real disability is not believing in yourself.

continued——▶

(Said by the child to herself)

> Whenever I hear myself saying "I can't," I replace it with "I'll try."

> I try my best.

> I can figure this out.

> I know how to get help if I need it.

IN ACTION

Seven-year-old Jada had a mild case of cerebral palsy. After her first swimming lesson she became discouraged and wanted to stop the lessons. Fortunately, her parents responded, "You can learn to swim. If you keep trying, you will learn."

Taking heart from her parents' encouragement, Jada plodded on for a few weeks. Then one day, she noticed a few small improvements. Seeing these tangible results inspired Jada to say, "I am getting better. I am improving." The lessons continued and more improvement followed. Soon she became a capable swimmer.

The Way Out of Helplessness— Through Making Choices

Another strategy for overcoming learned helplessness is to give kids choices. Choices empower children to become responsible for their lives. When children are given options, they experience themselves as acting upon their environment. Here are some statements that adult caregivers can make which will provide choices and options to the child with a disability:

- "You can wheel your chair (instead of having me push it). Would you like to do it on the way to lunch or coming back from lunch?"

- "Which type of adaptive equipment (tray, mobile arm support, foot rest) would you like to use today?"

• "Would you like your tray higher or lower? You can try it out and see what happens."

If a child continues to say "I can't," the adult can say, "Show me what you find difficult and I'll help you."

Overcoming learned helplessness requires a whole new way of thinking and behaving. It's a relearning process that takes time. But once a child takes that step toward independence, she will rarely want to return to the old way.

IN ACTION

Mikayla had a hard time feeding herself. She started to think of herself as helpless and asked others to feed her. Once she stopped feeding herself, she started to feel helpless to do other things—like going to the movies, using the bathroom, or picking out the clothes she wanted to wear.

With the help of her counselor, Mikayla learned that she had a choice as to how she wanted to think about herself. Mikayla decided that she didn't want to see herself as helpless anymore. Here are some affirmations she used to support her decision:

Mikayla's Affirmations

I can learn to help myself.

I can take part in feeding myself.

I want to become more independent.

As I practice being independent, I feel better about me.

As her program progressed, Mikayla noticed that sometimes she would go back to telling herself she was helpless, especially when she was struggling to feed herself crackers. As soon as she became conscious of this negative self-talk, Mikayla reminded herself that she could be independent, even though eating crackers was a hard thing to do. This gave her the confidence to try new things that she previously avoided.

Focusing on Strengths

Another way children can overcome the "I can't" syndrome is to focus on their strengths and recognize their areas of competence. A student with cerebral palsy who tutors classmates in English said, "As I give to others, I forget about my own problems and lacks. The joy I experience in giving is a blessing, especially when I am in danger of feeling sorry for myself." Please refer to Chapter 5, "Positive Talk to Build Self-Esteem," for some positive self-statements that children with disabilities can use to identify and celebrate their strengths.

Accepting Limitations

Along with their emphasizing strengths, kids with disabilities need to be realistic about and accept their limitations. It often takes children a while to appreciate what their disability is. Roy, a seven-year-old with spinal bifida, tells his parents, "I'll be a baseball player when I get older." At some point Roy will realize that he's not going to become an athlete. This does not have to be a depressing realization, for children with disabilities can still engage in fun and meaningful activities.

It's also important to allow the child to have his feelings about his disability. If the child expresses sadness about his disability and we say, "Oh, it's not so bad," we are denying him the right to experience his pain and grief. A response that validates the child's feelings is: "You have a right to feel sad about your disability It's a tough situation you are in. I understand that. Now let's figure out what we can do about it."

Acknowledging Progress

No matter what the child's level of disability is, she can make progress and expand the limits of what she can do. Acknowledging and celebrating this progress is part of building the child's self-esteem.

Once a month (or whatever time period you pick), set aside time when you and your child can chronicle her recent improvements. Focus on specifics—learning her numbers, learning new words, improving her walking, using words instead of hitting. The more areas in which she can see specific progress, the better she will feel. As children learn to evaluate and acknowledge their own progress, they will be more likely to think in terms of what they can do instead of what they can't.

IN ACTION

Lenny is a five-year-old child with Down's syndrome who has a mental age of nine to ten months. He cannot speak and can only walk with a walker.

One day he picked up a cup and showed it to his mother, signifying that he wanted water. This was an important step for him, one in which he and his parents took great pride. His mom and dad congratulated Lenny on his progress. Then he was ready to take his next step in learning.

IN ACTION

Estelle, the mother of a third grader with a learning disability was upset because her daughter was reading at the first grade level. A year earlier, however, the daughter wasn't reading at all. The teacher explained, "Look how far your daughter has come." Then she gave Estelle the following affirmations to review and repeat:

Estelle's Affirmations

My daughter is improving.

My child is moving forward.

I can rejoice with her about each step she takes.

I am proud of her.

After working with these affirmations, Estelle was able to accept her daughter at her reading level and acknowledge her progress.

Making Friends

Many students with disabilities are also delayed in their social and emotional development. They complain that they don't know how to make friends and fulfill their need for intimacy. They feel isolated, alienated, and cut off. A common refrain is, "No one likes me."

This sense of isolation is further compounded by the child's having a disability label or being in a special education program in school. If her home life isn't very supportive and she doesn't get help from her family in learning basic communication skills, her difficulties may be further exacerbated.

The impact of poor social skills is particularly felt during the adolescent years when peer group acceptance is so important. Kids with disabilities who can't bond with others become depressed and forlorn during this time. Others act out through disruptive behavior or gang involvement. Those who develop good social skills are more successful and happier, irrespective of the nature of their disability.

Fortunately, many school systems offer programs that teach specific social and communication skills to children. Such skills include how to make friends, how to express feelings, how to give "I" messages, and how to manage anger. Please refer to Chapter 16, "Affirming the School-Age Child," for friendship-building affirmations.

Teasing

Because they are perceived as "different," children with disabilities are vulnerable to teasing.

IN ACTION

Corey was a tall and clumsy child who also had a learning disability. At school, the other kids mercilessly teased him, calling him such names as "retardo." Corey also had a short fuse and frequently lashed out at his tormentors.

Fortunately, Corey found an ally in his school counselor. One day Mr. Grant sat down with Corey and asked him to list some names that really made him angry. After Corey compiled his list, Mr. Grant said, "When a kid calls you one of these names, here's what you can do. Ask the child, 'What was that you said?' When he repeats the name, look him straight in the eye and say, 'I can handle that.'" Then they role-played the scene.

Counselor: Hey, retardo.

Corey: What was that you called me?

Counselor: I said retardo.

continued⟶

Corey: That's what I thought you said—"retardo." I can handle that.

The counselor also taught Corey some deep breathing exercises to help him defuse his short temper (see the four-step anger management technique on pages 158–159). In addition, he gave Corey the affirmation, "No matter what others may say or do, I'm still a worthwhile person."

Two weeks later, Corey ran up to Mr. Grant on the playground and said to his classmates, "Here's the guy who helped me handle the teasing."

Please refer to Chapter 11, "What to Say When You Are Teased: Positive Talk for Responding to Put-Downs," for additional examples on how children can respond to teasing.

Positive Self-Talk
for the Child with Learning Difficulties

Many children are called "learning disabled" when a discrepancy exists between their overall aptitude and their ability in a specific area of learning—such as reading or math. In many cases, a child may have what might be better described as a learning difference—a way of learning that is different from the norm but doesn't mean she is incapable of learning. She can still learn the material when supported in her particular way of learning.

Some children are "language-impaired." These children experience a disruption in the way they understand and produce language. They struggle to understand what is said to them and to communicate their ideas to others. For example, a language-impaired child who had just returned from a vacation in Hawaii could not communicate how he had flown from Honolulu to his home in Portland.

The first step in working with kids who have learning difficulties is to affirm that every child is able to learn. Here are two affirmations which announce this truth: (1) All children can learn. (2) All children are learners.

In order to become a learner, the child with learning difficulties must discover her unique learning style. As one speech and language therapist explained to her students, "If you don't understand a concept, you need to raise your hand and ask to have it explained in a way that you do understand it. Maybe you need pictures. Maybe you need to be able to repeat it back to the teacher. Find out what works for you and then do it."

Children with learning difficulties who don't succeed in finding their learning style become frustrated and discouraged. Many develop behavior problems, get labeled as "bad students," drop out of school, and later engage in deviant behavior (see Chapter 21 on the acting-out child). Thus, it is paramount that we help children with learning differences to identify their style as early as possible and support them in seeing themselves as learners.

Make Your Affirmations Specific and Concrete

Affirmations for a child with a learning difficulty work best when they are paired with a concrete activity or behavior that the child has successfully performed. Then, when the child has mastered the task, the teacher can say, "Jasmine, you are a successful learner." Jasmine then self-reflects, "I am a successful learner."

Being specific and concrete also applies to general self-esteem affirmations such as "You're okay." Instead, specify what "okay" means—getting along with others, being willing to have fun, playing a game, sharing toys, talking about problems, or enjoying a joke.

Here are some very specific ways that Jasmine's teacher affirms to Jasmine that she is doing well:

- "Jasmine, people like to be around you." (Instead of "You are likable.")

- "You were able to write a good poem." (Instead of "You are a good writer.")

- "You let Patrick use the glue first." (Instead of "You are cooperative.")

- "You learned your numbers from one to twenty." (Instead of "You are smart.")

- "You drew an 'A.'"

- "You cut on the line."

Here is a list of affirmations for kids with learning disabilities that can be combined with success-oriented activities:

Affirmations for Children with Learning Difficulties

(Said by the adult to the child)

All children can learn.

Every child has a right to learn.

You can reach your potential.

You can learn in the way that works best for you.

(Said by the child to himself)

I am here to learn.

I can succeed using my own way of learning.

The more I read, the more I know; the more I know, the further I go.

What I can say, I can write.

I can remember my times tables.

I enjoy learning my numbers.

When I get stuck on a problem, I know how to get help.

IN ACTION

George was feeling frustrated in his math and reading. His teacher asked him to pick a "slogan" that would help him through. George looked over his affirmation list and chose, "The more I read, the more I know; the more I know, the further I go." Repeating his slogan helped motivate him to stick with his assignments.

Affirmations for Reducing Stuttering

Stuttering is defined as a genetic predisposition to produce sounds in an asynchronous, arrhythmic way that results in an interruption of speech flow. Stuttering is a normal part of speech development in preschool children. It goes away by itself if attention isn't called to it.

When listening to a stuttering preschooler, it is helpful to give them your undivided attention without helping them speak.

If stuttering becomes a serious problem, behavioral/mechanical techniques that focus on such processes as right breathing, the correct way of using the voice, and making smooth transitions between syllables can be helpful. But what the stutterer says to herself before and during stuttering also has a direct impact on her ability to produce controlled, normal-sounding speech. The use of positive self-talk helps stutterers gain fluency in a number of ways. First, it reminds the stutterer of her skills. Second, it focuses her attention on those aspects of speech over which she has control. And third, self-acceptance affirmations allow the child who stutters to become tolerant of her less-than-perfect speech.

Self-talk techniques for stuttering work especially well with older children (age twelve and up). They can be quite helpful for the self-conscious teenager for whom stuttering is a problem in her social life.

Many children who stutter fail to successfully use their speech control and fluency-enhancing techniques because of irrational beliefs that get in the way. Here are four such irrational beliefs and the affirmations that can replace them:

Irrational belief #1: "It is important that everyone approve of me all of the time." A child who has this belief will be reticent to use her fluency skills because of the fear of disapproval. An affirmation to counter the belief is, "I approve of the way I talk, and that is enough."

Irrational belief #2: "It is important that I excel in everything I do." Even after completing a fluency program, a person will still stutter now and then. Two affirmations that give her permission to be human are, "It's okay if I make a mistake" and "I accept myself."

Irrational belief #3: "If things don't go quite as well as they should, it's a catastrophe." To counter this irrational thought, the person who stutters can say, "Even if I mess up (as one man did by stuttering on the punchline of a joke) I will survive. I can find out what I need to focus on the next time."

Irrational belief #4: "Things that I fear should be a matter of great concern and worry." To alleviate the panic and anxiety that arise from this belief, one can say, "Whatever happens, I can handle it" and "I relax and let go."

IN ACTION ➤

Levi, a teenager who stutters, was nervously preparing to give a speech. Upon examining his self-talk, he heard the words, "I just can't cope. What if I stutter in front of the group?" Realizing that this negative self-talk would only worsen the stuttering, Levi created the following affirmations:

Levi's Affirmations

I'm nervous, but I know what I have to do to give a good speech.

I take a few slow breaths so I am comfortable and at ease.

I've spoken before in situations such as this and I can do it again.

This is a good opportunity to stretch my comfort zone.

Levi proceeded to give a fine talk.

IN ACTION ➤

Brianna, a seventh grader who stuttered when saying words that contained the letter "m", is understandably apprehensive about going to McDonald's and ordering a McChicken sandwich. The fast-clipped pace of the speech at the restaurant also worried her, as quick speech normally made her stutter even more. Here are some affirmations she used to address her negative self-talk as she placed her order:

Brianna's Affirmations

I feel nervous right now, but this is an opportunity to use my speech control.

It's okay if this person notices I'm working at my speech.

It's okay if I stutter.

No matter what happens, I'm still a worthwhile person.

Brianna combined her affirmations with her speech techniques to successfully order her lunch.

Positive Self-Talk for the Child with an Emotional or Behavioral Disability

In Chapters 19 and 20, we will explore the stress and abuse that children experience who grow up in severely dysfunctional families. A portion of these children develop emotional and behavioral problems that severely interfere with their ability to function in the world. Such problems include:

inappropriate anger
loss of control
learning problems
acting out
poor coping skills
inability to relax
blaming
condemning
being the victim
problems with boundaries

helplessness
yelling
interpersonal conflicts
pouting
manipulating
gossiping
perceptual distortions
harming themselves
low tolerance for frustration

Clinical terms for describing the child with an emotional disability include "severely emotionally disturbed" (SED) and "severely emotionally impaired" (SEI). Bear in mind, however, that such a child is not "disturbed at the core" but, like any child with a disability, is a normal person dealing with an abnormal situation.

The goal in working with the child with an emotional disability lies in teaching her to understand and modify her thoughts, feelings, and behavior so that she can function in a social context. This means learning to become responsible for her thoughts and actions so that she no longer reacts to the world as a victim.

The Role of Positive Self-Talk in the Healing Process

Positive self-talk can be a powerful tool to help the emotionally disturbed child to master and direct her emotions and behavior. After a year of using affirmations in her class, a special-ed teacher concluded, "Affirmations have become a way of life for my kids. They subtly change the way my children think about themselves. Most importantly, the habit of affirming stays with them after they leave the class. When faced with future challenges, they can use this tool again and again."

Let's now turn to a few areas where affirmations can make a difference in the lives of children with emotional disabilities.

Learning to Control Anger

Anger is a major problem for the child with an emotional disability. All children get angry, but the emotionally disturbed child's anger is more violent, lasts longer, and occurs more frequently. At the same time, she feels powerless and helpless to express her feelings any other way. The child doesn't act, but reacts. If Jeff pushes Dave, then Dave thinks, "I have to hit him. What else can I do?"

A second way that emotionally disturbed children express their anger is to turn it in on themselves (also called low-arousal anger). These shame-based kids see themselves as bad and worthless. When something negative happens to them, they say, "I deserved this." Often they become suicidal.

Whether the anger is acted out or acted in, healing lies in focusing the anger on the appropriate source and feeling the grief below the anger. Individual therapy and support groups provide safe environments where healing can take place. In addition, the anger management techniques and affirmations found in Chapter 10 can be directly applied by the child with an emotional disability. Please refer to them.

IN ACTION

Paco, a sixteen-year-old special-ed student, worked hard on his anger management with his counselor and teacher. One day he was attacked from behind and kicked by another student several times. Using the four-step process explained on pages 158–159, Paco got up and walked away without retaliating. Paco became an instant hero and role model to his classmates.

IN ACTION

Often children get angry so quickly that they cannot control themselves unless an adult is present to stop them. When a child does act out, the adult and child can debrief the incident afterwards.

Eleven-year-old Roy punched a kid who had teased him. Afterwards, his counselor asked Roy to draw a picture of what happened.

continued⟶

"Was losing control helpful to you?" the counselor asked.

"I guess not," Roy sheepishly replied.

"Why don't we see if you can draw a picture of another way that you can handle the situation next time."

Roy picked up the crayons and drew a picture of his new response. The drawing showed Roy walking away from his provoker while saying his affirmations.

Learning Social Skills and Appropriate Behavior

Managing anger fits into a broader issue that children with emotional disabilities must master—learning appropriate social skills. Mastering these skills becomes an important factor in determining when the child in a special education environment can be "transitioned" into a mainstream setting. At one residential facility, the director and staff ask that children demonstrate certain competencies before they are mainstreamed. They must:

- know what school expectations are
- know what good classroom conduct means
- be organized
- follow directions
- be able to take homework back and forth to class
- express anger appropriately
- not require physical restraint

As children learn to act more responsibly toward themselves and others, they gain the freedom to move from more restrictive to less restrictive environments. The following affirmations can help children learn and internalize their new behaviors. Many students find it helpful to post their affirmations at their desk or in places where they can view them on a daily basis.

Affirmations for Responsible Behavior
(Said by the child to herself)

> I am responsible for my school behavior.

> I learn how to get along with other kids.

> I get attention from the teacher by raising my hand.

> I ask for help when I need it.

> I follow directions.

> I behave in the lunchroom.

> I take care of myself.

IN ACTION

Hailey, a seventh grader, was sexually abused by her stepfather. When people asked Hailey to follow a direction, she acted out her rage by screaming, "You can't make me. I'll call my lawyer. My mother is going to kill you."

One day, after a typical time-out, her teacher said, "Hailey, can you think of some other way to respond?"

"I could probably ask for what I want," she replied. That answer became an affirmation, "I can ask for what I want." Here are some others she came up with:

Hailey's Affirmations

> I can stop yelling.

> People will listen to me.

> I can ask for what I need.

> People will respond to me.

One day, as a fit began to mount, the teacher asked: "Are we going to have a Hailey fit today?"

"I haven't decided," Hailey replied.

continued ⟶

"Do you have a choice?" asked the teacher.

"Yes, I do."

"What do you choose?"

"I don't need to have a Hailey fit," Hailey answered. "I am growing and growing. I am growing and growing."

The trauma of sexual abuse also shows itself through bodily symptoms. When Hailey complained of headaches and pains in her legs, she and her teacher made up the following affirmation for Hailey to repeat: "I am whole, well, and healthy, and feeling better all the time." Hailey set the words to a tune which she sang to herself. She also played affirmation-music tapes which her teacher brought to class. By the time she reached ninth grade, the physical symptoms had disappeared.

The Power of the Support Group

As a rule, children with emotional disabilities were raised in family systems where their feelings were not honored or validated. In their recovery process, they learn to label and give words to the emotions they feel such as fear, anger, sadness, and joy. Support groups are a wonderful way to help children identify and express their feelings. When Carole Allison, a middle-school special education teacher, first asked her class of fifteen emotionally disturbed children to sit together and talk about their feelings, they were too embarrassed. "The kids had so much shame, self-hate, and feelings of inferiority and anger, they couldn't handle being in a group," Carole reported.

By mid-year, however, the children couldn't get enough of group time. The group had become a place where they could talk about their pain and receive the support that was lacking in their lives.

One day Timothy, a lanky, soft-spoken ninth grader, arrived at the group very upset. The day before, his father wouldn't pick him up from school after he had taken ill. Timothy blurted out, "I hate my dad. He doesn't care about me." The group members acknowledged Timothy's right to be angry. They said, "Timothy, it's okay to be mad at your dad. He tries to love you, but he can only do it the way he was taught. You can get love from other places. We care about you in this group."

Then Carole gave Timothy the following affirmations to practice: "I am loved," "I have friends who care about me," and "I can talk about my hurt in my support group."

Affirmations for Self-Esteem

Like most children with emotional disabilities, Timothy and his group members have low self-esteem. Carole introduced special self-esteem affirmations, like those found in Chapter 5, that focused on things the kids did well and on what they liked about themselves. Typical affirmations included, "I can run fast," "I can draw a picture," and "I have a nice smile."

Carole also introduced a group exercise in which "a special person" receives a compliment from each of the other members. One afternoon, Sherry was chosen to be that special person. Here are some statements of appreciation she received from the group:

"Sherry, I like you because . . . you listen to me."

"Sherry, I like you because . . . you are a good worker."

"Sherry, I like you because . . . you take good care of yourself."

"Sherry, I like you because . . . you are you! I don't have a specific reason. I just like you."

Then Sherry was asked to give herself some compliments. She responded:

"I like me because . . . I am special"

"I like me because . . . I am a nice person."

"I like me because . . . I am considerate."

"I like me because . . . I work hard."

"I like me because . . . I look nice."

Sometimes, the self-image of children is so low that they can't think of positive words to say about themselves. When Bill was asked to give himself a compliment, he said, "This is hard. I can't give myself a compliment. I can't think of anything good to say."

"That's okay," the group replied. "Bill, you have a good mind. You can think of good things to say about yourself. We will wait." The group waited for five minutes. Finally, Bill did find something to say, but it was difficult. "It seems like bragging," he noted.

Later on, Carole had Bill fill in the following sentence. "I am wonderful; therefore I deserve _____." Bill said he deserved to have a pizza party with his group. Two weeks later, he got the party he had asked for.

The Healing Power of Music and Visual Imagery

Teachers, social workers, and therapists who work with emotionally disturbed children have long observed that they are especially receptive to "right-brained" modes of processing information such as music and visual imagery. Each morning, Carole leads her class in a progressive relaxation process and then plays the song "I Love Myself the Way I Am." Children become mesmerized as they listen to the music and its message of self-love and self-esteem. As one child put it, "Songs like this help me get back in touch with myself."

A large percentage of children with emotional disabilities are more visual than verbal (especially those who are language-impaired). Instead of hearing the words, they see pictures. Affirmations for these kids should be accompanied by pictures that symbolize the content of the affirmation.

For example, when Curt heard the words "I like myself," he saw a picture of himself smiling. He then drew a portrait of that image and looked at it each time he said the affirmation. In this way, Curt was able to internalize the affirmation by pairing it with a visual image.

Children with emotional disabilities often feel discouraged and hopeless. A second visualization exercise seeks to break the cycle of despair and hopelessness by asking children to imagine something greater than what now exists. After Christmas vacation, Carole Allison asks her students to draw what they would like to have happen in the coming new year. Each child also writes an affirmation below his or her picture. Carole collects the images and displays them where they can be viewed.

At the end of the school day, each child looks at his affirmation-portrait and says, "My dreams for _____ (the current year) are coming true. May this or something better happen to me this year."

Affirming Children with Behavioral Disorders

Some children who consistently exhibit severe behavior problems are diagnosed with behavioral disorders. For example, children with attention deficit hyperactivity disorder (ADHD) tend to be highly aggressive, unable to sit still, and unable to listen. Because actions such as these irritate and anger others, a child with a behavioral disorder may be told, "You're a bad girl." Soon she begins to reason, "If I'm a bad girl, I'll show those people how bad I can really be!"

This vicious cycle may sometimes be broken through medications such as Ritalin. Then, as the child's behavior improves, her teachers and students begin to reach out to her.

Behavior management employed over a long developmental period also produces positive results. This may include:

- setting up the environment so that the child receives ongoing feedback and monitoring

- giving the child a lot of external structure and keeping her attention focused

- providing explicit rules that the child can clearly understand

- following up with consequences that she can learn from

- providing one-on-one attention and lots of encouragement

Children with behavioral disorders may have difficulty using cognitive techniques, such as positive self-talk, to manage their behavior if they aren't able to focus easily. Nonetheless, as they make progress and become more able to focus, these children can learn to apply the affirmations listed throughout this chapter.

Letting Go of Parental Guilt and Shame

Parents of a child with a behavior disorder also become victims of their child's disorder. After being called down to the principal's office for the tenth time, one mother remarked, "Perhaps I am a bad parent. Maybe it's my fault that my child is out of control." Here are some helpful affirmations for parents:

Affirmations for Parents of Children with Behavior Disorders

(Said by the adult to herself)

I can learn ways to help my child.

With my help, my child has the ability to improve her behavior.

I am a good parent.

I have a good child.

continued ⟶

> I can find the resources I need to show me how to help my child.

> I can get help for my child's problem.

> We can work together to manage her problem.

> I love and accept myself as a parent.

IN ACTION

Mom was on the phone when Charlie, her five-year-old child with ADHD, began pulling at her pants and throwing a tantrum. Since overtly punishing the child leads to more aggressive behavior, she found an alternative solution.

Mom hung up the phone, called a recorded time message, and pretended to continue her original conversation. A few minutes later, Charlie took a break from the tantrum. Mom immediately turned to him and said, "Charlie, you settled down. That's exactly what Mommy wanted you to do. Thank you for helping Mommy."

Using this strategy, the mother positively reinforced the desired behavior (Charlie remaining calm while she talked) instead of negatively reinforcing the undesired behavior. She repeated this method over time and noticed that Charlie demanded less attention while she was on the phone.

Other Affirmations for Parents of a Child with a Disability

The family environment is a critical factor in determining how a child copes with her disability. With loving and supportive parents, a child can learn to live with and even transcend her disability. When the family system works against her, however, the child grows up with a double handicap.

In many respects, being the parent of a child with a disability is a more intensive version of regular parenting. Aside from the normal parenting duties, parents must gather and integrate a huge amount of information about their child and her disability. Meetings with professionals such as doctors, psychologists, and educators take up more time and energy.

Two powerful affirmations that the parent of a child with a disability can use to affirm herself and her child are:

I can help my child get what she needs.

I can be a good parent to my child.

Here are some others:

Affirmations for Parenting a Child with a Disability

(Said by the parent to herself)

I can be an effective advocate for my child.

The opportunity to serve my child brings me great joy.

Because I love and support my child, I can handle the extra responsibility.

I find opportunities for my child to develop within her limits.

I am supportive of my child at her developmental level.

I can share what I have learned to help other parents who have children with disabilities.

Please refer to Chapter 4, "Positive Talk for the Adult Caregiver," for a full range of parenting affirmations.

Preventing Burnout

Even with the extra time and effort devoted to caring for their child, parents of a child with a disability can find ways to nurture themselves if it's a priority. But many parents become overworked and neglect their own needs, resulting in burnout, depression, and poor parenting.

One factor that contributes to overwork is *guilt*. The parent who believes, "I did something that caused my child's disability," will work extra hard to try to make it up to the child. Forgiving oneself antidotes this unnecessary self-punishment. See pages 31–32 for affirmations that help parents release guilt.

Parents can also avoid burnout by discriminating between what they can do and what they can't do for their child. This discernment is beautifully described in the serenity prayer written by Reinhold Neibuhr: "God, grant me the serenity to accept the things I cannot change, the courage to change the things I can, and the wisdom to know the difference."

In Chapter 4, we offered strategies and affirmations that all parents can use for self-care. Here are some affirmations that are specifically adapted for parents of children with disabilities:

Affirmations for Self-Care
(Said by the parent to herself)

I can find time to nurture myself.

I can take breaks from parenting.

I deserve to take time for myself.

I accept my limitations in helping my child.

I have the courage to do what I can do, and the wisdom to know what I cannot.

I turn my child and her welfare over to God (Great Spirit, Allah, Higher Power).

Some Final Thoughts on the Resiliency of Children

Parents and clinicians who work with children with disabilities invariably comment on their positive mental attitude. Compared with adults, many children cope remarkably well with disabilities and serious illnesses. Instead of getting depressed, kids maintain a level of joy and optimism in the face of adversity.

An eleven-year-old with a terminal case of Deshene's muscular dystrophy was asked what he saw for his future. "I want to be a baseball player," he replied. "If they find a cure for what I've got, it's important to think about what I want to do." A teenage girl who was dying of leukemia went to school every day, even if it was for only ten minutes, so she could see her friends and connect with the community.

CHAPTER 19

Positive Talk for the Child from a
Chemically Dependent Family

> I believe a child can survive a family crisis
> as long as he or she is told the truth
> and allowed to share the natural sequence of feelings
> that people experience when they suffer.
>
> *Claudia Black, therapist and author*

One out of every four to five children in a typical elementary school classroom has an alcoholic parent.[1] The disruption to these children's lives and negative effects on their overall well-being are tremendous. Affirmations have long been an important tool for adults in recovery. In the following pages, we will explore how affirmations can also facilitate the recovery process for kids growing up in chemically dependent households.

The Effects of Living
in a Chemically Dependent Family

The stresses of growing up in a chemically dependent family affect a child in a variety of ways:

- **Abandonment/neglect.** Children need their parents' time, attention, and direction. When their dad is a drug or alcohol addict and their mom is trying to take care of him (or the dad is caretaking the mom), no one has time for the child. Teachers report that children from such households often come to school improperly nourished or clothed. They get sick more frequently than their peers and lag behind in language and social skills.

- **Abuse.** Children living in chemically dependent families are often abused by their parents or relatives. Alcohol in particular seems to bring out a dark, violent side of the user, which leads him to engage in verbal, physical, or sexual abuse.

- **Enmeshment.** If Daddy is absent on alcoholic binges, Mom looks toward her son to be her "surrogate husband." Likewise, if Mom is always out of it, the husband will look to "Daddy's little girl" to fill the role of his wife. In each case, the child becomes inappropriately bonded to the mom or dad. This is a form of emotional incest.

- **Hypervigilance.** Chemically dependent households create an atmosphere of uncertainty and lack of predictability. One day Dad is nice; the next day he explodes in a drunken rage. Mom picks you up from school on Monday; on Tuesday she arrives two hours late and loaded. The stress of having to be constantly vigilant in order to survive often results in a host of physical and psychological symptoms—difficulty sleeping, nightmares, bed-wetting, and the inability to concentrate at school.

- **Inability to delay gratification.** Because drug-affected parents don't follow through on commitments, their children feel they have to grab a reward now because it might not be there tomorrow. This impulsive behavior makes it difficult to finish schoolwork or engage in any form of self-discipline.

- **Development of a false self.** Children living in a chemically dependent household cannot be themselves. In order to survive, they must play certain roles such as that of the hero, lost child, placater, mascot, and scapegoat. They also may exhibit codependent behavior such as the smoothing out of conflict, "mothering" other kids, and taking responsibility for other people's pain.

These patterns are not limited to the alcoholic family but can occur in any poorly functioning family system. Fortunately, children living in these families do not have to wait until midlife to get into recovery. We can give them an early start on their healing journey by providing them with the opportunity to explore their feelings in a safe and supportive setting.

The Role of the Witness in Validating the Child's Feelings

The trauma of growing up in a chemically dependent family causes children to feel:

- fear (of abandonment or of being hurt)
- anger (at the parents for betraying them)
- embarrassment (because Mom showed up drunk at school)
- guilt (that they are causing the problem)
- sadness/hurt (that no one is there for them)

More than anything else, a child raised in a chemically dependent family needs a confidant or ally who will listen to and validate these feelings. This "witness" that we spoke of in Chapter 4 can be almost anyone—a neighbor, relative, baby-sitter, minister, coach, teacher, scout master, youth leader, school counselor, psychologist, or friend. The witness can even be the addict or codependent if he is in recovery.

The witness says to the child: "I'd like to hear your story. I believe what you have to say." Then he listens carefully to what the child has to say, letting him talk as much as he needs to, and reflecting the child's feelings back to him—for example, "That must have been scary to see your daddy pass out" or "Sounds like you feel sad about your mom being drunk."

Play therapy is one way to help children tell their story. One therapist places a group of toy bunnies on the floor and asks, "Which bunny is the one who drinks?" The child will then point to a bunny and say, "That's my mom/dad," and begin to tell his story. This process is especially effective for preschoolers and younger school-age kids.

Giving children permission to talk about their feelings is an affirmation in itself. As children voice their hurt, shame, fear, anger, and sadness, they can start to let go of the pain. When children don't believe they have any safe place to tell their story, they repress their feelings. This unresolved pain lies dormant for years and gets acted out in inappropriate ways. Please refer to Chapter 3, "Introducing Positive Talk to Children," for affirmations that validate a child's feelings.

IN ACTION

Ten-year-old Clyde's father is an alcoholic. Clyde constantly worries about his father's drinking. He is nervous, restless, and can't concentrate in school.

Through talking with his counselor, Clyde got in touch with two feelings. The first was fear. Clyde was scared that his father might die and no one would be left to care for him. Clyde was also angry that his father was acting without regard for his needs or feelings.

Clyde felt better after expressing his feelings. Here are some affirmations that gave him permission to feel his pain:

Clyde's Affirmations
(Said by the counselor to the child)

It's okay to be angry at your dad.

Expressing your anger helps you feel better.

It's okay to feel afraid.

No matter what happens to your dad, you can find support.

There are people who care about you.

Telling the Child It's Not His Fault

Any child who has, in its early years,
been overloaded with fears and pains . . . believes
"If such things are inflicted on me, it must be my fault.
There must be something wrong with me.
I am the cause of my sufferings."

Alice Miller, psychotherapist, researcher, and author

As early as the age of three, children can tell when something is wrong in the family. Unfortunately, their nonlogical, egocentric thinking leads them to believe that they have caused the problem. This belief often gets reinforced by one or both parents. For example, the dad may say, "Stop being so noisy. No wonder your mother is driven to drink."

As a result of such messages, the child develops the erroneous belief that "I am the cause of my mom's drinking." Because he feels responsible for his parent's addiction, he also believes that he can get the abuser to change his or her behavior. He will act cute, smart, helpful—anything to induce the parent to change.

The assumption that "I am responsible for my parent's pain and am therefore to blame" is clearly false. A child cannot cause his parent to become an alcoholic; he is not and cannot be responsible for an adult's behavior. A simple reality statement to replace this false belief is "It's not your fault." The power of this realization cannot be overemphasized. Once a child understands he is not at fault, he can begin to release the belief that he is a bad and unlovable person.

Statements such as "It's not your fault" are reality-based assertions that can be used side by side with affirmations. Here are some additional reality statements you can use to reinforce that it's not the child's fault:

Affirmations and Reality Statements That Say, "It's Not Your Fault"

(Said by the witness to the child)

It's not your fault.

You cannot make someone an alcoholic.

It's your parents' problem, not yours.

You are not responsible for Daddy (Mommy) being drunk.

It's not your fault that Dad and Mom are fighting.

It's not your fault that they are not taking care of you.

You are lovable.

Another way for children to release responsibility for their parents' behavior is to say the Serenity Prayer, which is widely used in Alcoholics Anonymous. Children love the Serenity Prayer. It is easy to learn and, when repeated, functions like an affirmation.

Serenity Prayer
God grant me the serenity to accept the things I cannot change,
the courage to change the things I can,
and the wisdom to know the difference.

IN ACTION

Devin was a ten-year-old who was torn between his workaholic dad and codependent mom. During their arguments, first he took his father's side and then his mother's. Afterwards, he felt angry and confused. With the help of his counselor, Devin realized that his primary responsibility was to his own happiness. Here are some affirmations Devin created:

Devin's Reality Statements and Affirmations

My parents' fighting is not about me.

I can let go of my parents' problems and let them take care of their own troubles.

I didn't cause their problems.

By detaching from the situation, I can work out my own problems and take care of me.

Breaking Through the Denial

One of the classic symptoms of a chemically dependent family is denial. For example, seven-year-old Suzie sees her drunk mom pass out on the living room sofa. The next morning she asks, "Why did Mom sleep on the sofa?" Her father replies, "Mom was so tired, she couldn't make it upstairs to the bedroom." Or ten-year-old Zach wakes up in the middle of the night to the sound of a violent fight his mom and dad are having upstairs. The next day the family goes to the zoo as if nothing had happened. No one says a word about the argument.

This type of communication is crazy-making. In both instances, the child knows very well that something is wrong, but no one else will validate his reality. Consequently, he starts to doubt the validity of his own perceptions. He no longer trusts what he sees, hears, and feels.

As the witness, you can help the child break through his family's denial by listening to his story and reflecting his feelings back to him. For example, after hearing about the above situations, the witness might say, "That must have been scary to see your mom passed out" or "Sounds like you are confused that Mom and Dad can be so angry one moment and calm the next." When the child hears his perceptions validated, he thinks, "Someone believes me. Maybe I'm not crazy after all." Once his perceptions are corroborated, he can begin to trust himself again.

Affirmations for Overcoming Denial
(Said by the witness to the child)

You see reality clearly, even if your mom and dad deny it.

You can trust what you see and feel.

You can trust what you know.

You can trust yourself.

Helping the Child to Care for Himself

In a chemically dependent family, the parents are unable to meet the child's needs. Thus the child must ask, "How can I find ways to take care of myself even when Daddy or Mommy can't take care of me?" Here are some helpful strategies that the witness can communicate to the child:

- The most important skill to learn is how to ask for help. Find a safe person to talk to. Develop relationships with other adults who you can trust.

- Find safe places and people to go to when the family environment gets out of control, such as to a relative or a neighbor. Have a list of phone numbers you can call for help, such as that of the school counselor or a crisis hotline.

- When your home is too chaotic to get any studying done, ask the teacher if you can work an hour or two after school. Or go to a friend's house and do your studying there.

- Carry fifty cents in your pocket so when you're at a bar or restaurant with a parent who is drinking too much, you can call someone to drive you home.

- Attend Twelve Step groups for kids such as Alateen, Alatot, or a similar support group.

- Find positive resources and activities outside the home where you will get strokes and support—such as athletics or joining a club.

- Take care of your body. Give it proper rest and nutrition. Avoid drugs, especially if drug abuse runs in your family.

The following affirmations are designed to strengthen the child's belief in his ability to reach out and get help. Given the ever-present danger of living in a chemically dependent household, knowing and internalizing these affirmations can be a matter of life or death.

Affirmations for Coping and Self-Care

(Said by the witness to the child)

You can find safe people to talk to.

You can find safe ways to get home when Mom or Dad is drinking.

You can reach out for help, even if Mom and Dad do not.

You can make healthy choices.

(Said by the child to himself)

I can learn to take care of myself.

I can find ways to reach out for help.

I can find safe people to talk to.

I can find help outside the family.

Learning to Be a Child

Earlier we mentioned that when a parent becomes nonfunctional, one of the children will take over the missing parent role and will "parent" the addict or the other kids in the family. This overly responsible child is called the "hero child." Because he is so busy acting like an adult, the hero never gets to be a child. As one teenage hero remarked, "I'm fifteen going on twenty-six."

The witness adult who is aware of this imbalance can encourage the child to play more and engage in fun activities with children his own age. In order to help her third-grade hero clients break out of their "responsible mode," a counselor asked them to finger-paint with pudding on a clean table. After overcoming their initial inhibition, they got into the process and made a big mess. Next, they raked a bunch of leaves in a pile and jumped in. They marveled at how much fun they had.

Afterwards, the counselor repeated the following affirmations with the children:

Affirmations for Being a Child
(Said by the counselor to the group)

It's okay to be a kid.

It's okay to have fun and play.

You can find time to have fun.

You don't have to be the mommy all the time.

You don't have to be the daddy all the time.

The above affirmations are ones you can use yourself if you were one of those hero children who is now an overworked parent or helping professional. As a caretaker, it's okay to take a break and attend to your own needs!

Validating Recovery

Children can start recovery when they are children and thereby free themselves from carrying unresolved pain into the future. We can help kids to choose recovery in a number of ways:

1. **Model recovery for them.** If you are a parent in a chemically dependent family, choose recovery for yourself. Finish your unfinished business and become an example of a person who can get his needs met. As suggested in the Twelve Steps, make amends to your children. Apologize for not having been there for them; then start to meet their needs in a way that you couldn't earlier. Children are very forgiving. They love you and will respond favorably once you reach out.

   The first year of their parent's recovery can be hard on children. The old system may have been painful, but at least it was familiar. In addition, parents put a lot of time into their recovery, going to many meetings and working on their own personal healing, so they are often as unavailable as before. If you are such a parent, assure your family that in the long run this work will benefit everyone.

2. **Educate the child about the nature of alcoholism and addiction.** Explain to him that the people who drink and use are not bad people; they are ill people who do hurtful things.

3. **Help children to develop an image of what a healthy, functional family is like.** Ask them, "What is it that you see in other families that you like?" Encourage them to spend time with nurturing, stable families. This gives them a model of health to internalize and apply when they create their own families.

4. **Encourage kids to seek support in therapy or in Twelve Steps groups such as Alateen and Alatot,** where children engage in the therapeutic act of telling their stories and listening to the stories of other kids. This validation and mirroring by the group supplements the support of the adult witness.

Never before has so much information been available about how healing can occur in family systems. Although the problems are great, they are matched by the marvelous tools that are available. Here are some affirmations that can guide kids through the recovery process:

Affirmations for Recovery

(Said by the witness to the child)

There is recovery.

You can feel better about yourself.

You can find new ways to handle your feelings.

You can choose healthy and happy relationships.

It may be hard and confusing now, but things will improve.

IN ACTION

Very often, children are tempted to drink in order to medicate the pain brought on by their parents' drinking. When the aunt of sixteen-year-old Crysten noticed that Crysten had started to use alcohol, the aunt said, "Drinking is not a way to feel better, as you learned from your mom and dad. When unpleasant feelings come up, you can talk to me or a friend or hit a pillow. You can cope with your feelings in healthy ways." Then she gave Crysten the following affirmations to repeat:

Crysten's Affirmations

I can cope with my feelings in healthy ways.

I no longer need to drink to cope with my pain.

I can seek treatment.

I make a commitment to attend AA.

I can reach out for support.

With her aunt's encouragement, Crysten began attending Alateen and later moved on to AA to control her drinking.

CHAPTER 20

Positive Talk for the **Abused Child**

> Our sensitivity to the cruelty with which children are treated
> and to the consequences of such treatment
> will as a matter of course bring to an end
> the perpetuation of violence from generation to generation.
>
> *Alice Miller, psychotherapist, researcher, and author*

In this chapter, we will explore ways to affirm children who are being abused. Child abuse is any act of commission or omission that endangers or impairs a child's physical or emotional health and development. Such acts include:

- sexual abuse and exploitation

- physical abuse and unreasonably severe corporal punishment

- physical neglect and inadequate supervision

- verbal and emotional abuse

Let's explore these in detail.

Sexual Abuse

An estimated 89,000 cases of child sexual abuse were substantiated in 2000.[1] Sexual abuse can be divided into two categories—overt and covert.

Overt sexual abuse is defined as inappropriate sexual behavior, brought about by coercion, deception, or psychological manipulation. The abusive behavior includes inappropriate touching, fondling, oral sex, or intercourse. Sexual abuse is usually perpetrated by an adult family member or older sibling with a minor child.

Covert sexual abuse is more subtle and includes parents talking about specific sexual acts, chronic nudity, forcing children to watch sex, inappropriate sexual comments, and making disparaging remarks about someone's sexual identity such as "All men are only after one thing."

Physical Abuse and Neglect

Physical abuse is the inappropriate use of physical force against a child such as pushing, shoving, smacking, hitting, whipping, slapping, pinching, punching, burning, or beating. Physical neglect occurs when the parents fail to provide the child with adequate food, clothing, shelter, or medical attention or when they leave the child alone for long stretches of time.

In her classic book, *For Your Own Good*,[2] Alice Miller demonstrates that the rationale for physical abuse comes from "poisonous pedagogy"—300 years of outdated parenting rules that view a child as an object to be owned, controlled, manipulated, and punished at a parent's discretion. Miller argues that in order to end this multigenerational violence, we must become sensitized to the abuse we received as children, so that we don't unconsciously pass it on to our own kids.

Verbal and Emotional Abuse

Like physical abuse, verbal and emotional abuse are a form of violence. Over time, they will beat a kid down as surely as the blows of a hand. Examples of emotional abuse include:

- constant criticism, judgment
- yelling, screaming
- humiliating the child
- threatening the child
- comparing the child to another
- invalidating and shaming feelings
- lying to a child
- manipulating a child's sense of reality

- neglecting to provide a child with consistent love, support, and guidance

Please refer to the verbal abuse section in Chapter 4 (pages 40–43) and to Chapter 11 for a full description of how to affirm the verbally abused child.

Finally, let us remember that a child is abused simply by witnessing abuse. The non-abused sibling who sees her sister or brother get slapped around may feel terror (that it may happen to her), helplessness (that she can't stop it), outrage (at the abuser), and guilt (that she escaped the punishment). She may also adopt a "good boy" or "good girl" facade in the hopes of escaping future abuse. Witnessing abuse also teaches a child that when she grows up and gets the power, she can play the part of abuser.

The Effects of Childhood Abuse

The effects of abuse are deep and pernicious. Children who are abused are likely to exhibit the following symptoms as they grow up: shame, addiction, eating disorders, chronic depression, dissociation from bodily pleasure, low-grade chronic anger, poor boundaries, hypervigilance, hypersensitivity, low self-esteem, feelings of lack of safety, inability to trust, suicidal thoughts, sexual acting out, and the inability to form intimate relationships.

Here are some of the adult symptoms of childhood abuse:

- You find it difficult to develop or maintain close personal relationships.

- You have a strong desire to isolate or "hide out" from life.

- Physical ailments like neck, back, and stomach problems repeat and persist despite your efforts at good self-care.

- Feelings of sadness, fear, and anger often seem unmanageable and even overwhelm you.

- Panics, rages, depressions, sleep disorders, or suicidal thoughts interfere with efforts to reach your cherished goals.

- You find yourself depending on alcohol, drugs, or food to cover and buffer feelings of humiliation, shame, and low self-esteem.

- You experience sexual problems such as low sexual self-esteem, avoidance of sex, promiscuity, or an inability to experience orgasms or erections.

- Signs of trauma like panic attacks, numbing of body areas, and feelings of being disconnected from your body limit your ability to fully participate in life.

How severely a child is affected by abuse depends on how early the abuse happened, how often it happened, and how long the abuse took place. Although all abuse is injurious, clinicians agree that sexual abuse is the most damaging. As one victim of sexual abuse described it, "Physical abuse leaves scars on the outside but sexual abuse makes you feel ugly inside." Sexual abuse tends to produce more shame than any other type of abuse.

The harmful effects of abuse are perhaps best summarized by the words of a fourteen-year-old who said to one of this book's authors, "I want you to tell parents that all abuse hurts. No matter what type of abuse it is, it hurts."

Beginning the Recovery from Child Abuse

In the previous chapter, we learned that children from chemically dependent families can begin recovery early on. The same holds true of abused children. With the right support from adults and peers, they can begin to heal from the abuse even as the abuse is occurring.

Since two-thirds of all physical and sexual abuse occurs in alcoholic families, many of the issues and affirmations we discuss will parallel those of the previous chapter.

Breaking the Silence by Telling the Secret

> Emotional access to the truth
> is the indispensable precondition of healing.
> Alice Miller, psychotherapist, researcher, and author

The most important survival skill for any victim of child abuse is the ability to reach out for help. Telling does two things:

- It liberates the child from her painful isolation.

- It can stop the abuse (assuming the adult witness takes action). Violence and sexual abuse can only occur in an atmosphere of secrecy.

Remember, it is not the trauma alone that wounds the child, but the repression of the trauma. Having to keep the trauma to oneself is more hellish than the original betrayal. Unfortunately, a variety of factors make it difficult for a child to talk about the abuse:

- The abuser tries to keep his victim silent with bribes, threats such as "If you tell I'll send you away," or assurance to the child that no one will believe her story.

- The child is ashamed to tell.

- The child is afraid of being blamed.

- The child fears that her mommy or daddy may have to leave if she tells. Disruption of the family is often perceived as a greater threat than the abuse itself.

- The child feels protective of the offending parent and does not wish to get her in trouble.

- The child believes that the abuse is her fault.

Even when the child does not speak out, an observant adult can detect abuse by the child's unusual behaviors. For example, the child may protest, "I don't want to go to Daddy's (or Grandpa's) house any more," or may break down and cry upon seeing the abuser. Other behavioral signs of abuse include nightmares, bedwetting, not wanting to be left alone, outbursts of crying, trouble in school, age regression, seductive dressing, wearing many layers of clothes, gaining weight, decreased interest in grooming and personal appearance, a sudden discomfort around peers of the same sex as the offender, and sexual acting out.

If you suspect that a child is being abused, you can encourage the child to open up by using the following affirmations:

Affirmations for Telling the Secret

(Said by the adult to the child)

> You can tell the secret.

> When people tell you to keep a secret, it's because they know what they are doing is wrong.

> There are people who will believe you.

> I will help you find a person to trust

(Said by the child to herself)

> There are people I can trust.

> I can find help when someone hits me.

> I can find help when someone touches my private parts.

> Getting help is scary, but I can do it.

IN ACTION

Avette, a fifteen-year-old, was first sexually abused by her father and then physically abused by her mother. Feeling suicidal, she told her story to a friend on the way to school. Fortunately, the friend acted promptly and referred Avette to the school counselor. As Avette experienced other people's caring and support, her despair and suicidal thoughts lifted. At a later stage, she called an agency that helped her find an alternative living situation.

After the crisis had subsided, Avette gave her classmates the following advice: "If you are being abused, tell someone right away. If they don't believe you, tell someone else until you find help. I waited too long. You don't have to."

Trusting What You Feel

Before a child can seek out help, she first needs to trust herself enough to realize that something is wrong with the way she is being treated. This means trusting her thoughts, feelings, perceptions, and bodily reactions. Many times the abuser will try to manipulate the child's sense of reality and tell her that nothing is wrong. The abuser may say, "This is okay, you don't need to be afraid," when the child knows on a gut level that she is afraid. As one child said, "If what Daddy did was okay, why did he tell me to keep it a secret?"

Here are some affirmative messages that encourage children who are being abused to trust what they feel:

Affirmations for Trusting Yourself

(Said by the adult to the child)

You can listen to your body.

Your body will tell you if something is wrong.

If you get a real yucky feeling inside, pay attention to that.

If your body says the person is not safe, then he isn't safe.

(Said by the child to herself)

I can tell when someone touches me in a way that makes me feel bad or upset.

If I get a real bad feeling inside my gut, I can trust that feeling.

My body will tell me if something is wrong.

I can reach out for help.

Processing the Feelings Around the Abuse

Being sexually, physically, or emotionally abused brings up a variety of feelings such as shame, sadness, anger, and terror. Once these feelings are acknowledged and the child has taken the initial step of getting help, she can begin to talk about and release these feelings. For young children, play therapy allows them to tell their story and externalize their feelings through using dolls and other objects. Older children can talk in a group or with a therapist.

The following two statements, made by therapists to abused children, beautifully epitomize the therapeutic power of talking out one's feelings in a safe and supportive setting:

"If you feel bad about what happened, you can talk about that bad feeling until that feeling gets very little."

"Sometimes you feel sorry and the sorry gets so big it makes your body ache. When you talk about it, it lets the sorry out."

Let's now explore some of the most common feelings that arise in children who are abused.

Dispelling the Shame

> Whenever there is a major deficit in parental love,
> the child will, in all likelihood, respond
> by assuming itself to be the cause of the deficit,
> thereby developing an unrealistically negative self-image.
>
> M. Scott Peck, author and psychiatrist

When a child is abused, she automatically assumes she is responsible for the abuse. Rather than see her parents as bad, she believes, "I did something bad. There is something wrong with me. I deserve to be punished." The abuser also tries to place the blame on the child by saying, "You made me do it" or "You're so cute, I couldn't help myself." The best way to break the spell is to tell the child, "It's not your fault."

The belief that "it's my fault" takes time to change. Sometimes older children will rationalize the abuse by saying, "My dad had a hard life" or "My mom was abused by her mom." While these might be valid reasons for the parents' behavior, they cannot be used to excuse the behavior or keep the child feeling responsible for the abuse. Eventually, the child will come to accept that she did not cause the abuse—that it was her parents who had the problem.

IN ACTION ➤

Janie was sexually abused by her dad when she was four years old. At first she went along with it, thinking it was a special way to get close to him. Later she realized it was wrong and felt horribly ashamed. When the authorities found out, her dad was removed from the home. After listening to Janie blame herself for her dad's departure, the caseworker, said, "It wasn't your fault that your dad had to leave. I want you to know that you are a valuable person. When you go to bed at night, I want you to say that you are a valuable and lovable person and that people do love you."

Please refer to Chapter 5, "Using Positive Talk to Build Self-Esteem," for other affirmations for the healing of shame (pages 63–66).

Fear and Terror

A child growing up in an abusive household lives in constant fear and terror. These fears include:

- fear of abandonment

- fear of physical harm

- fear of sexual harm

- fear of losing a parent

- fear of being removed from the family

If you are the supportive adult in the child's life, assure her that you will do your best to keep her safe and to protect her. One counselor said, "I wish this hadn't happened to you. I'm sorry that you got hurt. I'm sorry that you were scared and that no one was there to help you. Now you have someone to help." You might also want to share with a child who has been abused some of the affirmations for overcoming fear listed in Chapter 8.

Sadness

Childhood is meant to be a treasured time in which the child is kept safe by the adults around her. Abused children experience grief over the premature loss of their childhood and innocence. As one sexually abused girl put it, "I am sad that I didn't get to choose the first person I had sex with. I am sad that I didn't get to make it a special event."

A second emotion related to sadness is that of longing, a deep yearning for things to be different than they are. Examples include wishing for the parent who is never there, longing for the peace and security that has long ago vanished, and a longing for a heroic figure who can take the child away from the traumatic situation. Chapter 9, "What to Say When You Are Sad: Positive Talk for Coping with Loss, Divorce, and Depression," contains affirmations on helping children cope with loss.

Anger

> If a child is beaten, then it should be able to shout and rage
> to defend itself against idiocy and wickedness.
> Such protest would save the child's psychic health and dignity.
>
> *Alice Miller, psychotherapist, researcher, and author*

Abused children are angry children. They feel angry about being violated, betrayed, taken advantage of, and unjustly treated. Children can constructively express their anger by talking it out (using their "big voice") or by getting it out physically (hitting a pillow and making a loud noise). When a child expresses her anger, she gets in touch with her power, which can protect her from future abuse. Therapists call anger "the backbone of healing."

Conversely, when anger is not constructively expressed, it gets acted out destructively or turned in on the self. Kids who internalize their rage can become physically ill, accident-prone, suicidal, or self-mutilators. Cutting or hurting themselves gives children the feeling that they are alive or is used as a symbolic way to connect with the abusive parent whom they associate with pain.

Here are some affirmations that will support the child to get in touch with and express her anger about her abuse:

Affirmations and Reality Statements for Anger

(Said by the adult to the child)

> You can be angry.

> You have something real to be angry at.

> You're right to be angry at both parents.
> They both let you down in their own way.

(Said by the child to herself)

> I am mad at my dad/mom.

> I hate them when they hit me.

> I hate them when they don't protect me.

> I don't want them to touch my body.

> I want them to keep me safe.

The first and most obvious source for the child's anger is the offending adult—the parent or other person who hit, sexually molested, or emotionally abused the child. The second and less obvious culprit is the "silent" or "complicit" adult who allowed the abuse to take place. It is difficult to get a child to acknowledge her anger and rage at the complicit person, who often is the child's main source of love. To cut that person off would mean losing the last vestige of support.

In some instances, the silent partner didn't act because she didn't know about the abuse (at least not consciously). For example, untreated survivors of sexual abuse often fail to recognize that their own children are being abused. In other instances, the silent partner knew but was unable to do anything about it because she, too, was a victim of abuse. Examples of silent partners who are victims include the verbally abused father who can't protect his son against a mother's rage and the battered wife who can't stop her spouse from beating her son.

Numbing Out

A final way that children respond to abuse is to numb out. When abuse has reached a certain point, when the pain, rage, and fear are too much to handle, the emotional body goes on "overwhelm" and shuts itself down to protect itself from total breakdown. The child becomes numb—feelingless—as a way to survive. As one counselor observed, "We have to teach these kids to feel all over again."

Some kids try to access buried feelings by using drugs as a way to feel; others use drugs to numb out the pain when it comes up to the surface. This is why abuse is a setup for addiction. The alternative to addiction is recovery. Abused children can use peer support groups and individual counseling to gain the vocabulary to name and verbalize their feelings—and then process their pain without the use of chemicals.

Strategies to Keep a Child Safe

In the previous chapter, we listed specific strategies that a child living in a drug-affected family can use to keep herself safe. In addition to those strategies, here are some others that abused children can use to keep themselves safe:

- Note where and when the abuse is happening. If the abuse occurs at the same place and the same time, go someplace else.

- Notice the events that lead up to the abuse. If your dad hits you when he's drunk, make yourself scarce when he starts drinking.

- If you come home late from school and a parent starts yelling at you, yelling back will only accelerate the cycle. Instead of pushing your parent's buttons, find something else to do.

- Carry a list of numbers of people who are safe when there's violence in the home—a friend, neighbor, relative, or school counselor. Plan ahead. Have your suitcase packed and be ready to leave at a moment's notice.

- Seek out counseling or join a support group where you can talk about and work through your feelings.

Children have an inherent right to be safe and to be protected. Unfortunately, molested or abused children interpret the fact that they weren't protected to mean, "I was not deserving of protection" or "I should have been able to protect myself." We need to tell these children that it is never the child's responsibility to protect herself from the abuser. It is always the adult's job to keep the child safe.

Learning to Set Boundaries

Setting boundaries is an important strategy to keep oneself safe. Physical and sexual abuse are a major violation of a child's physical boundaries. Emotional abuse is a violation of a person's psychic or "inner self" boundaries. Protecting oneself from abuse means strengthening one's boundaries and learning how to say no. Abused children either develop weak boundaries (everyone walks all over them) or overly rigid boundaries (they retreat into themselves and don't allow anyone to get close).

To help protect kids from sexual abuse, we can teach them to name their body parts so that they will have the correct words to talk about their sexual organs. Then they can have a language to describe what doesn't feel right.

Kids can also use affirmations to define their boundaries. One particularly effective affirmation is, "I am the boss of my body; my body belongs to me!" Even if such assertions do not stop the abuse, they will increase the child's self-esteem so that she is more likely to reach out for help.

Affirmations for Setting Boundaries
(Said by the child to herself)

My body belongs to me.

My body is mine.

I am the boss of my body.

No adult has the right to touch me where I don't want them to.

No one has the right to physically hurt me.

No one has the right to scream at me or put me down.

I can say no.

I have a right to be safe and to be cared for.

If the person won't listen, I can get help.

Creating a Positive Self-Image

One of the major consequences of abuse is low self-esteem. Abused children internalize messages such as "You're bad," "You're stupid," "You're worthless," "You're no good," and "It's your fault." Rebuilding damaged self-esteem is accomplished by replacing this abusive self-talk with loving self-talk. Chapters 5 and 6 contain a variety of affirmations for building self-esteem and a positive body image that can promote healing in abused children.

Because of the intense sense of shame that sexually abused children feel, it is important not to introduce these affirmations too early. When a survivor of sexual abuse is initially told that she is good, lovable, or can do great things, the concept is so unbelievable that it can reinforce her feeling of being worthless. Wait until the child is far enough along in her recovery before you introduce self-esteem affirmations to her.

Breaking Out of the Victim Role

Children who are victimized or abused often unconsciously play the role of victim in other areas of their life. Children's victim behaviors include finding others to take advantage of them, not sticking up for themselves, always being the scapegoat, and getting into trouble at school. These behaviors reinforce the belief, "There is something wrong with me."

The child who is a victim of abuse does not have to live out the victim role forever. With the help of a supportive adult or peers, she can become conscious of her victim behaviors and learn to make new choices.

IN ACTION

Liang, a victim of physical abuse, reenacted his victim role by repeatedly getting sent to the principal's office. One day his counselor said to him, "Liang, try to see how you are setting yourself up for failure. When you are kicked out of class, ask yourself, 'What made me the only one who got in trouble?' If the teacher seems to pick on you, ask yourself, 'Why does she go after me? Could there be any way in which I am provoking her?'"

continued ⟶

After giving the matter some thought, Liang acknowledged the subtle ways he attracted trouble to himself such as talking in class and arriving late. The counselor then showed him that by making different choices, he could attract a new set of results. Later on she gave him a list of affirmations that he could repeat to reinforce his decision to break out of the victim role. Here is the original list:

Liang's Affirmations for Letting Go of the Victim Role

I can make new choices.

I no longer play victim.

I am a powerful person.

I am going to seek out people who will be kind to me.

I get to decide whether I want a problem or not.

I attract good into my life.

Liang chose two affirmations from the list and wrote them on a three-by-five-inch card that he carried with him. Focusing on these empowering statements helped him choose the new behaviors that he and his counselor had outlined.

Liang's counselor also helped him see how his current acting-out behaviors were linked to the abuse he received at home. "Oh yeah, maybe that's why I act this way," he responded. He also realized that he would need to get more intensive help to break the abuse cycle.

Regaining a Sense of Hope

An important part of recovering from abuse involves regaining a sense of hope. Because they have been beaten down for so long, abused children think that nothing is ever going to change and that they are "damaged" for life. Such hopelessness is a major barrier to the healing process.

The support of an adult witness is often the first step to turning this despair around. As the child realizes that someone truly cares about her, she thinks, "Someone is concerned about me. Maybe I am worth caring about. Maybe there is hope after all."

If you are the witness, it is important that you provide hope that has some basis in reality. For example, it is not supportive to tell a child, "Your dad will change," when the child's dad is a sexual offender deep in denial. What you can say is, "You no longer need to suffer alone. I will do all I can to help. Together, we can make the situation improve." Then, take action to help the child.

Children are resilient beings. Even the faintest glimmer of hope will rekindle their spirits. Here are some affirmations that can create a sense of hope:

Affirmations for Regaining Hope
(Said by the witness to the child)

There is hope.

Things can change.

There are people who will listen.

You can get through this.

I am here to support you until things get better.

Emerging a Triumphant Survivor

What doesn't kill me makes me stronger.
Friedrich Nietzsche, philosopher

When children heal from abuse, they do more than just "get over it." They actually emerge with new strengths. As one counselor said:

You have learned some things about yourself and life that some people never get to learn. You now possess strengths, knowledge, and tools that you can take with you for the rest of your life. When future crises come up, you can draw upon these strengths.

continued ⟶

> You have had the courage to confront something very painful. Like iron that has been tempered into steel, you have become a stronger person. You are living a life that is richer and more full because of the awareness you have gained.

This kind of realization usually occurs in the teenage years when the child achieves a detachment and perspective that allows her to see the good that emerged from an otherwise negative experience. Here are some affirmations that reflect this awareness:

Affirmations for Triumphant Survivors
(Said by the witness to the child)

Congratulations!

As bad as it was, you survived.

You can make a new life for yourself.

You are a stronger and wiser person.

You are a more understanding person.

Now you can reach out and help those who are going through what you went through.

When the Abused Child Becomes an Abuser

One of the sad aspects of child abuse is that the untreated abused child will often do to others exactly what was done to her—a sort of perversion of the golden rule. When a child is beaten or witnesses abuse, she learns how to be an aggressor as well as a victim. Psychiatrist Bruno Bettelheim observed this phenomenon in the concentration camps and called it "identification with the oppressor." This reenactment can occur when the abused child grows up or it can take place when she is still a child.

To the dismay of clinicians around the country, the number of children who are sexually abusing other children is increasing at an alarming rate. Without early intervention, such abuse will continue into adulthood and becomes virtually impossible to treat. When treatment occurs early enough, children can:

- learn to talk about their feelings about sexually touching other children
- develop a sense of self-esteem by controlling those sexual feelings rather than acting them out with other children
- learn to develop empathy for others
- learn to take responsibility for their actions

IN ACTION

Six-year-old Marcus was brought into treatment after he sodomized his younger brother. He also had been physically and verbally abusive. Unlike other children in his situation, Marcus said he felt bad about what he had done. Marcus had been molested by three different people before he was five years old. His parents also admitted there was a problem and were willing to cooperate with treatment.

Over two years of therapy, Marcus gained self-esteem by learning to control his impulses and developing empathy for other people. Since leaving the treatment program, Marcus has not molested other children, has stopped acting aggressively, and has done well in school.

IN ACTION

Twelve-year-old Scott is verbally abusive in the classroom. When his teacher explained that it was not okay to swear at other students, Scott said, "If you lived with my lousy parents, you'd talk like I do."

At this point, the teacher responded, "It must be hard to live at home. If I were in your shoes, I would be sad and I would feel bad and I would feel angry, but I would want to learn not to take it out on someone else. You can choose to talk about your feelings with me or your counselor instead of yelling at the other kids."

After a few conversations such as this, Scott began to catch himself whenever he started using abusive language. As his negative

continued⟶

words diminished, his relationships with peers and teachers improved. Later on his teacher told Scott, "This abuse is like a monkey on your back. You may have to do more work on it later on, in order for you to be healthy inside and outside. At some point, it would be smart to go to a counselor or join a support group."

These examples leave us an empowering thought. We can help children break the abuse cycle when they are young. They are not doomed to harm others because of the harm that was done to them.

Help for the Abusive Adult

In the previous application we saw how Scott's verbal abuse in the classroom was a reenactment of the abuse he received at home. During a parent-teacher conference later that year, Scott's teacher said to his parents, "I know you want Scott to succeed at school and I know that some of his problems relate to what is going on in the family. Is there something we can do to improve things at home?"

Scott's parents replied, "You may be right. Sometimes we get carried away with Scott. We really don't like yelling at him."

The teacher replied, "Would you like to learn how to improve the way you and Scott communicate and get along?" The parents agreed and enrolled in a parenting class that taught them alternatives to using verbally abusive language with Scott.

Few parents consciously wish to abuse their children. The harm they do comes from unconsciously acting out the abuse patterns they experienced in childhood. Other high risk factors for parents who engage in child abuse include:

- being a single parent
- drug or alcohol abuse
- unemployment
- heavy child-care responsibilities
- the inability to control rage and frustration
- involvement with the police

Many adults abused as children are concerned that they will in turn abuse their own children. This does not have to be. If the parent is aware of the potential danger and is willing to seek treatment, she can free herself from her negative conditioning. The desire to seek help is most often found in adults who engage in verbal or physical abuse rather than in sexual offenders. The latter are almost always locked into denial and unwilling to take responsibility for their behavior.

Physical or verbal violence is learned—and thus can be unlearned. People can find new strategies to manage anger, release frustrations, and resolve conflict. When there is a willingness to change, one can always find a way. Here are some affirmations that support the adult abuser's desire for change:

Healing Affirmations for the Abusive Adult
(Said by the adult to herself)

I am learning new ways of dealing with my feelings.

I am choosing positive alternatives to abuse.

I recognize when I may lose control, and take appropriate action.

I control my anger instead of letting my anger control me.

My child needs me to be an adult; I am the adult with her.

Please refer to the section on anger management in Chapter 4 (pages 37–47) for specific strategies for changing abusive behavior.

CHAPTER 21

Positive Talk for the
At-Risk and Acting-Out Child

> Nothing more than the opportunity to talk openly and freely
> about their lives, to people who would listen without judging,
> and who were interested in them as human beings
> rather than as problems to be solved or disposed of,
> has totally remade the lives and personalities
> of a number of confirmed and seemingly hopeless
> juvenile delinquents.
>
> *John Holt, author and teacher*

In this chapter, we will explore children who express their anger and pain through engaging in "antisocial" behaviors. Such behaviors include:

dropping out of school
truancy
teen pregnancy
vandalism
minor assault
gang involvement

classroom disruption
running away
drug and alcohol abuse
shoplifting
robbery
sex offenses

Most often, but not always, children who "act out" or are "delinquent" have grown up in very troubled homes. Many come from disorganized or chaotic environments where parents fail to set limits or teach self-control. Others are raised in chemically dependent households and become involved in drug and alcohol abuse. They also may have been subjected to neglect, abandonment, geographical instability, parents who are in trouble with the law, poverty, physical abuse, sexual abuse, and/or verbal abuse. Sometimes, despite the best efforts of concerned parents, children engage in antisocial behavior because of other influences on them, such as media or peer pressure.

Finally, it is helpful to remember that acting-out behavior is often a cry for help. Many children get into trouble in order to bring attention to the abuse they are receiving at home or elsewhere. At other times, the child may act out in order to draw attention to a crisis involving his parents. Thus, the entire family, not just the child, must be involved in treatment.

The Role of Behavioral Disorders

Many children in the juvenile justice system are diagnosed with a behavioral disorder. They end up in jail because of their poor impulse control. They are easily provoked and react violently, often engaging in assault. They also have difficulty making the link between cause and effect so that the negative consequences of breaking the law fail to deter their antisocial acts.

The child with a behavioral disorder experiences social problems as well. If he cannot control his inappropriate touching or hitting, he is shunned by other kids and made a social outcast—a setup for anti-social behavior.

To prevent children with these disabilities from ending up in the courts, we need to diagnose their disorders at an early age and teach them how to cope with the social problems that arise from their disability. The other way to support these children is to treat their families. For example, many parents are not prepared to raise a hyperactive child. Family therapy and intervention can help the family cope with the disorder until it ameliorates on its own.

Let's explore some of the issues faced by the acting-out child.

Working Through the Anger

It is clear that acting-out children cannot control their anger. Most of the behaviors that get them in trouble with the law—vandalism, stealing, assault, robbery—are the inappropriate expressions of their anger and rage.

What are these children angry about? They are angry about the abuse, neglect, and abandonment they have experienced in their lives. Thirteen-year-old Delsin, for example, repeatedly broke the law and got arrested in order to humiliate his over-controlling father, the town sheriff. In other instances, these children are imitating the angry and violent behavior of the adults at home or the kids on the street.

How do we help the acting-out child to break his anger-offender cycle? The first step is to give him a safe space to talk about and work through his rage and pain. This needs to be done in a gradual way so that the child does not become overwhelmed by his anger all at once.

In addition to going through therapy, children can learn anger management tools such as affirmations. For example, thirteen-year-old Steve took a three-by-five-inch card and wrote: The next time I feel like punching out a wall, here's what I can do instead. I can:

- jog
- take a shower
- breath deeply
- speak my anger into a tape recorder in private
- hit a pillow

Acting-out children can also be taught assertiveness training. Instead of aggressively pursuing their desires, they can learn how to state their needs and ask for what they want. Progressive relaxation and regular exercise help kids on the edge to discharge their pent-up tension before it erupts in inappropriate anger. Please refer to Chapter 10 for anger management strategies and affirmations.

Feeling the Sadness Below the Anger

When acting-out children begin to talk about their pain, they often discover that below their anger lies sadness about not having a functional family. The process of experiencing these core feelings of sadness and grief is know as "original pain" work.

Phillip is a twenty-year-old sex offender. In therapy, Phillip recounted the time his father abandoned him when he was nine. As Phillip hugged his teddy bear and let his tears flow, his angry, belligerent demeanor transformed into the face of a sad little boy. As Phillip got more and more in touch with his hurt and pain, his anger and acting out diminished. A more detailed description of the power of "original pain" work can be found in John Bradshaw's book *Homecoming*.

Constructing a Grief Line

A powerful technique to help delinquent kids access their grief is the "grief line." The child creates his grief line by listing all the major disappointments and losses that have occurred since birth. Here are the first three events on Phillip's grief line:

- At age 5, I was sexually abused by my mom, a heroin addict.

- At age 7, my mom was removed from the home by children's services.

- At age 9, my father was put in prison.

By reviewing these traumas and losses, Phillip can begin to become conscious of the pain, sorrow, and anger about his past.

Overcoming Hopelessness and Discouragement

Behind the bravado and antisocial actions of acting-out kids lies a deep core of hopelessness and powerlessness. Abuse at home, failure at school, and a string of disappointments have led them to abandon their hopes, desires, and dreams. Without a vision of the future, these children have no motivation to improve their lives.

Here are some common ways that discouraged children talk to themselves:

- "Nothing is ever going to change."

- "The world is against me."

- "There is nothing out there for me."

- "I have no future."

- "Why bother?"

- "What's the use?"

In order for children to regain their hope, they need to be shown a future that is based on achievable alternatives. One entrepreneur responded to the call by approaching an inner city elementary school class and offering a college scholarship to any student who graduated from high school. In a school system that had one of the highest dropout rates in the country, over 90 percent of that class graduated.

IN ACTION

One way that children can gain hope is to see their parents change. Parents don't need to make major breakthroughs—just small changes like learning to listen, not getting into power struggles with the child, or being more consistent. After years of physically abusing his son, Kevin's father learned to express his frustration without hitting his son. As Kevin saw his dad change, he became more willing to participate in his group therapy and to control his own impulses. Hearing his dad say "I was wrong" also allowed Kevin to release the belief that the abuse was his fault.

Developing a New Vision of Themselves

Acting-out children do not like themselves. When they look inside, all they can see is someone who is worthless and no good. They have failed at home, failed at school, and maybe even failed again by getting into legal trouble. Like all shame-based people, they inherited their low self-image from their parents, or in the case of many children of color, from the dominant culture.

The first step to breaking out of the cycle of shame, hopelessness, and despair is for children to get a new vision of themselves. Initially, this vision must be reflected through someone else's eyes, someone who they trust and respect.

Children who are subjected to early trauma or difficult family backgrounds can develop high self-esteem—if they have one or more caring adults to serve as a source of unconditional positive regard for the child. When we read stories of at-risk children who overcame their backgrounds and went on to lead fulfilling and productive lives, we find that the common denominator in every success was the presence of one adult who believed in the child; became that child's ally; empowered, inspired, and encouraged him to manifest his potential.

More than ever, young people are crying out for validation and affirmation from adult allies. As one athlete and mentor said, "These kids need good examples, somebody they can look up to besides the drug kingpins."

Here is a profile of a typical adult mentor. He is street-smart, balanced, firm, and consistent. He can roll with the punches and hang in there until he gains the trust of these kids. He also possesses the time and energy to maintain ongoing contact with these children, who, because of their low impulse control, may need frequent feedback, constant monitoring, or attention.

Here are some affirmations that adult mentors can use to help children develop a new vision of themselves:

Affirmations for Developing a New Vision
(Said by the adult to the child)

You have the mark of greatness on you.

You can become what you set your mind to be.

The only limits to what you can do reside in your imagination.

I see you making a difference in the future.

You can operate your own business.

You can help the environment.

You can help create a brand new tomorrow.

Setting Goals

Once a child has a larger vision of what he can become, his next step is to translate that vision into a plan of action. This can be difficult for the acting-out child who typically lacks direction and focus. Goal setting is a way to get things back on track. When children write down their goals and review them daily, it helps them stay on course with their purpose, stick with their new choices, and evaluate the results of those choices. Because they have a sense of participation in the process, they are more likely to follow through on their commitment.

Goals, like affirmations, work best when they are stated in the positive rather than the negative. Thus, instead of creating the goal, "I won't steal," the child can state, "I will ask before using Alim's radio." Rather than vowing, "I won't hit Noel," Bobby can say, "I will count to ten and walk away when I am angry."

IN ACTION

Miguel was an impulsive child who came to his therapy group one morning and said, "Why am I here? Why am I here?" The group leader replied, "Miguel, why don't you take out your goal card and read it?" Miguel took a three-by-five-inch card from his pocket and read it and said, "Oh yes, I am here to learn better communication."

Here are some other goals that Miguel wrote down in the form of affirmations:

Miguel's Affirmation Goals

I am going to have a good week.

I will finish my schoolwork.

I will follow the rules.

I will control my anger.

I will have a good weekend at home.

Breaking Out of the Victim Role

If you can determine what a man shall think,
you never have to concern yourself with what he will do.
If you can make a man feel inferior, you never have
to compel him to seek an inferior status, for he will seek it himself.
And if you can make a man feel like an outcast,
you never have to order him to go to the back door.
He will go without being told, and if there is no door,
his very nature will demand one.

Carter Woodson, teacher, historian, and publisher

Acting-out children see themselves as having no choices and no power. Here are some examples of victim thinking, taken directly from the words of acting-out kids:

- "My dad went to prison, so that's where I will end up."

- "My mom drinks, so that's why I'm an alcoholic."

- "Because my family is nuts, I can't do my homework."

- "My friends made me do the robbery. I just happened to be there."

- "It's all their fault."

- "The teacher hates me."

To help children escape this pattern of thinking like a victim, they must be shown that they have the power to choose. As one counselor told his group:

> I know you've got problems; everybody does. When you get up in the morning you are faced with a simple choice. Are you going to make your problems better or worse? If you choose the gang lifestyle or engage in destructive behavior, you make things worse. If you act responsibly, you make them better. Only you can decide.

Then he handed out the following affirmations:

Affirmations for Letting Go of Victim Thinking
(Said by the child to himself)

I can choose a different way.

I can learn from the mistakes of my parents.

I can review all the options, and choose one that will make things better.

I am more than my circumstances.

The most powerful person in the room is me.

IN ACTION

Twelve-year-old Evan approached his counselor and said, "James picked on me. He's an idiot." The counselor asked, "What did you do about it?" Evan replied, "I didn't hit him. I don't have to let his stupidness get me in trouble!" The counselor then acknowledged Evan for keeping his cool and not reacting. Later he showed Evan how to change his behavior so that he would not set himself up to be teased.

Working with the At-Risk School Child

School is one of the first places that acting-out behavior becomes visible. At-risk children get in trouble because of drugs, violation of rules, smoking in the halls, unruly behavior, skipping class, and tardiness. Many end up in detention (a time-out for older children) where they are isolated from the rest of the school for a period of time.

Typically at-risk school children exhibit low self-esteem, are angry at authority (especially the teachers), and don't feel they are respected. Academically, they see themselves as incompetent.

Transforming their self-talk is a two step process:

1. Build self-esteem through success experiences.

2. Help them realize that they are not victims and can take responsibility for their behavior. Here are some affirmations that reflect this change in thinking:

At-Risk Child's Negative Self-Talk	Replacement Affirmations
I am not good in school.	I can improve my grades.
I am dumb.	I am smart.
No one respects me.	I can get along with others.
I'm no good.	I'm okay.
I don't get enough attention.	I can get attention in positive ways.

IN ACTION

Jeremy was a fourteen-year-old student who was failing all his subjects. His academic problems were compounded by not having friends (he just moved to the school). Jeremy was also overweight and saw himself as a geek.

Fortunately, Jeremy's detention teacher Ms. Quigley took an interest in him. She approached him and asked, "Do you think you can get straight Ds?"

"Maybe," Jeremy replied.

"Well I think you can," said Ms. Quigley.

The next day Jeremy asked, "Do you really believe that I can get straight Ds?"

"I believe you can get Cs," she replied, "but let's start with Ds." Jeremy then created the affirmation: "I am changing my Fs to Ds." Here are some others he came up with:

Jeremy's Affirmations

I do positive things to get attention.

I believe in myself.

I have something to offer.

How I look is okay.

I can learn.

In addition to his poor grades, Jeremy was writing at a third-grade level. His English teacher assigned him a short book report.

"I can't do it. I can't do it," he complained to Ms. Quigley later that day.

"Yes you can," she said. "It doesn't have to be like the others. Do what you can do. You can learn to write."

The next day Jeremy wrote one paragraph and handed it in as his assignment. The English teacher was astonished as Jeremy had never turned in anything before. With this positive feedback, Jeremy started to do more assignments. He eventually turned in a seven-page term paper, which Ms. Quigley helped him to edit. Later Ms. Quigley said, "My faith in Jeremy inspired him to have faith in himself." All it takes is one adult to believe.

Positive Peer Support Groups

Most acting-out kids start to get in trouble with the law shortly before or during adolescence. This is also the time when the influence of the peer culture becomes powerful. Peers are a child's main source of identity, dispensing advice, encouragement, and criticism. A fifteen-year-old is more apt to listen to a sixteen-year-old than to an adult.

Peer support groups take advantage of this reality. They combine the normal advantages of a support group—validation and support from people in similar circumstances—with the power of peer bonding and peer pressure. This structure creates an ideal alternative to the norms of the street culture.

For example, if a child in a positive peer culture engages in a behavior, such as taking drugs, that opposes the group norm, he quickly finds himself ostracized by his peers. Or he may steal—an action which violates the norm that says, "All kids have the right to be safe and respected." Once again, his peers will make him aware that his behavior is inappropriate.

Positive peer support groups can be found in schools, community organizations, and worship communities. Many acting-out youth may be introduced to them within a treatment setting. They are organized by adults and run by the children, with adult oversight. Kids stick with the program because of the support and caring they receive from one another. The exchange of love and appreciation keeps them strong and prevents them from reverting back to the old patterns of the past.

All children have a need to be needed. As troubled kids reach out and support each other, they begin to experience that they matter. In the past, the only way they could matter was in a negative way—by acting out. Now, they see that it is possible to make a difference by cooperating with their peers and contributing to the larger whole.

The positive feelings that arise from being needed and appreciated by the group help motivate the acting-out child to act in socially appropriate ways. No longer does it make sense to antagonize people or get in trouble. For the first time in his life, he experiences what it is like to interact in a mutually, caring supportive environment.

Overcoming the Influence of Gangs

All children need to grow up in an intact structure where they can belong and receive guidance and direction. When the family system or school fails to provide that intact structure, kids look for it else-where. Those children who feel no love at home, see no future in school, and have few positive role models in their neighborhood are naturally drawn to gang life. The appeal of gangs is multifaceted:

- Gangs provide the alienated child with identity, structure, direction, power, money, and status.

- Gangs are like family; they look out for the child and let him know they care.

- Gangs provide a structure with explicit and rigid rules which children from chaotic backgrounds desperately crave.

- Gangs offer antisocial kids a way to rebel.

- Gangs are a path to excitement, recognition, and thrills.

Gangs are the peer groups of the dispossessed. The key to over-coming the lure of gang life is to provide kids with an alternative peer group where they can matter in a positive way. Two such alter-natives are:

- positive peer support groups (see previous section)
- community/neighborhood centers that provide a haven of recreational activity and peer companionship

Another factor in any anti-gang program is that of the adult men-tor. Unfortunately, adult male mentors are few and far between, espe-cially in the inner cities. As one Detroit police officer observed, "These kids not only don't live with a responsible male; they've never even met one." Fortunately, more and more organizations are bringing adult mentors into the community to become role models for the acting-out child.

We have a stake in teaching the acting-out child how to become a responsible, powerful force in the world. If we don't show disaf-fected children how to participate in the system, they will create their own system and become entrepreneurs without morals. Hence, it is imperative that society choose to teach its youth to use their creativ-ity, resourcefulness, and organizational skills in a socially construc-tive way.

The Unbonded Child

In their book *High Risk: Children Without a Conscience,* authors Ken Magid and Carole McKelvey chronicle a disturbing social phenomenon—the unbonded or unattached child. Due to a disruption of the bonding process during the first two years of life, unattached children are unable to trust and unable to love. As a result of this lack of trust, they construct a false self to manipulate, charm, and control the adults in their lives. Invariably, these children grow up to become thieves, con artists, drug users, psychopaths, and gang members.

Many unbonded kids pass through the foster care system. One of the early signs of the unattached child is his avoidance of direct eye contact. If you have a foster child who is hesitant to look you in the eye, you can begin to establish eye contact by "gazing" at the child in the same way that a mother lovingly gazes at her infant. Also touch and hold the child as much as he will allow. This gazing and touching replicates early mother-child bonding and therefore can facilitate bonding between you and the child. One caution here is to realize that in some cultures, notably within Native American communities, direct eye contact is considered rude, and is not encouraged. Therefore, lack of eye contact in children from these cultures may not reflect a lack of parent-child bonding.

When a child is unattached, he is difficult to reach. Traditional therapies are minimally effective. Some therapists believe that behind the child's sociopathic behavior lies a reservoir of unconscious rage. A good example of this can be seen in the case of Andy, a ten-year-old child who molested other children. As a baby, Andy had been abandoned repeatedly for days at a time by his drug-addicted mother. The therapist who interviewed him said that the boy had been damaged so badly that he couldn't trust anybody. He had lost his ability to care. His rage was so great that later on he imagined he was beating the therapist in the head with a baseball bat and watching her brains roll out. Meanwhile, he was laughing all the time.

Proponents of "rage reduction" therapy say that children like Andy need to release this bottled-up rage or they will act it out on society. The love and consistency of an adult mentor are also a key to possibly "saving" this child. There are support groups for parents and professionals that provide information on how to relate to this unique and challenging child.

"There Is No Bad Boy"

The majority of acting-out children are not unbonded. Their behavior is a cry for help, not a vicious act. It is true that children who act dangerously need to be placed in controlled circumstances. But even children in controlled circumstances can be treated with dignity and respect.

Children in pain need more than anything to be told that they are loved and okay. When they work through their shame and realize that they are lovable, their true beauty can emerge. Previously destructive energy becomes constructive when it is given an alternative way to express itself. To repeat the motto of Father Flannigan, child advocate and the founder of Boystown, "There is no bad boy!" (or bad girl).

CHAPTER 22

Positive Talk for the Adopted and Foster Child

In this chapter, we will explore ways to affirm those children who have been separated from their family of origin and live with a new set of parents. We will also see how the non-biological parents of those children can get the support they need. Let's begin with looking at the needs and challenges of the adopted child.

Affirming the Child Adopted at Birth

Most children begin to understand they were adopted into their families between age two or three, but they do not fully grasp the concept until a few years later. Parents are encouraged to explain the adoption to the child from infancy on, through books, stories, lifebooks or lifeline journals, and pictures. Gradually, as the child begins to understand that she grew in someone else's body, questions emerge. Sometimes the questions reflect the child's assumption that she was responsible for her parents giving her up:

- "Why didn't my mother keep me?" (I must have been ugly, I cried too much.)

- "Did I do something bad to be adopted?" (It was my fault.)

- "What was it about me that caused my parents to give me away?" (They didn't love me.)

Adoptive parents can answer these concerns by explaining, "It wasn't your fault that your parents couldn't keep you. Your parents love you, and so do we." Then they can explain the exact circumstances of the child's adoption to show her that she is not to blame.

Here are some healing affirmations that will help the adopted child understand that she is not to blame for her adoption:

Affirmations for Releasing Shame About Adoption

(Said by the adult to the child)

It's not your fault that your parents didn't keep you.

You didn't do anything wrong.

Your birthparents loved you but couldn't take care of you, so they made sure you had a family who could do both.

You were placed with your new parents so you could be cared for.

Your birthmother loves you and so do we.

IN ACTION

On the playground, Lou overheard some of his classmates making snide comments about his being adopted.

"What's wrong with being adopted?" he asked.

"It's different," they replied.

"Yes, it *is* different," Lou said. "It's special. I have two wonderful families who love and care about me. You should see my presents at Christmas."

Afterwards, the other kids stopped their teasing.

Answering Questions About Birth Parents and Identity

Once a child realizes she has been adopted, it is natural for her to wonder about her birthparents. "What was my birthmom like? What was my birthdad like? Do my birthparents think about me on my birthday? Do I have any brothers and sisters I don't know about?"

The adoption process used to be cloaked in shame and secrecy. Hence, these questions were difficult, if not impossible, to answer. With "open adoption," children now have access to information about their birth family and thus their roots and heritage. Many adoptive children receive a scrapbook containing pictures of their birthparents, information about their heritage, and the reasons for their adoption. Birthparents also stay in touch through gifts and letters. An increasing number of adopted children from U.S. birth families enjoy a totally open relationship with their birthparents, and adoptive families plan visits with birth families on a regular basis.

In addition, older children and adopted adults have the freedom to search out and meet their birthparents. Upon making this connection, it is not uncommon for children to become more confident and accepting of themselves. As one child put it, "Finding my birthparent was like filling in a missing gap in me. I needed to learn where I came from. Now I know."

Here are some affirmations that affirm an adoptive child's right to learn about her roots and heritage:

Affirmations for Learning About One's Birthparents
(Said by the adoptive parents to the child)

It's okay to wonder about your birthparents.

It's okay to want to meet them.

It's okay to wonder where you came from.

Your curiosity is healthy and normal.

Becoming a Permanent Part of the New Family

A common fear of adopted children is that their adoptive parents will give them away, just as their birthparents did. To help eight-year-old Eric gain a sense of belonging and permanency, his mom showed him the adoption decree: "This was signed by a judge and is permanent. It means I am officially your parent, now and forever."

Sometimes a child experiences confusion as to the identity of her true parent. "Who is my real mommy—my birthmommy or the mommy who has me now?" she asks. Here are two examples of how adoptive parents responded:

"I'm your mom because we made a promise to forever take care of you. Although you didn't grow in my tummy, your dad and I grew you in our hearts."

"I'm your dad because I made a promise to forever take care of you. When we signed the paper, you found a permanent home. You are my daughter, and nothing can ever change that."

Here are some other affirmative statements that will reassure the child that she has a permanent home with her adoptive family:

Affirmations for Creating a Sense of Permanency

(Said by the parent to the child)

You will always be our child.

Adoption is for always.

This is your home.

We will keep you forever.

We are your forever family.

(Said by the child to herself)

Being adopted means being in my family forever.

I am wanted by my parents.

This is my family.

I am happy with my adoptive family.

Adoption means I have more people who love me.

IN ACTION

After not being allowed to go to her friend's party, eleven-year-old Celeste shouted angrily at her adoptive mother, "You're not my real mommy! I don't have to listen to you." Although her mother was initially stung by the comment, she also realized that her daughter was reacting from anger and disappointment. Later in the evening, mother and daughter had a reconciliation in which they reaffirmed the love between them.

Affirming the Foster and Special Needs Adoptive Child

The majority of foster children come from homes where they were abused, neglected, or abandoned. The combination of this unhealthy background and the trauma of being removed from the home creates serious stress for the child. Consequently, a foster child has more than a 50 percent chance of exhibiting a serious mental, behavioral, or physical problem during her life.

Ideally, foster care provides a temporary refuge for a child until her home life stabilizes again. In many instances, the family situation is such that it cannot be rectified and the child cannot return to her original home. In the past, these long-term foster children became "lost in the system," growing up in multiple, relatively unsupervised foster homes. Alienated from biological kin, they had no permanent ties with a substitute family. Now, many of these "special needs" children are finding permanent homes with families who are eager to have them.

Joey is a sociable, smiling eighteen-month-old who has made significant progress, but is still developmentally delayed by three to five months in most areas. Joey has mild cerebral palsy and future neurological problems are a possibility. Joey, who is an African-American child, needs a family who can support his African-American heritage, is realistic in their expectations, and can accept his limits.

Fifteen-year-old Charles is interested in almost any activity, from woodworking to sewing. He sometimes has difficulty in relating to peers, but he is eager to please adults who show an interest in him. Charles, who has come from an inconsistent and abusive background, has made much progress in the areas of self-control and self-esteem. He now needs a family to provide a structured, stable environment with consistent limits and clear consequences.

While foster care was originally short-term, today the average child remains in a foster home for two years, while many never find a permanent residence. Those who are fortunate enough to be adopted are known as "special needs" adoptive children.

Let's explore how we can affirm foster and special needs adoptive children and help them cope with the many challenges they face.

Dealing with the Grief of Moving

Like the adopted child, the foster child's main trauma revolves around loss. Because her birthparents were either unwilling or unable to care for her, her first loss occurs when she is removed from her family of origin.

A second type of loss occurs when the foster child faces the added trauma of being moved from one foster home to another, or from foster care to adoption. Since the average stay in a foster home is two years, the pain of separation from the foster family can equal that of the separation from the original family. This separation trauma may be repeated again and again, depending on how many times the child is placed.

As the adult caregiver (caseworker, foster parent, teacher), you can support a foster child in her grieving in a number of ways:

- **Listen to her story**. Let her talk; let her cry; let her know that the upset feelings she is experiencing are normal.

- **Recognize that children have strong feelings about moving.** Validate those feelings of sadness, anger, fear, shame, guilt, anticipation, and hope by giving her the words to express how she feels ("I bet it makes you sad to leave this home," "You are probably pretty mad right now.")

- **Love her unconditionally.** Let her know that someone cares.

- **Explain to her the reasons for the move** and what you will be doing to support her.

- **Make sure that the move is done in a planned, gradual way** after preparation and visits with the new parents. During these visits, the foster family can gradually transfer parenting duties to the new family.

- **Expect the child to show distress before the move.** Some kids regress to earlier stages of development. Others get angry or rejecting, believing that it is easier to say good-bye when the other person is angry at you. Realize that these behaviors are a response to the stress of change and do not reflect her feelings toward you.

- **Have a good-bye party** on the day that the child is officially transferred to the new family. Invite the child, both families, friends, and the social worker. Have the previous parents give their blessings for the move. The parents can say, "You are special and we love you, but now the time has come for you to move. We wish you only the best in your new home."

A foster parent once said that children are like eggs; each time we move them they crack a little. If children are moved patiently, slowly, and sensitively, we can keep the egg from breaking.

Validating the Sadness

In order to grieve, children must feel their sadness. When children are allowed to grieve and feel their hurt, the pain can begin to diminish. Please refer to Chapter 9 for affirmations that support grieving.

Sometimes children don't want to talk about their feelings. When eleven-year-old Nathan was asked how he felt about his mom who abandoned him, he replied, "It's a private matter." In such an instance, we need to respect the child's wishes and not pressure him to talk. Let him know you are available to listen if he needs to talk. When he is ready, he will reach out.

Affirmations for Validating the Foster Child's Sadness
(Said by the adult to the child)

It's okay to feel sad.

You can tell me whatever is bothering you.

It's hard to leave people you love.

Children need safe homes where they will not be hurt or neglected.

You are going to a home where you will receive loving care and attention.

All of your feelings are okay.

IN ACTION

Art therapy is a wonderful way to help children express their deepest feelings. A seven-year-old foster girl drew two pictures about her family. In describing the first picture she said, "This is my house. I'm picking up my mom from Chicago." However, the house is crooked and no people are in it. In addition, the colors are somber—dark purple, black, and blues. The rain also adds to the sad and lonely feelings.

The second drawing is the house of her birthmother. The girl said, "I like it because she's kind of nice. She's inside the house. She's cooking dinner for us." Once again, however, the house is empty. "Where is my mother?" the picture cries out. A spider is dangling nearby, indicating that the child feels scared and threatened. At some point the counselor will help this girl put words to her feelings of loneliness and despair.

Validating the Anger

The second dimension of a foster child's grief is her anger. The same events that make her sad—being abandoned, neglected, or abused—also make her angry. This anger can get "acted out" through lying, hitting, being disruptive, being unable to concentrate in school, cutting classes, and running away.

The alternative to acting out anger is to "work it out"—through writing, talking, drawing, painting, and sculpting the feelings, or by expressing them in play therapy. Group therapy is especially valuable in providing a safe and supportive environment where children can experience their rage and pain.

Because children tend to idealize their parents, it is difficult for foster kids to express their feelings of anger at their birthparents. Too often this anger is displaced onto the caseworker or foster parent. It takes time before the child can feel safe enough to direct her anger at its true source. Here are some affirmations that can help the child to own and express her anger in a healthy way:

Affirmations for Validating the Foster Child's Anger
(Said by the adult to the child)

It's okay to be angry.

I can understand why you are upset with being moved around.

It must be very frustrating.

I'd be upset, too, if I were in your situation.

It's okay to be angry, but it's not okay to hit your brother.

It's okay to be angry, but it's not okay to destroy the furniture.

It's okay to be angry, but it's not okay to skip school.

You can find healthy ways to express your anger.

IN ACTION

Stephanie is a twelve-year-old girl whose mother is a heroin addict and whose father is an alcoholic. A few weeks after arriving at her foster home, she began to punch her new sister.

One day, her caseworker remarked, "You know, Stephanie, I bet you really miss your mom. I think you must feel very lonely sometimes." Stephanie immediately broke down and sobbed as she experienced the sadness and hurt which lay behind her anger. As she continued to grieve for the loss of her mom, her anger and abusive behavior also subsided.

Dealing with the Shame

When a young child is removed from her home, she automatically assumes that "I must have done something bad to be taken away from my parents. It must be my fault." Many foster children carry this shame as they move from home to home.

In addition, foster children who get moved from home to home rapidly develop a rejection complex. At the core of this complex lies the belief, "Nobody wants me; nobody loves me." Even when these children find a permanent home, they can feel that their adoptive parents love them less than their own birth children.

Once again, it is up to an adult witness to be present for the child. Over time, the child will know that you really "see" her, that you care about her, and that she is a valuable person. Here are some shame-reducing affirmations to share with the foster child:

Affirmations and Reality Statements for Releasing Shame

(Said by the adult to the child)

You didn't cause being taken from your parents.

Even though your mom (dad) loves you, she (he) has many problems.

You are still lovable.

You are important enough to me that I will spend time alone with just you.

I'm glad you are in my life.

Trust and Safety Issues

Most foster children don't trust adults. There is good reason for this. In the past, adults have abused them, failed to protect them from abuse, abandoned them, or let them down in some other way. Consequently, the foster child comes to believe that adults are unsafe and undependable. To regain these children's trust takes time, patience, and the willingness to stick out the tough moments when children test you to see if you really do care.

In addition to not trusting adults, foster kids don't trust life. Experience has taught them that the world is unsafe, that they cannot depend on anyone, that "nothing lasts." These beliefs will persist until the child finds a safe and healing family environment.

IN ACTION

Because of their mistrust of adults, foster children will often resist a self-esteem affirmation that is said directly to them. One parent solved this problem by posting an envelope on her daughter's bedroom door and periodically depositing an affirmation in it. Tahira would then peek at the affirmation when her mom was not looking. Making the affirmation process into a game allowed Tahira to internalize her mom's positive messages without the usual resistance.

Staying in Contact with the Biological Parents

To mitigate the trauma of separation, it is important to keep the foster child's connection with her biological parents intact. This helps integrate the child's past into the current life experience.

Despite their previous experience of abuse or neglect, foster children remain closely bonded to their birthparents. When foster children have some contact with their parents or see their parents' lives improving, they feel much better about themselves. When the parents don't visit or don't work to stabilize their lives, the child's self-esteem declines.

Although a caseworker cannot control the parents' actions, she can keep the child posted on the parents' progress or their lack of progress—for example, "Your mom is finding a job, but your dad is not attending his anger management classes." The caseworker can also arrange visits with the birthparents when possible.

Affirmations About Parents' Progress
(Said by the adult to the child)

We are working to help your parents succeed.

We are helping your mom find a house.

We are helping your dad to manage his anger.

It's up to your parents how they do.

It's okay to be angry with them if they let you down.

It's okay to be sad if they let you down.

IN ACTION

Like all kids, foster children tend to idealize their parents and selectively forget about the abuse and neglect they received. Peers can be instrumental in helping a child to let go of her illusions.

For example, when Sam told his support group how his father would pick up a chair in a fit of rage and throw it at his mom, Brooke replied, "I bet you're glad he's gone!" Sam responded, "I guess you're right. My dad is a dangerous person. I miss him, but he's dangerous."

Because Sam's father lived in another city, it was easy for Sam to keep up an idealized picture of him. Wisely, his caseworker arranged for the alcoholic father to visit. After spending two days with his inebriated dad, Sam once again realized why he couldn't live with him.

The Lifeline Journal

A foster child can keep a lifebook or lifeline journal that helps her look back at her life and chronicles the major events and transitions. She starts with a description of her parents and family, and traces her life up to the present. The journal process helps her to grieve those unresolved separations and to deal with critical identity questions—*Who am I?* and *Where did I come from?* It also starts a process that can lead her to seeing her life as valid, meaningful, and purposeful.

Affirming the Foster Parent and Special Needs Adoptive Parent

Becoming a foster parent or a special needs adoptive parent is a challenging and life-changing experience. The child you adopt will likely bring with her heavy emotional baggage from the past such as emotional, physical, or sexual abuse; neglect; and the effects of parental drug abuse.

The parent who takes on this role will benefit if she:

- has a healthy relationship with herself and her partner
- has good parenting skills

- has a sense of humor, flexibility, and high self-esteem

- has a comfortable working relationship with professionals such as social workers, therapists, and school personnel

- has a good support system for herself

In addition, because so many foster and special needs children have been sexually abused, parents need to feel comfortable with their own sexuality and receive some training in the issues of sexually abused children.

Let's now explore some of the important challenges of being a special needs adoptive or foster parent.

Responding to Loss

Like the foster child, foster parents are experts at dealing with loss. Not only must they grieve each time a child moves out of their home, they must attend to the child's grief brought on by her own transition. No wonder that grief is the primary issue that foster parents talk about in support groups. Here are some suggestions on how to make transitions easier for you and for your child if you are a foster parent:

- Before you even discuss the move with the child, **sort out your own feelings** with someone you trust, such as a friend, therapist, or the members of a support group.

- **Acknowledge your sadness** about having to let go. Maybe you feel the new family's values and philosophy are different from yours.

- **Acknowledge your anger** at the forces or circumstances that are taking the child from you. Note where the anger is directed—at the birthparents, the new foster parents, the caseworker, or the system. Behind the anger and frustration is the deep pain about having to say good-bye to your child. As one foster parent said, "I was so angry when they moved Benjamin. It took me several weeks before I realized that the caseworker didn't have any other choice in the matter."

- **Ask to be part of the team that helps the child move.** Participating in the process helps you release your feelings of powerlessness.

Affirmations for a Foster Parent's Grief

(Said by the foster parent to herself)

I can let my child go.

I can accept the fact that she must move on.

I can get support for working through my own grief.

I can help my child work though her grief.

It's okay to feel sad and angry.

All of my feelings are okay.

Responding to the Child's Acting-Out Behavior

When a child first arrives in a foster or special needs adoptive home, she is initially on her best behavior. During this "honeymoon" period, the parent may think, "I wonder why the agency called Alicia a problem child. She's nothing of the sort."

Then, without warning, the child's old hurts and pains emerge with a vengeance. She may:

- act out her anger through fighting, yelling, and destructive behavior

- lie, steal, or cheat

- sexually act out through provocative behavior, masturbating in public, or initiating sexual contact with other children in the home

- withdraw, sulk, or become depressed

- demand excessive amounts of attention

- be dependent or overcontrolling

- regress to a previous developmental stage (for example, engage in bedwetting and soiling)

When your child acts out or gets in trouble, it may be easy to feel that you are a bad parent or that you are the cause of the problem. Don't take it personally! Your foster or special needs adoptive child came to you with her own emotional history and problems that have nothing to do with you.

Earlier we alluded to a major reason a foster child acts out—to test you to make sure that you really care. When your child seems to be doing everything she can to get you to reject her, hang in there. Love her enough to say, "I'll never give up on you no matter what you do!"

There is an old saying in foster care, "If it works, it also hurts." Here are some affirmations that will support you to get through the tough times and come through the other side:

Affirmations for Responding to Acting-Out Behavior
(Said by the parent to herself)

My child is acting out because of the trauma she experienced.

I did not cause the trauma and I can't undo it.

My child is testing me to see how much I care.

I can respond with understanding when I am tested.

I have the love and patience to stick with my child through her acting out.

I can wait and see this through.

IN ACTION

Adrian, an eleven-year-old foster child, was caught stealing around the house. His parents expressed displeasure toward the behavior, but kept affirming their love for Adrian. In addition, they let Adrian know that there would be consequences assigned to his behavior. If he stole, for example, he would be asked to scrub the kitchen floor. After scrubbing the kitchen floor six times, Adrian decided that he didn't want that consequence any more. In a short time, his stealing dropped off.

Reaching Out for Support

Conventional parenting classes will not prepare the special needs adoptive or foster parent for what lies ahead. Fortunately, many sources of support exist. They include:

- foster parent associations that provide numerous workshops and training opportunities on issues specific to foster parenting

- foster parent support groups that offer parents the chance to talk with and learn from other foster parents

- therapists

- friends and neighbors

Like all parents, it is essential to take breaks from your children and nurture yourself and your primary relationship. Taking time to relax is another important survival skill. Please refer to the "Self-Care" section in Chapter 4 (pages 32–33) for more information and affirmations on how to get your own needs met.

Learning to Cope with the System

Much of a foster or adoptive parent's time is spent dealing with professionals and the institutions they work for. At times, parents may feel uncomfortable about communicating their needs to the system, especially when they disagree with the system's recommendations. Here are some affirmations that support the parent's right to speak up for herself and work out differences of opinion with those in authority.

Affirmations for Coping with the System
(Said by the parent to herself)

I can ask for what I want.

I have a right to be heard.

I can stand up for myself and my children.

I can communicate my needs to my caseworker.

I can make the system work for me.

A Final Note

The social problems that are placing children in foster care are not going away soon. When the parent-child bond is broken early on, lasting and sometimes irreversible damage can occur. To reverse the trend of family dissolution, more and more states are turning to "family preservation," a short-term intervention program where social workers and counselors teach parents and children the skills they need to resolve family conflicts. When families are given the opportunity to learn new coping skills, they can and do stay together. Families in crisis can change when they are given the support and the tools to do so.

Emily's Story:
The Reason for Hope

> One discovers that destiny can be directed, that one
> does not have to remain in bondage to the first wax imprint
> made in childhood. One need not be branded
> by the first pattern. Once the deforming mirror is smashed,
> there is a possibility of wholeness; there is a possibility of joy.
>
> *Anaïs Nin, author*

It is not an easy time to be a child. The bonds that once held families and communities together are changing and loosening. The choices for parents and children are more complex and fraught with anxiety than ever before. And, yet, there is reason for hope because we know what a child needs to grow into a healthy, alive, and fully functioning person.

The unchanging nutrients are love, dignity, and respect. Given these, a person can overcome even the deepest multi-generational patterning. A child's ability to attach himself to even the slimmest of hopes and to use that hope to stay healthy is truly remarkable. Sometimes all we have to do is smile back.

This movement toward health and wholeness is illustrated by the story of Emily. Emily's grandparents spent their lives shooting at each other in the Ozarks. Her mother was physically abused, and she then abused Emily and her siblings.

Emily was placed in a class for emotionally disturbed children. Through the encouragement of her ninth-grade teacher, she began to express her feelings of pain and reach out for support. Later, she entered therapy to deal with her childhood trauma. She is now working and raising a family.

Every so often Emily visits the one person who believed in her. "I don't know how you put up with me," she tells her teacher, "but I'm glad you did. Now that I have worked through some of my original pain, my children will have it better. I know they will."

We take a vow as parents, grandparents, teachers, counselors, or mentors never to take for granted our ability to powerfully affect the life of a child, no matter how small the effort may seem. The hope that our witnessing brings is the most precious of gifts.

Suggested Reading

Bass, Ellen, and Laura Davis. *The Courage to Heal: A Guide for Women Survivors of Child Sexual Abuse.* New York: HarperPerennial, 1994. This comprehensive guide for women healing from child sexual abuse includes personal experiences, practical suggestions, and an abundance of resources.

Benson, Peter L., Judy Galbraith, and Pamela Espeland. *What Kids Need to Succeed: Proven, Practical Ways to Raise Good Kids.* Minneapolis: Free Spirit Publishing, 1998. Find information on forty developmental assets that children need to grow into healthy, caring, and successful adults. Practical, concrete suggestions for building assets at home, at school, in the congregation, and in the community are supplemented with further resources.

Biddulph, Steve. *Raising Boys: Why Boys Are Different—and How to Help Them Become Happy and Well-Balanced Men.* Berkeley: Celestial Arts, 1998. This resource for parents focuses on the specific challenges that boys face growing up. Examining psychological, emotional, and physiological factors, this research-based book is a comprehensive and practical resource for helping boys become healthy young men.

Bloch, Douglas. *Healing from Depression: Twelve Weeks to a Better Mood.* Berkeley: Celestial Arts, 2002. Sharing his own experience with a depressive illness, Douglas Bloch describes how a holistic approach aided his recovery. Examining alternative healing methods, this comprehensive manual on depression offers practical suggestions for feeling better.

Bloch, Douglas. *Listening to Your Inner Voice: Discover the Truth Within You and Let It Guide Your Way.* Center City, MN: Hazelden, 1992. Using a holistic approach, this resource encourages readers to look within themselves to discover the things most important to them. The book promotes spiritual growth and a sense of purpose which can guide readers to a more fulfilling life.

Bloch, Douglas. *Words That Heal: Affirmations and Meditations for Daily Living.* Portland, OR: Pallas Communications, 1988. This book of affirmations is a great resource for anyone experiencing a tough day. Find wisdom and advice for daily healing and encouraging words that promote a healthy sense of self.

Bradshaw, John. *Bradshaw On: The Family: A New Way of Creating Solid Self-Esteem.* Deerfield Beach, FL: Health Communications, 1996. This book offers an explanation of family dynamics and of how roles and attitudes taken by individual family members can create perpetual problems for everyone. Bradshaw offers advice for breaking detrimental cycles that keep both individual members and family units from living happy and fulfilling lives.

Bradshaw, John. *Healing the Shame That Binds You.* Deerfield Beach, FL: Health Communications, 1988. This resource examines how shame can lead to compulsive behavior, addiction, and perfectionism, all conditions that cause stress in family life. Practical suggestions show the way to healthier attitudes that will benefit all family members.

Bradshaw, John. *Homecoming: Reclaiming and Championing Your Inner Child.* New York: Bantam, 1991. Bradshaw, a conductor of workshops on the inner child, offers practical suggestions for building confidence and making sense of life. Inspiring insight and affirmative words make it clear that emotional damage sustained during childhood need not hamper the possibility of a fulfilling adult life.

Clarke, Jean Illsley. *Self Esteem: A Family Affair.* Center City, MN: Hazelden, 1998. Offering profiles of real families, Clarke examines the critical role family relationships play in children's emotional development. This is a practical resource for establishing positive communication in the home and helping all family members feel better about themselves.

Clarke, Jean Illsley, and Connie Dawson. *Growing Up Again: Parenting Ourselves, Parenting Our Children.* Center City, MN: Hazelden, 1998. Parents will find a wealth of information in this book for effective parenting. Focusing on personal habits, attitudes, and feelings, this resource illustrates how parents can fulfill themselves through the love and care of their children.

Denham, Susanne A. *Emotional Development in Young Children.* New York: Guilford Press, 1998. This comprehensive resource for fostering healthy emotional development in young children includes research on children's needs and methods for meeting them. Offering a thorough overview of a child's emotional world, this book provides insight for arming children with the emotional assets they need.

Elias, Maurice J., Steven E. Tobias, and Brian S. Friedlander. *Emotionally Intelligent Parenting: How to Raise a Self-Disciplined, Responsible, and Socially Skilled Child.* New York: Harmony Books, 1999. This research-based book illustrates the world that today's children face and examines their emotional reactions. Specific parenting tactics offer advice for tackling common family problems, helping kids become aware of their feelings, praising children, and helping them to make responsible decisions.

Faber, Adele, and Elaine Mazlish. *How to Talk So Kids Will Listen and Listen So Kids Will Talk.* New York: Avon, 1999. This guide offers a step-by-step approach for improving family relationships. Practical exercises help parents communicate effectively with children and help them solve problems.

Gardner, Howard. *Frames of Mind: The Theory of Multiple Intelligences.* New York: Basic Books, 1993. The theory of multiple intelligences has revolutionized the way parents and educators raise and teach students. This guide offers methods for addressing children's learning strengths at home and in the classroom.

Garrabino, James. *Lost Boys: Why Our Sons Turn Violent and How We Can Save Them.* New York: Free Press, 1999. Based on extensive research, this book examines why some boys become violent and offers parents advice for helping boys to become caring and emotionally balanced individuals.

Gil, Eliana. *Outgrowing the Pain: A Book for Adults Abused as Children.* New York: Dell, 1988. Parenting can be difficult, and adults who experience abuse as children often encounter further complications in their relationships with children. This resource offers former abuse victims information for understanding the ways that their personal experiences influence interactions with their own children.

Goleman, Daniel. *Emotional Intelligence: Why It Can Matter More Than IQ.* New York: Bantam, 1995. This research-based book examines how self-awareness, altruism, empathy, and personal motivation are often stronger factors in determining happiness and success than IQ. Parents will find practical suggestions for increasing emotional intelligence in children, allowing kids to grow into capable adults.

Gordon, Thomas. *Parent Effectiveness Training: The Proven Program for Raising Responsible Children.* New York: Three Rivers Press, 2000. This time-tested resource offers parents practical, step-by-step guidance for communicating effectively with children, learning how to support children, and teaching them problem-solving skills that will help them make responsible decisions.

Holt, John. *How Children Fail.* New York: Perseus, 1995. Originally published in 1964, this resource has proven a timeless classic for parents and teachers looking to improve student success at home and in the classroom. Focusing on the needs of all children, this is a practical and straightforward guide for raising smart and resilient kids.

Kaufman, Gershen, Lev Raphael, and Pamela Espeland. *Stick Up for Yourself! Every Kid's Guide to Personal Power and Positive Self-Esteem.* Minneapolis: Free Spirit Publishing, 1999. This practical guide helps children raise their self-esteem. Real-life examples, affirmative language, and activities for building assertiveness help kids feel good about themselves and form healthy and lasting relationships.

Krementz, Jill. *How It Feels When a Parent Dies.* New York: Knopf, 1988. Focusing on the stories of children ages 7–17, this affirming book helps kids cope with the loss of a parent. Real-life stories and photographs help kids realize that they are not alone in their grief.

Krementz, Jill. *How It Feels to Be Adopted.* New York: Knopf, 1988. This book features interviews with children ages 8–16 from all social backgrounds. Kids learn about the experiences and feelings of other adopted kids.

Lamb, Sharon. *The Secret Lives of Girls: What Good Girls Really Do—Sex Play, Aggression, and Their Guilt.* New York: Free Press, 2002. Research-based, this book offers insight into traditional notions of femininity and how those ideas affect the development of girls. Parents and teachers will find a practical model for understanding and nurturing the strengths that girls carry, but often mask.

Miller, Alice. *The Drama of the Gifted Child: The Search for the True Self.* New York: Basic Books, 1996. This resource examines how gifted children are often unhealthily driven toward unrealistic achievements by feelings of worthlessness and excessive parent expectations. Readers discover how to reconcile their feelings and gain insight into stopping the cycle of unhealthy expectations.

Miller, Alice. *For Your Own Good: Hidden Cruelty in Child-Rearing and the Roots of Violence.* New York: Noonday, 1990. Miller explores the background of violent and self-destructive individuals and shows how childhood experiences affect adult behavior. For those who experienced abuse as children, Miller provides a process for getting in touch with the child in the adult and opening an emotional life previously repressed.

Miller, Alice. *Thou Shalt Not Be Aware: Society's Betrayal of the Child*. New York: Noonday, 1998. This book explores how children suffering abuse, unable to express their feelings, carry pain and anger inside. Read about how the unconscious retains internalized pain from childhood, and how it can cause poor mental health and destructive decision making in adulthood.

Pipher, Mary Bray. *Reviving Ophelia: Saving the Selves of Adolescent Girls*. New York: Ballantine, 1995. This research-based resource offers the stories of real adolescent girls and examines how an appearance-obsessed culture keeps them from discovering their full potential. Parents will find strategies for helping adolescent girls to combat prevalent cultural images and feel good about themeselves.

Pollack, William S. *Real Boys: Rescuing Our Sons from the Myth of Boyhood*. New York: Random House, 1998. William Pollack explains how boys struggle with conflicting societal expectations of masculinity. Parents learn about the causes of male behavior problems and discover how to build and maintain boys' self-esteem and emotional intelligence.

Roehlkepartain, Jolene L. *Raising Healthy Children Day by Day: 366 Readings for Parents, Teachers, and Caregivers, Birth to Age 5*. Minneapolis: Free Spirit Publishing, 2001. Based on forty developmental assets that all young children need, this book of daily readings provides parents with a year's worth of practical advice and inspiration. Readings emphasize building social skills, family support, and positive values.

Saarni, Carolyn. *The Development of Emotional Competence*. New York: Guilford Press, 1999. This research-based book provides information on the wide range of skills that contribute to a child's emotional intelligence. Included are discussions of self-awareness, sensitivity to others, expressing emotions, coping with disappointment, and confronting adversity.

Seligman, Martin. *The Optimistic Child: A Proven Program to Safeguard Children Against Depression and Build Lifelong Resiliency*. New York: HarperPerennial, 1995. Parenting toward a child's emotional health begins with affirmative words and loving actions. This book goes further by providing information on and strategies for teaching children to think and perceive their world in a positive way.

Spock, Benjamin, and Stephen Parker. *Dr. Spock's Baby and Child Care*. New York: Pocket Books, 1998. This classic book offers information on a wide array of parenting issues. General advice is supplemented with practical suggestions for dealing with a host of situations.

Verny, Thomas, and John Kelly. *The Secret Life of the Unborn Child: How You Can Prepare Your Unborn Baby for a Happy, Healthy Life*. New York: Delta, 1994. This book examines the ways that parents can respond to and care for their child when it is still in the womb. Based on two decades of medical research, the exercises are intended to ensure that children grow into healthy and caring individuals.

Additional Resources

Alcoholics Anonymous (A.A.)
Grand Central Station
P.O. Box 459
New York, NY 10163
www.aa.org
A.A. is a fellowship of men and women who share their experience, strength, and hope with each other that they may solve their common problem and help others to recover from alcoholism. Look for "Alcoholics Anonymous" in any telephone directory. In most urban areas, a central A.A. office, or "intergroup," staffed mainly by volunteer A.A.s, will be happy to answer your questions or put you in touch with those who can.

American Academy of Child and Adolescent Psychiatry (AACAP)
3615 Wisconsin Avenue NW
Washington, DC 20016
(202) 966-7300
www.aacap.org
The AACAP provides information about developmental, behavioral, and mental disorders of children and adolescents, including fact sheets for parents and caregivers, current research, practice guidelines, managed care information, and much more.

Children's Defense Fund (CDF)
25 E Street NW
Washington, DC 20001
(202) 628-8787
www.childrensdefense.org
CDF is a private, nonprofit organization that provides a strong, effective voice for all the children of America who cannot vote, lobby, or speak for themselves, especially poor and minority children and those with disabilities.

Federation of Families for Children's Mental Health
1101 King Street, Suite 420
Alexandria, VA 22314
(703) 684-7710
www.ffcmh.org
The Federation is a national advocacy organization for families of children and youth with mental health needs and provides an opportunity for family members to work with professionals and other interested citizens to improve services for their children.

National Council on Child Abuse and Family Violence (NCCAFV)
1025 Connecticut Avenue NW, Suite 1012
Washington, DC 20036
(202) 429-6695
www.nccafv.org
NCCAFV is a nonprofit corporation serving as a resource center on family violence prevention services, and providing public education materials, program and resource development consultation, and technical assistance and training to agencies and volunteers.

National Foster Parent Association (NFPA)
7512 Stanich Avenue, #6
Gig Harbor, WA 98335
1-800-557-5238
www.nfpainc.org
NFPA is a nonprofit, volunteer organization that strives to bring together foster parents, agency representatives, and community people who wish to work together to improve the foster care system and enhance the lives of all children and families.

National Institute on Mental Health (NIMH)
6001 Executive Boulevard, Room 8184
Bethesda, MD 20892-9663
(301) 443-4513
www.nimh.nih.gov
NIMH's mission is to reduce the burden of mental illness and behavioral disorders through research on mind, brain, and behavior, and to generate information that is needed to better understand, treat, and prevent mental disorders.

National Mental Health Association (NMHA)
2001 North Beauregard Street, 12th Floor
Alexandria, VA 22311
1-800-969-6642
www.nmha.org
NMHA is a nonprofit organization addressing all aspects of mental health and mental illness. It works to improve the mental health of all Americans, especially those suffering from mental disorders, through advocacy, education, research, and service.

PACER Center
8161 Normandale Boulevard
Minneapolis, MN 55437
(952) 838-9000
www.pacer.org
PACER identifies the resources and services available to help expand opportunities and enhance the quality of life of children with disabilities and their families.

Parents Anonymous® Inc.
675 West Foothill Boulevard, Suite 220
Claremont, CA 91711
(909) 621-6184
www.parentsanonymous.org
A national family strengthening program, Parents Anonymous® encourages all parents to ask for help early, whatever their circumstances, to effectively break the cycle of abuse to protect today's children and strengthen tomorrow's generation of parents.

Prevent Child Abuse America
200 South Michigan Avenue, 17th Floor
Chicago, IL 60604-2404
(312) 663-3520
www.preventchildabuse.org
This organization provides leadership to promote and implement child abuse prevention efforts at both the national and local levels. With the help of state chapters, their mission is to strengthen families and engage communities nationwide.

Endnotes

Chapter 1: Sticks and Stones Will Break My Bones, But Words Will Wound Me Forever

1. Vissing, Yvonne M., et al. "Verbal Aggression by Parents and Psychosocial Problems of Children." *Child Abuse and Neglect* 15:3, 1991: 223–238.

Chapter 3: Introducing Positive Talk to Children

1. Miller, Alice. *The Drama of the Gifted Child: The Search for the True Self.* New York: Basic Books, 1996.

Chapter 4: Positive Talk for the Adult Caregiver

1. Information on Parent Effectiveness Training (PET) and Family Effectiveness Training (FET) is available online at *www.thomasgordon.com.*

2. Child abuse information from the National Council on Child Abuse and Family Violence is available online at *www.nccafv.org.*

3. Rosenthal, Robert, and Lenore Jacobson. *Pygmalion in the Classroom: Teacher Expectation and Pupils' Intellectual Development.* New York: Irvington Publishers, 1992.

Chapter 6: Positive Talk for Physical Health, Body Image, and Athletic Performance

1. Benson, Herbert. *Timeless Healing: The Power and Biology of Belief.* New York: Scribner, 1996.

2. Pert, Candace. *Molecules of Emotion: The Science Behind Mind-Body Medicine.* New York: Simon and Schuster, 1997.

3. Weber, D.O. "The Power of the Mind." *University of California, Berkeley Wellness Letter* 12:12, 1996: 2–3.

4. Birkimer, John, et al. "Predictors of Health Behaviors from a Behavior-Analytic Orientation." *The Journal of Social Psychology* 136:2, 1996: 181–189.

Chapter 8: What to Say When You Are Scared

1. Nansel, Tanja, et al. "Bullying Behaviors Among U.S. Youth: Prevalence and Association with Psychosocial Adjustment." *Journal of the American Medical Association* 285:16, 2001: 2094–2100.

2. Ibid.

3. Borba, Michele, and Michael Borba. *Building Moral Intelligence: The Seven Essential Virtues That Teach Kids to Do the Right Thing.* San Francisco: Jossey-Bass, 2001.

4. National Center for Educational Statistics and Bureau of Justice Statistics. *Indicators of School Crime and Safety 2001.* Washington, DC: National Center for Educational Statistics and Bureau of Justice Statistics, 2001.

Chapter 9: What to Say When You Are Sad

1. Miller, Alice. *The Drama of the Gifted Child: The Search for the True Self.* New York: Basic Books, 1996.

2. Schrof, Joannie, and Stacey Schultz. "Melancholy Nation." *U.S. News and World Report*, March 8, 1999: 56–63.

3. "Suicide in the United States," compiled by the National Center for Injury Prevention and Control, a division of the Centers for Disease Control, is available online at *www.cdc.gov/ncipc/factsheets/suifacts.htm*.

4. Ibid.

5. Schrof, Joannie, and Stacey Schultz. "Melancholy Nation." *U.S. News and World Report*, March 8, 1999: 56–63.

6. Knickerbocker, Brad. "Young and Male in America: It's Hard Being a Boy." *Christian Science Monitor*, April 29, 1999.

7. Wingert, Pat, and Barbara Kantrowitz. "Young and Depressed." *Newsweek*, October 7, 2002: 52–61.

8. Taylor, Kate, et al. "3 to 6: The Teen Alone Zone: Kids Write Their Own Rules When Adults Aren't Around." *The Sunday Oregonian*, June 20, 1999.

9. Ibid.

10. "Suicide in the United States," compiled by the National Center for Injury Prevention and Control, a division of the Centers for Disease Control, is available online at *www.cdc.gov/ncipc/factsheets/suifacts.htm*.

11. Ibid.

Chapter 11: What to Say When You Are Teased

1. Information on Fighting Fair from the Peace Education Foundation is available online at *www.peace-ed.org* or by telephoning 1-800-749-8838.

Chapter 12: Prenatal Positive Talk

1. Verny, Thomas, and John Kelly. *The Secret Life of the Unborn Child: How You Can Prepare Your Unborn Baby for a Happy, Healthy Life.* New York: Delta, 1994.

2. Chamberlain, David. *The Mind of Your Newborn Baby.* Berkeley: North Atlantic Books, 1998.

3. Verny, Thomas, and John Kelly. *The Secret Life of the Unborn Child: How You Can Prepare Your Unborn Baby for a Happy, Healthy Life.* New York: Delta, 1994.

4. Standley, Jayne. "The Effects of Music and Multimodal Stimulation on Responses of Premature Infants in Neonatal Intensive Care." *Pediatric Nursing* 24:6, 1998: 532–538.

Chapter 13: Affirming the Infant

1. Wirth, Frederick. *Prenatal Parenting: The Complete Psychological and Spiritual Guide to Loving Your Unborn Child.* New York: Harper Collins, 2001.

Chapter 14: Affirming the Toddler

1. Becker, Ernest. *The Denial of Death.* New York: Touchstone Books, 1997.

Chapter 17: Affirming the Adolescent

1. Terry, Elizabeth, and Jennifer Manlove. *Trends in Sexual Activity and Contraceptive Use Among Teens.* Washington, DC: National Campaign to Prevent Teen Pregnancy, 2000.

2. Reported on the Web site of the National Campaign to Prevent Teen Pregnancy (*www.teenpregancy.org*), this information is an analysis of S.K. Henshaw's *U.S. Teenage Pregnancy Statistics* (New York: Alan Guttmacher Institute, 1996) and J.D. Forest's *Proportion of U.S. Women Ever Pregnant Before Age 20* (New York: Alan Guttmacher Institute, 1986).

3. Children's Defense Fund. *The State of America's Children Yearbook 2001.* Washington, DC: Children's Defense Fund, 2001.

4. National Center on Addiction and Substance Abuse at Columbia University. *Dangerous Liaisons: Substance Abuse and Sex.* New York: National Center on Addiction and Substance Abuse at Columbia University, 1999.

5. Hawsey, David. "Picking a Major: Finding an Academic Program as Unique as You." Article appears on the College Confidential Web site (*www.collegeconfidential.com*).

Chapter 19: Positive Talk for the Child from a Chemically Dependent Family

1. Morey, Connie K. "Children of Alcoholics: A School-Based Comparative Study." *Journal of Drug Education* 29:1, 1999: 63–75.

Chapter 20: Positive Talk for the Abused Child

1. These projections by the Crimes Against Children Research Center at the University of New Hampshire are based on estimates from *Children Maltreatment 2000: Reports from the States to the National Child Abuse and Neglect Data System.* Washington, DC: U.S. Department of Health and Human Services, Children's Bureau, 2002.

2. Miller, Alice. *For Your Own Good: Hidden Cruelty in Child-Rearing and the Roots of Violence.* New York: Noonday, 1990.

Subject Index

Sexual exploration by preschoolers, 209, 213
Shame
  of acting-out child, 309
  antidotes to, 10
  of being abused, 288, 292–293
  of being adopted, 319–320
  of being sexually abused, 288, 293
  of foster child, 327–328
  healing, 64
  is root of addictions, 10
  of parent with child with disabilities, 270–272
  protecting against with unconditional love, 65
  reinforcing with self-talk, 64, 249
  as result of divorce or separation, 144
  types of, 63–64
Siblings, 136–137, 202–203
Social skills. *See* Making friends
Spock, Benjamin, 341
Sports. *See* Athletic performance
Stepparents, accepting, 144–146
Stick Up for Yourself! (Kaufman), 340
Stuttering, 260–262
Suicide, 150–153
Support groups
  for acting-out children, 315, 316
  for alcohol abuse, 283, 342
  for children in chemically dependent families, 283
  for children with behavioral or emotional disabilities, 267–268
  for teenagers, 315, 316
Systematic desensitization, 105, 127

T
Teachers
  accepting own limitations, 55
  classroom management and, 54
  creating optimal learning environment, 52–53
  creating put-down-free zones, 172–174
  detachment is necessary for, 55–56
  exhibiting patience, 53–54
  influence of expectations on, 57
  lesson for accepting mistakes, 101–102
  school phobia and, 129
  self-acknowledgment by, 57–58
  self-care for, 56–57

Teasers, 170–172
Teasing
  by bullies, 11
  of child with disabilities, 257–258, 269
  coping with, 112, 113
  counteracting, 165–170, 172–174
  identifying, 164–165
  self-esteem and, 167
  visualizations for, 167
Teenagers
  body image of, 232–234, 245
  breaking up by, 235–236
  creating positive futures, 241–242, 245
  dating by, 234–235, 245
  depression and, 149–150
  developmental overview of, 225–226
  divorce and, 140–144
  drug and alcohol use by, 239–241, 240
  fears of, 104
  letting go of, 242–244
  peer acceptance and, 227–229, 245
  peer pressure and, 229–232, 245
  peer support groups for, 315, 316
  pregnancy and, 237–239
  safe sex and, 237–239, 245
  suicide and, 150–152
  using affirmations with, 226
Test-taking
  overcoming anxiety about, 84–86, 87–88
  visualization for, 86–87
Thou Shalt Not Be Aware (Miller), 341
Time-outs for adults, 37–38
Tobias, Steven E., 339
Toddlers
  development of
    exploration by, 194–195, 206
    saying no by, 196–198, 206
    separation from parents by, 196, 206
    "terrible twos" of, 198–201, 206
  divorce and, 140–144
  fears of, 104
  letting child develop at own rate, 205
  siblings and, 202–203
  toilet training and, 203–205, 206
Toilet training, 203–205, 206
Toxic shame, 64
Trauma, need to feel pain of, 26

About the Authors

Douglas Bloch, M.A. (shown with his goddaughter, Amy Mae), is an author, teacher, and counselor who writes and speaks on the topics of psychology, healing, and spirituality. He earned his B.A. in psychology from New York University and an M.A. in counseling from the University of Oregon. In addition to writing *The Power of Positive Talk,* Bloch is the author of the inspirational self-help trilogy *Words That Heal: Affirmations and Meditations for Daily Living; Listening to Your Inner Voice;* and *I Am With You Always,* as well as *Healing from Depression: 12 Weeks to a Better Mood,* which has been acclaimed as "a lifeline to healing" for those suffering from mental disorders.

A former radio talk show host and popular public speaker, Bloch has given hundreds of lectures and workshops to businesses, schools, church groups, recovery centers, and national psychology conferences. He has also appeared on radio and television shows across the country.

Bloch lives in Portland, Oregon, where he facilitates ongoing support groups for people who suffer from depression and anxiety. He is joined by his partner Joan, his cat and muse Gabriel, two parakeets (Sebastian and Sabrina), and a box turtle named Vishnu.

You can learn more about Douglas's work by visiting his Web site: *www.healingfromdepression.com.*

Jon Merritt, M.S. (shown with his grandson, Alex), has worked with children and families for thirty-five years as a teacher, elementary school principal, counselor, and consultant. Currently he supervises student teachers at Linfield College in McMinnville, Oregon. He lives in Portland, Oregon, with his wife and has three children and four grandchildren.

You may contact the authors in care of Free Spirit Publishing at:

217 Fifth Avenue North, Suite 200
Minneapolis, MN 55401-1299

Or email them at help4kids@freespirit.com

Other Great Books from Free Spirit

Problem Child or Quirky Kid?
A Commonsense Guide
by Rita Sommers-Flanagan, Ph.D.,
and John Sommers-Flanagan, Ph.D.
The authors suggest remedies for parents to try at home, then offer ideas for getting professional help. The message throughout is clear: What's best is when our children are neither normal nor abnormal, but simply able to live well. For parents. *$15.95; 232 pp.; softcover; 6" x 9"*

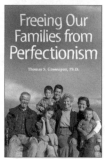

Freeing Our Families from Perfectionism
by Thomas S. Greenspon, Ph.D.
In this encouraging, insightful book, Tom Greenspon explains perfectionism, where it comes from (including influences outside the family), and what to do about it. His healing process can work for anyone who is concerned about perfectionism and its harmful effects on children and adults alike. For parents. *$14.95; 128 pp.; softcover; 6" x 9"*

Raising Healthy Children Day by Day
366 Readings for Parents, Teachers, and Caregivers, Birth to Age 5
by Jolene L. Roehlkepartain
Daily readings support adults who live and work with infants, toddlers, and preschoolers and who want to build young children's developmental assets—positive things all kids need in their lives. *$10.95; 416 pp.; softcover; 4¼" x 6¼"*

What Kids Need to Succeed
Proven, Practical Ways to Raise Good Kids
Revised, Expanded, and Updated Edition
by Peter L. Benson, Ph.D., Judy Galbraith, M.A.,
and Pamela Espeland
Our new edition of a proven best-seller identifies 40 developmental "assets" kids need to lead healthy, productive, positive lives, then helps them build their own assets at home, at school, in the community, and in the congregation. *Parents' Choice* approved. For parents, teachers, community and youth leaders, and teens. *$6.95; 256 pp.; softcover; 4⅛" x 6⅞"*

To place an order or to request a free catalog of SELF-HELP FOR KIDS® *and* SELF-HELP FOR TEENS® *materials, please write, call, email, or visit our Web site:*

Free Spirit Publishing Inc.
217 Fifth Avenue North • Suite 200 • Minneapolis, MN 55401-1299
toll-free 800.735.7323 • local 612.338.2068 • fax 612.337.5050
help4kids@freespirit.com • www.freespirit.com

Fast, Friendly, and Easy to Use
www.freespirit.com

Browse the catalog **Info & extras** **Many ways to search** **Quick check-out** **Stop in and see!**

Our Web site makes it easy to find the positive, reliable resources you need to empower teens and kids of all ages.

The Catalog.
Start browsing with just one click.

Beyond the Home Page.
Information and extras such as links and downloads.

The Search Box.
Find anything superfast.

Your Voice.
See testimonials from customers like you.

Request the Catalog.
Browse our catalog on paper, too!

The Nitty-Gritty.
Toll-free numbers, online ordering information, and more.

The 411.
News, reviews, awards, and special events.

 Our Web site is a secure commerce site. All of the personal information you enter at our site—including your name, address, and credit card number—is secure. So you can order with confidence when you order online from Free Spirit!

For a fast and easy way to receive our practical tips, helpful information, and special offers, send your email address to upbeatnews@freespirit.com. View a sample letter and our privacy policy at *www.freespirit.com*.

1.800.735.7323 • fax 612.337.5050 • help4kids@freespirit.com

If you liked *The Power of Positive Talk,* you'll also like *Our Family Meeting Book* and *What Young Children Need to Succeed*

1-57542-120-8, $16.95

OUR FAMILY MEETING BOOK

Fun and Easy Ways to Manage Time, Build Communication, and Share Responsibility Week by Week

This colorful step-by-step guide helps busy families organize, prioritize, strengthen ties, and otherwise keep it together.

1-57542-070-8, $11.95

WHAT YOUNG CHILDREN NEED TO SUCCEED

Working Together to Build Assets from Birth to Age 11

Learn how to build developmental assets—family support, positive values, social skills, and more. Includes over 1,000 tips and activities.

Call **1.800.735.7323** to order anytime or mail this card for a FREE catalog!

Send me a Free Spirit catalog! (I am a ❏ parent ❏ educator ❏ counselor ❏ other)

name (please print) _____

street_____

city/state/zip _____

email _____

Order online at ***www.freespirit.com*** and download excerpts, quizzes, and more!

Want to know more about *successful strategies* to meet the social, emotional, and educational needs of *every child?*

Free Spirit can help! We're the home of SELF-HELP FOR KIDS®, SELF-HELP FOR TEENS®, and other award-winning materials used by educators, counselors, and parents. Our practical, ready-to-implement strategies help adults make a positive difference in the lives of children. Mail this card for a FREE catalog. (And have one sent to a friend or colleague!)

Send me a Free Spirit catalog! (I am a ❏ parent ❏ educator ❏ counselor ❏ other)

name (please print) _____

street_____

city/state/zip _____

email _____

Send one to my friend: (He/She is a ❏ parent ❏ educator ❏ counselor ❏ other)

name (please print) _____

street_____

city/state/zip _____

email _____

Order online at ***www.freespirit.com*** and download excerpts, quizzes, and more!

Two busy moms share the cure for over-scheduled families.

BUSINESS REPLY MAIL

FIRST-CLASS MAIL   PERMIT NO. 26589   MINNEAPOLIS MN

POSTAGE WILL BE PAID BY ADDRESSEE

free spirit PUBLiSHiNG®

Department 795
217 Fifth Avenue North, Suite 200
Minneapolis, MN 55401-9776

Free Spirit Publishing
Your SELF-HELP FOR KIDS®
and SELF-HELP FOR TEENS®
source for over 20 years.

BUSINESS REPLY MAIL

FIRST-CLASS MAIL   PERMIT NO. 26589   MINNEAPOLIS MN

POSTAGE WILL BE PAID BY ADDRESSEE

free spirit PUBLiSHiNG®

Department 795
217 Fifth Avenue North, Suite 200
Minneapolis, MN 55401-9776